Interdisciplinary Perspectives on Learning to Read

Interdisciplinary Perspectives on Learning to Read brings together different disciplinary perspectives and studies on reading for all those who seek to extend and enrich current practice, research and policy debates. The breadth of knowledge that underpins pedagogy is a central theme and the book will help educators, policymakers and researchers understand the full range of research perspectives that must inform decisions about the development of reading in schools. The book offers invaluable insights into learners who do not achieve their full potential. The chapters have been written by key figures in education, psychology, sociology and neuroscience, and promote discussion of:

- comprehension
- gender and literacy
- phonics and decoding
- digital literacy at home and school
- bilingual learners and reading
- reading difficulties
- evidence-based literacy
- visual texts.

This book encompasses a comprehensive range of conceptual perspectives on reading pedagogy and offers a wealth of new insights to support innovative research directions.

Kathy Hall is Professor of Education and Head of the School of Education at University College Cork.

Usha Goswami is Professor of Education at the University of Cambridge and a Fellow of St John's College, Cambridge.

Colin Harrison has a personal chair in Literacy Studies in Education at the University of Nottingham.

Sue Ellis is Reader in Literacy and Language in the Department of Childhood and Primary Studies at the University of Strathclyde.

Janet Soler is Senior Lecturer at the Open University, where she teaches and publishes on literacy education and literacy policy.

Routledge Psychology in Education
Edited by Karen Littleton

The new *Routledge Psychology in Education* series is interdisciplinary in nature, publishing cutting-edge research in educational psychology and education-based research from related areas, including cognition, neuropsychology and social psychology. Titles will take a broad and innovative approach to topical areas of research and will address the needs of both researchers and advanced students (Masters and Ph.D.) within both psychology and education programmes and related areas.

Titles in the series will:

- review the field to provide an interesting and critical introduction to the student;
- explore contemporary research perspectives, issues and challenges;
- signpost future directions and trends.

Interdisciplinary Perspectives on Learning to Read

Culture, cognition and pedagogy

Edited by Kathy Hall,
Usha Goswami, Colin Harrison,
Sue Ellis and Janet Soler

Routledge
Taylor & Francis Group

LONDON AND NEW YORK

First edition published 2010
by Routledge
2 Park Square, Milton Park, Abingdon, Oxon, OX14 4RN

Simultaneously published in the USA and Canada
by Routledge
270 Madison Avenue, New York, NY 10016

Routledge is an imprint of the Taylor & Francis Group, an informa business

Typeset in Galliard
by Keystroke, Tettenhall, Wolverhampton
Printed and bound in Great Britain
by CPI Antony Rowe Ltd, Chippenham, Wiltshire

British Library Cataloguing in Publication Data
A catalogue record for this book is available
from the British Library

Library of Congress Cataloging-in-Publication Data

Interdisciplinary perspectives on learning to read: culture, cognition
and pedagogy / edited by Kathy Hall . . . [et al.]. – 1st ed.
    p. cm.
    Includes bibliographical references.
    1. Reading (Elementary)—Social aspects. 2. Multicultural
    education. 3. Cognitive styles in children. I. Hall, Kathy, 1952–
    LB1573.I63358 2010
    372.4′044—dc22   2009035791

ISBN10: 0–415–56123–X (hbk)
ISBN10: 0–415–56124–8 (pbk)
ISBN10: 0–203–87566–4 (ebk)

ISBN13: 978–0–415–56123–5 (hbk)
ISBN13: 978–0–415–56124–2 (pbk)
ISBN13: 978–0–203–87566–7 (ebk)

Contents

Illustrations

Figures

Tables

Contributors

Kate Cain, DPhil, is a Reader in the Department of Psychology at Lancaster University. Her research and publications focus on the development of language comprehension in children with a particular interest in the skill deficits that lead to reading and listening comprehension problems. Her work has been published in Journal of Experimental Child Psychology, Journal of Educational Psychology, Memory and Cognition, Journal of Child Language, and Language and Cognitive Processes. She is co-editor with Jane Oakhill of *Children's comprehension problems in oral and written language: A cognitive perspective* (2007), and is an associate editor for the *International Journal of Language and Communication Disorders* and the *Journal of Research in Reading*.

Barbara Comber is a key researcher in the Centre for Studies in Literacy, Policy and Learning Cultures in the Hawke Research Institute at the University of South Australia. Her particular interests include literacy education and social justice, teachers' work and identities, place and space, and practitioner inquiry. She has worked collaboratively with teachers in high poverty locations focusing on innovative and critical curricula and pedagogies which address contemporary social challenges. She has recently co-edited two books: *Literacies in place: Teaching environmental communication* (Comber, Nixon & Reid, 2007) and *Turn-around pedagogies: Literacy interventions for at-risk students* (Comber & Kamler, 2005).

Henrietta Dombey is Professor Emeritus of Literacy in Primary Education at the University of Brighton. Since the start of her teaching career, when she was confronted with a class of seven-year-olds with very little purchase on written language, she has been passionately interested in the teaching of reading. A central focus of this interest has been the interactions between teachers, children and texts. A Past Chair of the National Association for the Teaching of English and Past President of the United Kingdom Literacy Association, she has worked extensively with teachers and teacher educators to develop professional thinking and action.

Rose Drury is Senior Lecturer in Early Years at The Open University Faculty of Education and Language Studies and formerly Senior Lecturer in Early Childhood Education at the University of Worcester and Principal Lecturer in Early Years Education at the University of Hertfordshire. She worked for the Minority Ethnic Curriculum Support Service in Hertfordshire and has extensive experience of teaching bilingual children in the Early Years. Based on her ethnographic doctoral study, the recently published *Young bilingual learners at home and at school* examines the experiences of three four-year-old bilingual children as they begin school in three English nursery classes from a sociocultural theoretical perspective. Her work has been cited as a key reference in a recent 2007 DCSF publication *Supporting children learning English as an additional language: Guidance for practitioners in the Early Years Foundation Stage.*

Sue Ellis is a Reader in Literacy and Language in the Department of Childhood and Primary Studies at Strathclyde University. Her first degree was in Theoretical Linguistics and Language Pathology and her current work involves research, teaching and consultancy in literacy assessment, pedagogy and policy. She is interested in how children learn to become literate but also in how the literacy curriculum is framed, developed, taught and assessed. Recent research projects include a study of the impact of Literature Circles on reading engagement and a study of how indirect speech and language therapy can be used to support children with language impairment in primary schools. The latter project highlighted the systemic, resource and expertise issues that impact on the quality and quantity of support that children with language impairment in mainstream classrooms receive.

Usha Goswami is Professor of Education at the University of Cambridge and a Fellow of St John's College, Cambridge. She is also Director of the University's Centre for Neuroscience in Education, which uses EEG techniques to study the neural basis of dyslexia and dyscalculia. Usha Goswami is currently funded by the Medical Research Council to carry out a longitudinal investigation of the brain basis of dyslexia in children. This is a five-year study involving over 100 children. Prior to moving to Cambridge, she was Professor of Cognitive Developmental Psychology at the Institute of Child Health, University College London, 1997–2003, and before that she was a University Lecturer in Experimental Psychology at the University of Cambridge, 1990–1997. She received her Ph.D. from the University of Oxford in 1987; her topic was reading and spelling by analogy. Her current research examines relations between phonology and reading, with special reference to the neural underpinnings of rhyme and rhythm in children's reading. She has received a number of career awards, including the British Psychology Society Spearman Medal, the Norman Geschwind-Rodin Prize for Dyslexia Research, and Fellowships from the National Academy of Education (USA) and the Alexander von Humboldt Foundation (Germany).

Kathy Hall was Principal Investigator for the ESRC seminar series from which the chapters in this volume emerged. She is Professor of Education and Head of the School at University College Cork. She has published in the areas of literacy, assessment and pedagogy, drawing on sociocultural perspectives. Publications include *Listening to Stephen read* (2003); *Literacy, Schooling and Society* (2004); *Making formative assessment work* (2003) with W. Burke; *Learning and identity* (2008), with P. Murphy, *Pedagogy and identity* (2008), with P. Murphy and J. Soler and *The Reggio Emilia Experience and Loris Malaguzzi* (2010), with M. Horgan, A. Ridgway, R. Murphy, M. Cunneen and D. Cunningham. Kathy is Editor of UKLA's journal *Literacy*.

J. Richard Hanley took up a Chair in Neuropsychology at the University of Essex in 1998. Before that he was a Senior Lecturer in Psychology at the University of Liverpool. His interests in the psychology of reading include the study of acquired reading problems following brain injury. He is particularly interested in the effects of different writing systems on the way in which children learn to read with particular reference to the Welsh language and the Chinese language. He is on the editorial board of the journals *Reading Research Quarterly, Cognitive Neuropsychology* and *Memory*.

Colin Harrison has a personal chair in Literacy Studies in Education at the University of Nottingham, where he has worked since 1976. He has directed 33 funded research projects, in the fields of reading, evaluation and ICT. His publications have focused on literacy, curriculum evaluation and ICT, and have included three reviews of research commissioned by the English and Scottish national education departments. In recent years he has become increasingly interested in the intersection of research and policy, as well as in improving the dissemination of research findings. His most recent book is *Understanding reading development* (2004).

Dawnene D. Hassett is an Associate Professor in the Department of Curriculum and Instruction at the University of Wisconsin–Madison. She teaches courses on literacy and language development, and manages the licensure programs for reading teachers and reading specialists. Dawnene's research analyses the relationships between print literacy and new forms of emerging literacies by juxtaposing early literacy curriculum and instruction, as dominated by alphabetic print concepts, with new forms of text, as dominated by images, graphics, and multiple modes of representation. She studies how new technologies require different readers/writers, and therefore updated reading strategies and an updated theory of literacy learning. She has published most recently in the *Journal of Early Childhood Literacy*, the *English Journal*, and the *Journal of Curriculum Studies*.

James V. Hoffman, Ph.D. is Professor of Language and Literacy Studies at the University of Texas at Austin. He is Past-President of the National Reading Conference and the former editor of *The Reading Research Quarterly*.

Dr Hoffman's research interests are focused on teacher education and the qualities of texts that support literacy learning.

Jessica Hoffman is Assistant Professor of Teacher Education at Miami University, Oxford, OH. A former early childhood classroom teacher in urban and suburban schools, she completed her doctoral research on fostering literary read-alouds in kindergarten classrooms at the University of Illinois at Chicago. Her research interests include early literacy learning, instruction, and professional development, especially in higher-level literacy practices like analysis and criticism.

Jackie Marsh is Professor of Education at the University of Sheffield, UK. Jackie is involved in research which examines the role and nature of popular culture, media and new technologies in early childhood literacy, in both in- and out-of-school contexts. She has conducted a number of studies that have explored children's out-of-school learning in relation to their use of media and new technologies, including the 'DigitalBeginnings project', a survey of young children's use of media in England (http://www.digitalbeginnings.shef.ac.uk/). She is a past president of the United Kingdom Literacy Association (2005–07) and is an editor of the *Journal of Early Childhood Literacy.*

Melissa Mosley, Ph.D. is an Assistant Professor of Language and Literacy at the University of Texas at Austin. She draws on critical discourse analysis and ethnographic methods to study how preservice teachers construct critical literacy/culturally responsive practices. With colleagues, she authored *Designing socially just learning communities: Critical literacy education across the lifespan* (2009).

Gemma Moss is Director of the Centre for Critical Education Policy Studies (CeCeps) and Professor of Education at the Institute of Education, University of London. Current research interests include literacy and education policy; the study of texts in their contexts of use; and the shifting relationships between policy-makers, practitioners and other stakeholders that are reshaping the curriculum. Her most recent book is *Literacy and gender: Researching texts, contexts and readers* (2007).

Kathleen A. Paciga is a Ph.D. candidate at the University of Illinois at Chicago in the Literacy, Language and Culture program. She specializes in read-aloud research and has focused on traditional and electronic read-alouds, with emphasis on young children's story comprehension and their engagement during read-alouds. She also works as a Graduate Research Assistant on two Early Reading First projects and is an instructor in the College of Education.

Vivienne Smith moved into higher education after completing a doctorate on critical literacy and reading. She works as a lecturer in the department of Childhood and Primary Studies at the University of Strathclyde, where she teaches in the language team and pursues research interests in children's literature, critical literacy and the development of children as readers. She has published a number of articles, including, most recently, chapters in Goodwin (2008) *Understanding children's books*; Evans (2009) *Talking beyond the page*; and Styles and Arizpe (2009) *Acts of reading: Teachers, texts and childhood*.

Janet Soler has taught and published internationally in areas related to literacy education and literacy policy. She has held appointments as a teacher, university researcher, and lecturer in schools and universities in New Zealand and England. Janet's current research interests include the history and politics of literacy pedagogy and practice in England and New Zealand, and comparative investigations into the socio-historical construction of the curriculum and related policies. Recently published books include *Reading across international boundaries* (2007) and *Literacy crises and reading policies: Children still can't read* (2006).

William H. Teale is Professor of Education at the University of Illinois at Chicago. Author of over one hundred publications, his work has focused on early literacy learning, the intersection of technology and literacy education, and children's literature. He has worked in the area of early childhood education with schools, libraries, policy-makers, and non-profit organizations across the United States. He is a former editor of the journal *Language Arts* and a member of the Reading Hall of Fame.

Dominic Wyse is a Senior Lecturer in Primary and Early Years Education at the University of Cambridge and Fellow of Churchill College Cambridge. He was a primary teacher for eight years which included posts in London, Bradford and Huddersfield. Following his work as a teacher he lectured at Liverpool John Moores University for eight years, latterly as a Reader in Primary Education. Dominic's research focuses on primary and early years education, particularly in relation to curriculum policy and pedagogy for the teaching of English, language and literacy. His interest in educational innovation has led to research on creativity in the primary curriculum and innovation more generally, including in secondary schools. Dominic is a Deputy Executive Editor of the *Cambridge Journal of Education*. He is also editor of the Routledge Primary Education series. He is a member of the editorial boards of *Teaching and Teacher Education: An International Journal of Research and Studies* and *Writing and Literacy*.

Acknowledgements

The chapters in this book are the result of a seminar series which was funded by the Economic and Social Research Council (ESRC) and the British Curriculum Foundation (BCF).

Introduction

Chapter 1

Significant lines of research in reading pedagogy

Kathy Hall

Introduction

This introductory chapter explains the background to the book and the rationale for its focus and themes. It then goes on to map the terrain of reading pedagogy, drawing attention to significant lines of enquiry, some of which are picked up and developed more specifically in subsequent chapters in the volume. The chapter highlights the pedagogic steers arising from what could be classed as three recognized, though not discrete, traditions in reading education: psycholinguistic, cognitive, and cultural. The status accorded by policy and practice to these various aspects of reading pedagogy is also noted. Finally, the chapter outlines the main sections of the book.

Background and rationale

Few other areas of children's learning have had more research attention than reading development and pedagogy, and the disciplinary lines of research that have evolved on the subject are now many and diverse. Though not confined to these, reading research spans sociocultural, semiotic, educational, linguistic, historical, political, psychological, and neuro-scientific/biological traditions. It is difficult then for researchers and users to have an overview, much less an in-depth knowledge, of the theoretical and pedagogical implications of such a diverse field. And few opportunities are available for sustained cross-disciplinary engagement among reading researchers, practitioners and policy-makers, the tendency being for researchers from the same disciplinary background to communicate and work together in relative isolation from those coming from other disciplinary lines of enquiry. For example, the scholarly volumes *The Science of Reading* (Snowling and Hulme 2005) and *The Voice of Evidence in Reading Research* (McCardle and Chhabra 2004) as well as key research journals (e.g. *Scientific Studies in Reading*) draw almost exclusively on psychological and biological perspectives on reading and do not incorporate sociocultural or sociological ones. Equally scholarly volumes and journals, for example, the *Handbook of Early Childhood Literacy* (Hall et al. 2003) and the *Journal of Early Childhood Literacy*, tend not to incorporate work from experimental psychology or biology, being grounded primarily in sociocultural perspectives.

Education policies and practices would benefit from being informed by the full range of perspectives on reading and this in turn suggests a need for interdisciplinary dialogue among reading researchers, teacher educators, policy-makers, and education practitioners. These interested groups need to share perspectives on reading development so that they can at least acknowledge, and where appropriate integrate, perspectives from the existing knowledge base into their research and professional practices.

This volume stems from almost three years of seminars, reflection and conference presentations designed to support dialogue across disciplinary traditions. Supported by grants from the Economic and Social Research Council (ESRC) and the British Curriculum Foundation, leading scholars, research students, education practitioners, and policy-makers shared and debated discussion papers, perspectives, and professional concerns, and in so doing, sought to build bridges across reading research communities. Pedagogy was a central theme in that the aim was to help educators and policy-makers draw on a more comprehensive range of perspectives when making decisions about the promotion of reading in schools. This is especially important for those learners who are currently not achieving their full potential and so forming the long tail of underachievement which is characteristic of British schooling. The group had one interest in common: to further understanding of reading development and pedagogy, while the challenge set at its meetings was threefold:

1   to find ways of researching the teaching and learning of reading that recognise the achievements of reading research from different disciplinary traditions;
2   for practitioners, including teacher educators, to apply pedagogic approaches that are informed by a wider range of evidence; and,
3   for policy-makers to promote practices that are grounded in the best available evidence.

The origin of the book then stems from the premise that researchers and educators whose primary interest is in reading pedagogy benefit from networks that include all relevant disciplinary perspectives. The chapters seek to reflect a wide range of conceptual perspectives on reading pedagogy and to encourage cross-fertilisation and new insights to support practice and research directions. This chapter proceeds to highlight some key lines of enquiry and their impact on reading policy and pedagogy.

Pedagogic contribution of the psycholinguistic line of enquiry

Originating largely in the work of Noam Chomsky the psycholinguistic perspective on literacy exerted a considerable influence on professional practice, on policy, and on reading research. Among the names most associated with this tradition are Kenneth and Yetta Goodman and Frank Smith, and they along with many others, for example Don Holdaway, Margaret Meek, Lucy Calkins, and Donald Graves, were enormously influential in teacher education and in primary practice. Miscue analysis, emergent literacy, whole language, and real books are some of the pedagogic concepts deriving from their work.

How could one explain the remarkable oral language achievement of young children – a remarkable level of proficiency that did not require any direct teaching but developed from sheer exposure to the language in the environment? Since oral language was far too complex to be developed by means of imitation or linking up the various meanings of adjacent words, Chomsky postulated a nativist view of language acquisition, claiming that humans are innately predisposed to acquire the language of their environment. Could the observations, prompted by Chomsky, that children could work out the rules of oral language grammar for themselves also be applied to written language acquisition? Put another way, could learning to read and write be natural? This question is the basis of the psycholinguistic position on reading.

Let's take miscue analysis as an example. Goodman's close observation and analysis of actual reading behaviour led him to describe reading as a psycho-linguistic guessing game in which learners construct meaning from text, where the act of reading is viewed as a transaction between the reader's text, i.e. what the reader brings to the text in terms of world knowledge and expectations and the published text (Goodman 1992). He suggested that readers draw on three cue systems simultaneously to make sense of text: graphophonic, syntactic, and semantic. By using these cue systems readers could keep to a minimum of uncertainty about unknown words and meanings. Goodman (and others) saw learners as naturally motivated to make sense of text and they saw no reason to distinguish between a word identification phase in reading and a comprehension phase. Further, they saw no reason to isolate any cue system for separate training and development. Goodman said, 'We can study how each one works in reading and writing, but they can't be isolated for instruction without creating non-language abstractions' (1986: 38–9). Frank Smith's idea that the reader develops hunches about upcoming words in a text and samples only a few features of the visual text display – just enough to confirm or reject their hunches – advanced the controversial idea that reading was only incidentally visual. The accuracy of this view was to be challenged later by psychological studies.

A key message deriving from their theoretical work was that there was only one reading process, that is that all readers, whether beginner/inexperienced or fluent/experienced, use the same process, although they differ in the control they have over it. A non-stage reading process was assumed. Skilled readers it was thought relied less on orthographic information. What psycholinguists sought to get teachers away from was the notion that reading is a linear process of letter-by-letter decoding, sounding out, word recognition and finally text comprehension.

They insisted reading consisted of a meaning-building, problem-solving process (see Hall 2003a for full discussion).

The upshot for pedagogy of this line of inquiry included the following: use of texts that are rich in natural language and a focus on helping the reader attend to meanings and contexts. The use of language for authentic purposes was the hallmark, and ownership and choice for the learner and the integration of language modes were all evident in the range of practices advocated in textbooks for student teachers and in articles in professional journals (e.g. *Language Arts, The Reading Teacher, Reading* (now *Literacy*)). Activities that promoted meaning building, interpretation, and engagement on the part of the learner included the following:

- shared experiences through reading 'big books';
- sustained silent reading;
- reading aloud in class to facilitate the pleasure of reading;
- literature circles (discussion of one piece of literature that everyone has read, related texts, etc.);
- literature response activities (e.g. writing to characters in stories, dramatizing stories, painting, etc.).

Writers like Margaret Meek emphasized the richness of language and the satisfying plots in children's literature as opposed to the insubstantial characters, the lack of interest and suspense, the short sentences and simple vocabulary of commercially produced reading schemes. Commercial publishers changed considerably in the 1980s and 1990s in response to the groundswell of support within the teaching profession for literature-based reading and whole and meaningful texts. In addition, school and class libraries got a boost and became a significant resource for the reading curriculum. As a result of this perspective, isolating print from its functional use by teaching skills out of context and by focusing on written language as an end in itself came to be challenged, if not abandoned in practice.

Psycholinguistic ideas fitted historically with the 'language through experience' approach of the 1960s where originality, creativity, first-hand experience, self-expression, self-discovery, and imaginative spontaneity were the hallmarks. These ideas connected well with teachers' pedagogical philosophies, if not always their actual practices. And proponents were not just in teacher education institutions. Several official reports of literacy practice in England during the 1980s urged teachers to devote more attention to imaginative aspects of reading and texts. For example in 1982, referring to the fact that five-year-olds were introduced too quickly to published reading schemes, the inspectors stated: 'The children spent a good deal of time decoding print with the result that they read mechanically and with little understanding . . .' (DES 1982: 5). This same survey of first schools commented on the unproductive time spent by 50 per cent of the schools on English exercises which stifled individuality. Official reports in the late 1980s (DES 1988) confirmed the importance of children's literature and response to literature for the growth of imagination and the intellect. Such endorsements of meaning, literature and authentic activities from officialdom invited teachers' scepticism about decontextualized, work-book exercises on, say, letter–sound correspondences, syllabification and routine comprehension exercises.

Research in the UK in the 1980s revealed that teachers did not abandon more traditional methods of teaching early reading, including the use of schemes and the teaching of word attack skills and phonic knowledge. It would seem that very few teachers adopted the attitude that skills would emerge incidentally from exposure to children's literature; the vast majority of infant teachers taught the mechanical skills of reading through combinations of formal instructional routines, or mini-lessons on the so-called basics. Effectiveness research seemed to confirm the merits of such practices (see Hall 2003b; Hall and Harding 2004 for reviews). The most accomplished teachers understood that the beginner reader did not simply catch the alphabetic principle by exposure to quality texts, they understood that most children needed a balance of systematic skills instruction and contextually grounded activities using quality texts and activities.

The acknowledgement of the various cueing systems, through the reading searchlights model, was a striking feature of national policy in England in the 1990s and early 2000s. The searchlights model described how each of the four searchlights (phonic knowledge, knowledge of context, grammatical knowledge, and graphic knowledge) 'sheds a partial light, but together they make a mutually supporting system' (DfES 2001: 1). Although the policy (NLS) noted that, of these approaches, phonic and graphic should be prioritized, the searchlights model is where psycholinguists had their greatest policy and pedagogic influence. However, more recent policy initiatives, exemplified in the Rose Report on early reading, challenge this work by prioritising systematic phonics teaching and within that an emphasis on synthetic phonics.

Through this line of work, learner efforts and responses to work set acquired status in offering insights into thinking processes and reading strategies. Pupil responses, whether accurate or inaccurate, were now to be noticed, thought about and acted upon. Errors were no longer to be dismissed merely as negative but were to become part of the formative assessment process: the basis on which future tasks would be set and informative of the direction future teaching might take. In sum, by highlighting reading as a constructive process and by giving us miscue analysis, psycholinguists gave us at once a theory of reading and a way of examining pedagogy (see Pearson and Stephens 1994; Hall 2003a). In relation to pedagogy its contribution grew from the ground, from teachers themselves and from those involved in the education of teachers.

Pedagogic contribution of the cognitive line of enquiry

Studies from the more dominant, cognitive and experimental psychological perspective on early reading pedagogy and development attends to the individual child's mental functioning, motivations and capacities. It attends typically to print literacy and especially word recognition, although comprehension features increasingly.

Word recognition is considered to be the foundation of reading in cognitive psychology; it is one of the oldest and most enduring areas of research in the whole of psychology, and since the late 1970s tremendous strides have been made in terms of understanding the word recognition processes. A major finding that has emerged from experimental psychological literature is the assumption of considerable interactivity among the various types of lexical and semantic structures in word recognition. The role of phonology is key here and it is accepted that phonological coding is central to word recognition although there is no agreement as to how phonology is accessed and its possible importance in providing access to semantic information remains unclear (Snowling and Hulme 2005). However, recent cross-linguistic research by Usha Goswami demonstrates that the orthography of English, in comparison with all other languages, presents significant challenges for the beginning reader (Ziegler and Goswami 2005; also Chapter 8 of this volume) and Goswami's line of enquiry has led to a novel theoretical framework (psycholinguistic grain size theory) for understanding reading development.

A point that distinguishes those taking a cognitive view from those from the psycholinguistic view just noted is whether children progress through reading stages or whether the reading process is essentially the same for the experienced and novice reader. The former adopt a stage model showing that:

1   There are qualitative differences between experienced and beginner readers;
2   Word identification is key to comprehension;
3   Knowledge of the orthography is more important than syntactic or semantic knowledge;
4   Maximal orthographic information is used and the efficient use of this knowledge leads to better comprehension.

Here the alphabetic nature of written language is considered the major hurdle for the beginner reader. An example of one such stage model is that of Linnea Ehri, who distinguished the following chronological stages: pre-alphabetic, partial alphabetic, full alphabetic, and consolidated alphabetic.

Experimental psychological research using eye-movement technologies demonstrated that readers do attend closely to visual information, a finding that challenged Frank Smith's notion of how readers sample the text for visual information rather than attend to every visual clue. The evidence being assembled (see the *Handbooks of Research on Reading*, and *The Science of Reading*) leads to the conclusion that learning the cipher is neither easy nor natural and that explicit and some systematic teaching is helpful to nearly all beginner readers. The outcome of all this work on stages and models of reading acquisition has meant a tempering of the constructivist metaphor where the reader builds meaning and highlighted instead how the text itself constrains expectations and beliefs (Stanovich 1992).

In line with the increased understanding about the role of word recognition, phonological and phonemic awareness (or what some refer to as the new phonics) is a significant development in our understanding of the reading process in the past 20 years. In order to get to a point of automatic, context-free word recognition skill (Adams 1990) to store sight words in memory, children have to be able to connect up graphemes to phonemes in the word and then retain those connections in memory. Phonics teaching is a way of teaching reading that emphasizes the knowledge of the letter–sound correspondences and the ability to apply this knowledge to reading and spelling. Cognitive psychologists have furnished enough evidence to show the value and importance of early, explicit teaching in word recognition. And, as already noted, effectiveness studies have demonstrated how the most accomplished literacy teachers use a balance of approaches in the development of early reading (Hall and Harding 2003) by building on what the learner already knows and by integrating print knowledge with real reading for meaning.

The study of the nature and origin of reading comprehension is a more recent area of study and specific difficulties in reading comprehension is a relatively new focus of study in experimental psychology (see Cain *et al.* 2004 and Chapter 6 of this volume) and in education (Harrison 2004).

Reading difficulties and reading pedagogies to address them are beginning to be better understood also by investigations of the neurobiological underpinnings of reading. Neuroscientific data from several studies (e.g. McCandliss *et al.* 2003) show differences in the developmental trajectories of beginning readers and more competent readers, and between individuals with reading disability and non-impaired readers. Moreover, word accuracy and fluency/automaticity draw on different brain systems in reading development, indicating implications for a variety of pedagogic approaches. Such studies are leading some researchers to probe whether a given reading intervention, at a given age and for readers with a certain profile of reading disability, will support their learning. While considerable challenges remain in this work for investigating the difficulties encountered by children with developmental dyslexia (e.g. Price and McCrory 2005) those conducting pedagogic research and seeking to support learners with specific reading difficulties would benefit from having a critical understanding of this work.

The contemporary influence of the cognitive perspective is most noticeable in relation to the emphasis in current policy and practice on phonological and phonemic awareness training. This influence is partially explained by the increasing politicization of reading research, policy and practice and the push for measurable outputs to enhance accountability (see Ellis, Chapter 14 of this volume). Research grounded in numbers ('scientific' research) is accorded greater status than research emanating from ethnographies, case studies, or action research studies – research orientations that tended to characterize the psycholinguistic (and cultural) traditions. In the US two significant, government-funded reports heralded the way for a much stronger emphasis on quantitative and experimental psychological pedagogical research than heretofore. One was *Preventing Reading Difficulties in*

Young Children (Snow *et al.* 1998) and the second was the National Reading Panel Report (NICHHD 2000), the latter especially controversial because it privileged studies based on randomized or quasi-randomized control trials and ignored more qualitative research.

Pedagogic contribution of the cultural line of enquiry

The cognitive perspective on literacy curriculum and pedagogy tends not to engage with how texts are located within multi-modal practices, privileging instead print literacy and essentialist views of gender, race and other social categories. The psycholinguistic and cognitive lines of enquiry have in common an exclusive emphasis on the child as individual and the individual nature of the construction of meaning. A cultural perspective shifts the emphasis from an internal process located in an individual per se to the individual in relation to other individuals, and to the social and cultural context in which literacy occurs – a relational view of learning. Originating in Vygotsky's work, developed by Bruner (1996) and more recently Lave, Wenger (Lave and Wenger 1991, Wenger 1998), and Rogoff (2003) among others, and extended in the literacy arena by Bakhtin (see Holquist 1990), Gee (2003), Brice-Heath (1983), Dyson (2000), Solsken (1993), and Marsh (2007) and evidenced in, for example, the *Journal of Early Childhood Literacy*, this line of enquiry has hugely enriched our understanding of literacy learning.

From this perspective, learning to read is a process in which knowledge, understanding, and meaning are constructed through participation in literate communities, or more precisely, through active, meaningful engagement in practices mediated by artefacts, tools, theories, policies, technologies, and especially, other people. People learn to read by participating in whatever practice reading is deemed to be in their lived world. Similarly, people learn to write by participating in the practices that those around them demonstrate, through their actions, writing actually is. The nature of people's engagement or participation in these practices changes over time and these changes in the type and level of participation constitute identity changes. That is what learning is: changes and shifts in identity, brought about by the agentic repeated participation in activity. Repeated participation enhances the competences needed to do well in these practices, even when participants do not engage in them to enhance their competence. Participation does not merely facilitate or inhibit some kind of predetermined and fixed course of cognitive development; rather it gives rise to it.

Cultural studies of reading, and literacy more generally, show how learners appropriate what is available to be learned. Opportunity to learn and the factors enhancing and hindering those opportunities, with reference to the literate practices of peers, family, community, and institution or school are all highly relevant to this way of studying reading pedagogy and the process of developing competence. Studies show how children's engagements with new media, popular culture and digital technologies can be and indeed are being brought into effective learning experiences in the classroom as well as in other less formal learning environments (Britsch 2005; Comber and Hill 2000; Marsh and Millard 2003). Thus, the multiple nature of reading and writing practice becomes flagged. Moreover, such studies seek to recognise that what is salient to learners influences what they bring to and take away from the learning opportunities made available to them.

Cultural studies of literacy seek to engage with the diversity and complexity of learners' lived experiences. They examine, for instance, how views about gender, race, class, dis/ability and so on intersect with becoming competent in literacies, how identities conflict and require negotiation in order to make progress, and how learners' home and school literacy experiences may align or misalign with consequences for learners' educational success. Work from this tradition has established how children living in areas of economic disadvantage are more likely to engage with popular and media literacies than with traditional children's literacies, exemplified by the 'bedtime story' (Comber and Hill 2000; Luke and Luke 2001). Yet these same children depend more than their economically better off peers on their teachers and their schools for success in the kind of literacy valued by school and society (Taylor *et al.* 2000). The case for bridging across the various spaces where young learners live their lives is a strong feature of a cultural perspective on reading (see Part I of this volume).

It is not so much the ontological status that is at issue in a cultural view as the significance of what is on offer. A cultural perspective understands culture as more than 'in the head' phenomena (Bloome *et al.* 2005). Culture produces meanings, guides actions, assigns identities, makes particular events possible, structures social relationships and power relations among people, while people also produce and transform culture (Bloome *et al.* 2005; Hall 2008; Holland *et al.* 1998). A cultural perspective shifts the emphasis from cognitive psychology towards disciplines that are about the ways in which people behave in groups. This means that disciplines like sociology, anthropology and socio-linguistics become more relevant, and researchers have sought to explore literacy pedagogy through ethnographic studies of situated literacies, i.e. literacies in the context of their occurrence (e.g. Hall 2002). This has meant the use of open-ended styles of fieldwork over long periods, often years, to try to understand literacy from the perspectives of those inside particular communities of practice. Reports of such work appear in the form of learning biographies of the children, classrooms and communities studied (e.g. Brice-Heath 1983; Gregory 1998; Hicks 2008).

While such work is becoming better recognised and established in early literacy pedagogy, policy initiatives tend to lag behind these insights. Culturally framed research is sometimes overlooked by higher-level policy-makers and mandates calling for 'bias-free' and 'scientific' research, as noted already (see Ellis below).

The lessons from this line of enquiry have directed us to literacy interactions and practices in the home and the need for connecting home and school literacies and popular culture, viewing literacy as multi-modal and not just print-based. To become a better reader then is not merely about acquiring skills like decoding but coming to know how to be like a reader in the context of the literacy demands of the setting. A fundamental outcome of this line of enquiry is a recognition of what pupils bring with them in terms of cultural knowledge and experiences.

Conclusion and plan of the volume

Reading research and policy shape literate practices in classrooms. This chapter has shown how different lines of reading research have emphasised different practices with consequences for learners and representations of competence. Depending on the viewing frame, certain features of literacy are deemed to be relevant, to merit attention and so are carefully detailed, while other features are glossed over, consigned to the background and so rendered less relevant. What reading practices are available to pupils in school? Do they constrain or empower them? What status in policy do certain literacy practices have and what are the consequences for learners of such decisions? The chapters in this volume probe these and several other aspects in further discussions of the complexities of teaching and learning to read.

Five areas of work were brought together with a focus on reading development and pedagogy. Part I, entitled 'Families, communities and schools', contains three chapters explicitly drawing on sociocultural theory with direct reference to learning in schools. Jackie Marsh's chapter analyses the fit across homes and schools in relation to reading material and describes the actual practice of one teacher whose reading pedagogy aligns well with home and community practices. Place cannot be discounted, suggests Barbara Comber in her chapter, drawing attention to the notion of 'reading places' and how learners read places as they develop their literate repertoires. Rose Drury's chapter on bilingual children exposes learning that is often invisible to teachers and other learners in school and she offers a new interpretation of scaffolding. By attending to learners' lived worlds these chapters show the remarkable skills and potential of young learners and they expose the limitations of some traditional teaching practices.

Part II consists of three chapters on comprehension. The first, by Vivienne Smith, argues that meanings in texts are not fixed, but emergent, depending on individual and community experiences, and she develops the implications of this cultural perspective for practice in classrooms. Grounded in the psychological tradition, Kate Cain's longitudinal study shows how comprehension can be limited not just by word reading skill; she identifies a range of other variables that impact text comprehension and considers how the findings might influence assessment practices. Based on semiotic and sociocultural perspectives Dawnene Hassett's chapter proposes 'a pedagogy of multiliteracies' and updates the terrain of early literacy pedagogy by examining hypertextual, interactive, and visual elements of contemporary children's texts. Deriving from different lines of research, these chapters challenge traditional definitions of comprehension and invite new research questions, richer pedagogies, and more nuanced policies.

Educators have long appreciated the links between language and literacy development, though the nature of those links is quite another thing. Part III, 'Beginning to read print', offers valuable insights into acquiring the alphabetic principle in English. Attending to the developing brain of the beginner reader Usha Goswami explains how the quality of phonological representations determines literacy acquisition. She argues that as the beginner reader develops alphabetic knowledge, the brain restructures its earlier acquired phonological representations into 'phonemic phonology'. She goes on to show how a specific problem with phonology points to a child having specific literacy difficulties. Continuing earlier work (Ziegler and Goswami 2005) about the learning challenges posed to young readers by the deep orthography of English, Rick Hanley's chapter compares children's alphabetic development in English and Welsh. He confirms that English is an especially difficult writing system to learn; he also provides further insights on some of the intricacies of learning English, and concludes by recommending 'extensive phonics training' to overcome them. Next, Dominic Wyse, in a chapter entitled 'Contextualised phonics teaching', offers insights into effective phonics teaching and goes on to examine policies in several countries, finding limitations in England's contemporary policy.

Part IV – the longest part – challenges in various ways reading research, policy, practice or a combination of these. The authors here draw on research from a range of disciplines and they expose issues in the application of research to education. One overarching theme in this section is the manner in which current literacy policies and the uptake of research on literacy – at least in the UK and the US – may constrain pupil learning by endorsing narrow views of literacy curricula and pedagogy. William Teale and his colleagues argue that early literacy programmes need to be reoriented to stress what is foundational with respect to early literacy, their contention being that more systematic attention should be given to content, comprehension, child engagement, and complex interactions with text if students are to be successful with literacy, not only when they are in the early grades, but as they progress through the remainder of primary and secondary schooling. Henrietta Dombey's chapter on the forms that classroom interaction has taken in recent years highlights the uneasy fit between what we know about how reading develops and the dominance of a recitation mode of interaction in classrooms. Her illustration of a richer type of interaction prompts her to link types of interaction with different purposes of education. In an historical chapter, Janet Soler traces the controversies and debates surrounding dyslexia and its emergence as a professional discourse in the twentieth century and, offering an alternative reading, she notes how legacies of earlier times still lurk in current discourse and practice.

This book seeks to encourage a deeper and more extensive engagement with evidence and perspectives on reading. Sue Ellis addresses this head-on in her chapter: she complicates the notion of evidence applied to literacy teaching in order to understand it better. She describes some of the paradigms and problems associated with the use of evidence in relation to specific interventions and programmes. Her analysis points to how we have not given adequate attention to ways in which the different levels of the education system impact on teachers' classroom decision making. In a provocatively entitled chapter, Colin Harrison is deeply critical of England's interpretation of the 'simple view' of reading, showing how it is 'over simple'. He draws attention to what it ignores: fluency, vocabulary, cognitive flexibility, and morphology. In the final chapter in this section Gemma Moss considers the impact of policy-driven education reform on the social organization of reading in school. Drawing on ethnographic data collected in English classrooms before and after the introduction of the National Literacy Strategy, the chapter identifies some of the key dilemmas teachers face in managing pupils' transition into self-directed reading. The six chapters assembled in this section call for a deeper engagement, especially on the part of national policy-makers, with the range of perspectives and evidence now available on the complexities of early literacy development.

Various chapters in this book show how research and policy shape what is acceptable, doable and achievable in classrooms. In turn this shaping determines, at least partially, what is available to be learned by pupils. Teachers and their professional education are at the interface of what literacies learners can appropriate as they participate in what is on offer to them in classrooms. The concluding chapter deals with what teachers need to be able to do in schools and literacy classrooms, and more particularly, how they become competent in doing it. Set in the United States, Jim Hoffman and Melissa Mosley, in line with other authors in earlier sections, challenge the narrow and simplistic interpretation of what constitutes knowledge and competence, this time within the context of teacher education. They acknowledge the practical and political dimensions of teacher knowledge and strongly reject the contemporary move towards lists of inert competences and standards in teacher education. Their analysis shows the situatedness of literacy policies and practices. To enhance literacy teaching they advocate paying much greater attention to researching how student teachers use knowledge in dynamic and problem-solving ways in classrooms. In line with the messages in other chapters, they tend to the complex and away from the simplistic. Their metaphor is apt: they are less interested in tying up loose ends and much more interested in understanding the knot!

The lens through which one looks frames particular views. In this volume we have sought to look at reading development and pedagogy through a variety of lenses and the result is a more nuanced and layered perspective than is typically reflected in national policies. By bringing a range of perspectives to bear on early reading it is hoped that this book will encourage researchers, policy-makers and practitioners to look outside their own comfort zone when they make recommendations about how reading should be taught in our schools.

References

Adams, M.J. (1990) *Beginning to Read: Thinking and Learning about Print*, Cambridge, MA: MIT Press.

Bloome, D., Carter, S., Christian, B., Otto, S., & Shuart-Faris, N. (2005) *Discourse Analysis and the Study of Classroom Language and Literacy Events: A Microethnographic Approach*, Mahwah, NJ: Erlbaum.

Britsch, S.J. (2005) ' "But what did they learn?" Clearing third spaces in virtual dialogues with children', *Journal of Early Childhood Literacy*, 5, 2: 99–130.

Bruner, J. (1996) *The Culture of Education*, Cambridge, MA: Harvard University Press.

Cain, K., Oakhill, J., & Lemmon, K. (2004) 'Individual differences in the inference of word meanings from context: The influence of reading comprehension, vocabulary knowledge, and memory capacity', *Journal of Educational Psychology*, 96: 671–681.

Comber, B. & Hill, S. (2000) 'Socio-economic disadvantage, literacy and social justice: Learning from longitudinal case study research', *Australian Educational Research Journal*, 27, 3: 1–20.

DES (1982) *Education 5–9: An Illustrative Survey of 80 First Schools*, London: HMSO.

DES (1988) *Report of the Committee of Inquiry into the Teaching of English* (Kingman Report), London: HMSO.

DfES (2001) *The National Literacy Strategy*, London: The Stationery Office.

Dyson, A. (2000) 'On re-framing children's words: The perils, promises and pleasures of writing children', *Research into the Teaching of English*, 34: 352–367.

Dyson, A.H. (2003). ' "Welcome to the jam": Popular culture, school literacy, and the making of childhoods', *Harvard Educational Review*, 73, 3: 328–361.

Gee, J.P. (2003) *What Video Games have to Teach us about Language and Literacy*, Basingstoke: Palgrave Macmillan.

Goodman, K. (1986) *What's Whole in Whole Language?*, London: Scholastic.

Goodman, K. (1992) 'Why whole language is today's agenda in education', *Language Arts*, 69: 354–363.

Gregory, E. (1998) 'Siblings as mediators of literacy in linguistic minority communities', *Language and Education*, 1, 12: 33–55.

Hall, K. (2002) 'Negotiating subjectivities and knowledge in a multi-ethnic literacy class: an ethnographic–sociocultural perspective', *Language and Education*, 16, 3: 178–194.

Hall, K. (2003a) *Listening to Stephen Read: Multiple Perspectives on Literacy*, Buckingham: Open University Press.

Hall, K. (2003b) 'A review of research on effective literacy teaching', in J. Marsh, N. Hall & J. Larson (eds) *Handbook of Research on Childhood Literacy*, 315–326, London: Sage.

Hall, K. (2008) 'Leaving middle childhood and moving into teenhood: Small stories revealing identity and agency', in K. Hall, P. Murphy & J. Soler (eds) *Pedagogy and Practice: Culture and Identities*, 87–105, London: Sage.

Hall, K. & Harding, A. (2003) 'A systematic review of effective literacy teaching in the 4 to 14 age range of mainstream schooling', in *Research Evidence in Education Library*, London: EPPI-Centre, Social Science Research Unit, Institute of Education.

Hall, N., Larson, J. & Marsh, J. (eds) (2003) *Handbook of Early Childhood Literacy*, London: Sage.

Harrison, C. (2004) *Understanding Reading Development*, London: Sage.

Heath, S.B. (1983) *Ways with Words*, London: Cambridge University Press.

Hicks, D. (2008) 'Literacies and masculinities in the life of a young working class boy', in P. Murphy and K. Hall (eds) *Learning and Practice: Agency and Identities*, 133–148, London: Sage.

Holland, D. *et al.* (1998) *Identity and Agency in Cultural Worlds*, Cambridge MA: Harvard University Press.

Holquist, M. (2002 [1990]) *Dialogism: Bakhtin and his World, Second Edition*, London: Routledge.

Lave, J. & Wenger, E. (1991) *Situated Learning: Legitimate Peripheral Participation*, Cambridge: Cambridge University Press.

Luke, A. & Luke. C. (2001) 'Adolescence lost/childhood regained: On early intervention and the emergence of the techno-subject', *Journal of Early Childhood Literacy*, 1: 91–120.

Marsh, J. (2007) 'New literacies and old pedagogies: Recontextualising rules and practices', *International Journal of Inclusive Education*, 11, 3: 267–281.

Marsh, J. & Millard, E. (2003) *Literacy and Popular Culture in the Classroom*, Reading: University of Reading.

McCandliss, B.D., Beck, I., Sandak, R., & Perfetti, C. (2003) 'Focusing attention on decoding for children with poor reading skills: A study of the Word Building intervention', *Scientific Studies of Reading*, 7, 1: 75–105.

McCardle, P. & Chhabra, V. (eds) (2004) *The Voice of Evidence in Reading Research*, Baltimore, MD: Brookes.

National Institute of Child Health and Human Development (2000) *Report of the National Reading Panel. Teaching Children to Read: An Evidence-Based Assessment of the Scientific Research Literature on Reading and its Implications for Reading Instruction* (NIH Publication No. 00-4769), Washington, DC: U.S. Government Printing Office.

Pearson, P.D. & Stephens, D. (1994) 'Learning about literacy? A 30-year journey', in R.B. Ruddell *et al.* (eds) *Theoretical Models and Processs of Reading*, 22–42, Newark, DE: International Reading Association.

Price, C. & McCrory, E. (2005) 'Functional brain imaging studies of skilled reading and developmental dyslexia', in M. Snowling and C. Hulme (eds) *The Science of Reading*, Oxford: Blackwell.

Rogoff, B. (2003) *The Cultural Nature of Human Development*, New York: Oxford University Press.

Snow, C.E., Burns, M.S. and Griffin, P. (1998) *Preventing Reading Difficulties in Young Children*, Washington, DC: National Academy Press.

Snowling, M. and Hulme, C. (2005) *The Science of Reading*, Oxford: Blackwell.

Solsken, J. (1993) *Literacy, Gender and Work*, Norwood, NJ: Ablex Publishing Corporation.

Stanovich, K.E. (1992) 'The psychology of reading: An evolutionary and revolutionary development', *Journal of Research in Reading*, 18, 2: 87–105.

Taylor, B.M., Pearson, P.D., Clark, K. & Walpole, S. (2000) 'Effective schools and accomplished teachers: Lessons about primary grade reading instruction in low income schools', *Elementary School Journal*, 101: 121–165.

Wenger, E. (1998) *Communities of Practice: Learning, Meaning and Identity*, Cambridge: Cambridge University Press.

Ziegler, J. & Goswami, U. (2005) 'A psycholinguistic grain size theory of reading and reading development across languages', *Psychological Bulletin*, 131, 1: 3–29.

Part I

Families, communities and schools

Chapter 2

The ghosts of reading past, present and future

The materiality of reading in homes and schools

Jackie Marsh

Introduction

I have chosen this Dickensian title for the chapter because it characterises, albeit in a rather melodramatic fashion, the key argument made here that the present imaginaries for reading in homes and schools are haunted by spectres which shape specific understandings of reading, spectres that are very different in nature in both domains. I want to begin by sharing a recent reading experience of my own. Figure 2.1 is a screenshot taken inside the virtual world, *Second Life*. A virtual world is a computer-based simulated environment in which users may have avatars, which are virtual representations of themselves. In this screenshot, my avatar in *Second Life* can be seen floating through a sea of words in the '15 seconds of poetry – a game of words' virtual installation. In this installation, *Second Life* users can choose to let their avatars drift through a collection of poems that appear on the screen before them.

The experience of floating past and through poetry was enjoyable and was certainly a unique way to read poems. I was then able to share this reading experience through the chat messaging system in *Second Life* and reflect with others, in geographical locations very distant from mine, on the poems themselves. This experience offers an example of the way in which reading all types of texts, including poetry, is changing in an age of rapid technological change (Kress 2003). The aim of this chapter is to outline these developments and their impact upon young children and to examine how far the reading landscapes of home and school that they experience relate to each other. In the first part of the chapter, recent research relating to children's reading on screen in homes and communities is outlined. The chapter moves on to consider the outcomes of a material culture analysis of two early years classrooms and compares the findings to what we know about children's out-of-school reading experiences. The conclusion considers the implication of this analysis for reading curriculum and pedagogy. This focus is important, I argue, because of the need to ensure that the classrooms of the twenty-first century prepare children for the reading demands of the digital future.

Figure 2.1 Floating through poetry.

Reading on screen in homes and communities: the ghost of reading present

Reading in the twenty-first century is becoming an ever more diverse and screen-based process. The following vignette was developed for the QCA 'Taking English Forward' Consultation (available at: http://www.qca.org.uk/qca_5676.aspx), following an analysis of cumulative data from a number of studies I have conducted that have explored young children's use of media and new technologies in the home (e.g. Marsh 2003; Marsh *et al.* 2005). I use this composite picture to illustrate the way in which children in these studies move across a variety of texts in homes and communities.

> Yvette's family live on a publicly owned housing estate in a northern city. Yvette's father is employed in a local factory; her mother works as a part-time shop assistant. Yvette has an older sister, aged eight and an older brother, aged twelve. The family own two televisions (one with cable), one DVD player, one desktop computer, a PlayStation 2, two CD players and two mobile phones. The family connected to broadband about six months ago, as part of a package with the phone and television channels. When she was a very young baby, Yvette used to sit on her dad's lap as he played games on the PlayStation 2. She became interested in the games and, when she was two, began to sit next to her brother as he played on it, using a second set of controls which were not plugged in. Now she is three, Yvette can navigate a

vehicle on a track and can recognise some of the on-screen instructions, e.g. 'Wrong way'. She likes to look at the covers of the games and the computer magazines which feature her favourite games.

When Yvette was two, she began to use the desktop computer with her sister. In the first stages, Yvette simply banged the keys indiscriminately, but her sister introduced her to games on the website of a popular television channel and Yvette soon learned how to interact with them. Just before her third birthday, Yvette began to turn on the computer independently, use the mouse to find the Internet connection and then, once on the web browser, find her favourite Internet site by remembering where it was on the Favourites menu.

Yvette also uses the computer's word-processing package to input letters on the screen, and plays with a range of games which develop knowledge of letters, sounds and images. She has learned how to print out using the print icon on the tool bar and so prints off a range of texts and images for various purposes. Yvette has discovered the games on her brother's mobile phone and constantly pesters him to let her play some of them. She likes to tell her brother when he has a text message, as she recognises the bleep which means that a message has arrived. She asks him to read them to her, but he doesn't like to share all of them! Yvette also enjoys playing games on the interactive television set and can navigate some of those independently. She loves to watch television and especially likes to view her favourite DVDs repeatedly. Yvette can use the remote control for the television and DVD player in order to put her films on and rewind them when necessary. She can use the EPG (electronic programme guide) on the screen as she has memorised where her favourite channel is, which is perhaps easy for her as it is the same name she has to find on the Favourites menu on the computer!

Yvette owns lots of printed texts that relate to her favourite films and television programmes, such as books and comics, and is beginning to ask for some of the computer games which also link to these narratives. Yvette is looking forward to starting nursery next month as, on a recent visit, she saw a computer in the corner of the nursery.

At three, Yvette has already developed a range of skills, knowledge and under-standing in relation to media and new technologies, as this vignette illustrates. She has, from birth, been involved in a range of family social practices in which technology is an integral part, her family providing the sort of scaffolding which has enabled her to learn the meanings of these practices and the processes involved in them. Printed texts are still a central part of her life, but they integrate and overlap with other media in complex ways. The convergence of different kinds of media is requiring new sorts of skills, skills that Yvette has already begun to acquire through these emergent digital literacy practices.

Although Yvette is a fictional figure, this vignette is drawn from a range of data which indicates that there are many young children in England who have the experiences and skills that Yvette demonstrates and this is supported by further

Table 2.1 Reading in homes

Media	Texts read
Paper	Books, comics, magazines, notes, environmental print (leaflets, etc.)
Television screen	Words and symbols on remote control Electronic programming guide Text included in games Words, signs and symbols in programmes and advertisements
Computer screen	Alphabet on keyboard Text on websites Text instructions for programs Text in programs
Handheld computers	Text instructions for programs Text in programs
Mobile phones/ PDAs	Text on screen, e.g. text messages Signs and symbols on the keypad
Electronic games, e.g. LeapPad	Alphabet on keyboards and text on screen, e.g. alphabet games
Console games	Text instructions for programs Text in programs
Musical hardware, e.g. CD players/ radios/karaoke machines	Words and symbols on operating systems Words on screen with karaoke machines
GPS technologies, e.g. TomTom	Text on screen, e.g. navigation page
Other domestic electronic devices, e.g. microwave, washer	Words, signs and symbols on the devices

evidence from international studies (Rideout, Vandewater and Wartella 2003). Table 2.1 summarises the range of texts that young children encounter in their homes, drawn from data from a number of my own studies (Marsh 2003; Marsh *et al.* 2005). This correlates with the findings of other research that has examined children's use of new technologies in the home (Bearne *et al.* 2007; O'Hara 2008; Plowman, McPake and Stephens in press).

In summary, it can be seen that reading in homes involves a great deal of reading on screen. In addition, this reading is embedded in children's popular cultural interests and is central to children's identity construction and performance. What the cultural theorist Appadurai (1996) refers to as 'mediascapes' – flows of ideas, images, narratives and texts from the media that move across nations in an age of globalisation – permeate children's out-of-school reading. Whilst it would be unrealistic to expect that reading in homes and schools could ever be the same in nature, one would hope that there is sufficient overlap in order to ensure some continuity between the two domains. In the next section of the chapter, I move on to examine how far this is the case.

Material culture analysis

Evidence from a number of studies suggests that early years settings and schools offer a more limited repertoire of ICT practices than that experienced by children outside of school (Jewitt 2008; Marsh *et al.* 2005; O'Hara 2008; Rideout, Vandewater and Wartella 2003). It would seem, therefore, that opportunities for reading on screen are more restricted in classrooms than in homes. However, there is a need to look in further detail at the kinds of reading supported in both environments in order to determine how far the two domains support the same understandings of reading as a social practice. In the next section of this chapter, I outline a detailed material culture analysis of two classrooms in order to identify the ways in which the environments of home and school may differ. The classrooms were host to children aged four and five and the classes were known in the first school as the 'Foundation Stage 2' class and in the second school as the 'Reception' class. The two schools featured in this study were chosen because they served very different communities and because they had been graded 'good' by Ofsted in relation to their resources. They are not intended to be representational of schools generally, but may provide an indicative snapshot of what is considered to be sufficient resourcing for reading by Ofsted. They will be referred to as 'School A' and 'School B', both situated in a northern city in England. School A was a Church of England school that served an inner-city community diverse in terms of ethnicity. Sixty-four per cent of children spoke English as an additional language. The school had 255 pupils on roll, with 30 in the 'Foundation Stage 2' class. The second school, School B, was situated in a primarily white, working class, suburban community. The school had 446 pupils on roll, with 24 children in the 'Reception' class. There were no pupils at the school who spoke English as an additional language.

I undertook a material culture analysis of two classrooms in these schools. As Miller and Tilley suggest:

> The study of material culture may be most broadly defined as the investigation of the relationship between people and things irrespective of time and space. The perspective adopted may be global or local, concerned with the past or present, or the mediation between the two.
>
> (1996: 5)

Whilst of course objects themselves cannot tell us about how they are used in practice, an analysis of material culture can present us with some information about the resources on which people draw in the construction of culture. There have been numerous analyses of the content of books for children, for example, particularly in relation to gender representations (Baker and Freebody 1989; Gooden and Gooden 2001; Gupta and Lee Su Yin 1989). Children may not accept unquestioningly the discourses they are presented with in these reading resources (although there is some work which suggests that children do adopt stereotypical understandings of gender roles from a young age, such as Davies 1989), but nevertheless the analysis of these texts outside the context of the reading practice itself is important if we are to understand the nature of the lifeworlds being presented to children in classrooms.

The analysis reported in this chapter was undertaken when there were no children in the classrooms. I noted every artefact and text that was available to support the teaching of reading in both classrooms. I listed only artefacts and texts that were publicly available; I did not, for example, examine the content of teachers' desk drawers. I counted the number of books that were intended for children's use, both fiction and non-fiction. This included books accessible to children on bookshelves, and books that were stored by teachers for future use, such as on shelves that were not accessible to children. I then analysed each book in terms of its representations of technology. I noted when books featured types of technologies, such as televisions or computers and analysed in what context the technologies were featured, for example domestic use or use outside of the home, the gender of users and so on. In the following discussion, I outline how far both classrooms supported the construct of the reader as a competent user of multimedia, multimodal texts, given the extent to which this construct is sustained in the majority of homes. Here, I use the term 'digital literacy' to denote those literacy practices that are mediated by new technologies.

Reading in schools: the ghost of reading past

In both classrooms, the reading resources were primarily focused on traditional models of literacy. Table 2.2 outlines the reading resources available.

Whilst School A did have three computers in their Foundation Stage 2 classroom, the early years co-ordinator commented that they were underused because of the lack of confidence of practitioners in the setting at that time, a situation which she intended to address through training and support. The teacher in Setting B reported that the computer and the interactive whiteboard (which were linked) were primarily used by her for whole-class work, with the whiteboard being set at a height on the wall which made it comfortable for her to use it (and therefore not at a convenient height for children). This underutilisation of

Table 2.2 Reading resources available in classrooms

School A	School B
• Alphabet wall chart	• Alphabet display
• Magnetic and plastic letters	• Plastic letters
• High-frequency word cards	• Alphabet books and dictionaries (6% of
• Magnet boards	total books)
• Name cards	• Alphabet charts
• Alphabet books, dictionaries	• Name cards
(2% of total books)	• High frequency word cards
• 3 computers	• 1 computer
• 593 books (392 graded early	• 1 interactive whiteboard
reading/guided reading books)	• 382 books (148 graded early reading books)

technologies in early years classrooms has also been highlighted in a review of research in the area conducted for BECTA (Aubrey and Dahl 2008).

The focus in both classrooms in terms of reading resources was on the teaching and learning of phonics. Whilst it would not be sensible to suggest that this situation should have been otherwise, given the evidence outlined elsewhere in this volume that the systematic teaching of phonics is a necessary (but not sufficient) pre-requisite for reading, one would hope that phonics could be taught in a context which recognises the multimedia, multimodal nature of the contemporary communication landscape. This did not appear to be an inherent feature of these classrooms.

Following this assessment of the material provision for reading, I then went on to consider how far the books used in the classrooms represented the realities of children's daily lives in their homes, in which they would have been engaged in the use of a range of new technologies. I looked at all of the books in both classrooms. I identified whether any book contained references to or images of new technologies and if so, noted what the technologies were and what the context was in which they appeared. Table 2.3 indicates that only a minority of books contained references to technologies.

Television was the most frequent technology to be featured, followed by cameras, computers and music players. Whilst this sample was too small to develop any generalisations, there were gender patterns that emerged in that it was most often boys who were depicted using televisions and computers, whilst the technologies girls primarily used were telephones, music players and cameras. It was interesting to note that whilst new technologies were rather thin on the ground, the books did contain representations of outdated technologies. For example, both classrooms used a popular and frequently used alphabet dictionary for this age group, which under the letter 't' included an entry for a typewriter and under 'c', a cassette tape. It is unlikely that the generation taught in these classrooms had ever seen these technologies. Whilst this limited depiction of technologies in the lives of children might seem largely irrelevant to some to the teaching and learning of reading, I would concur with Baker and Freebody's comments on their assessment of the effect of the gender stereotypes they identified in early reading books:

> We view these contents as more than a reflection of young children's presumed natural interests. Rather, they provide the child-readers with a definition of what their identities, interests, attitudes and experiences are conventionally deemed to be.
>
> (Baker and Freebody 1989: 47)

Table 2.3 Analysis of books in relation to depiction of technologies

	School A	School B
Total number of books	593	382
Total number featuring ICT	9 (2%)	25 (7%)

In these two classrooms, therefore, there was little evidence that attention was being paid to the reading demands of the twenty-first century. How, then, had both schools been rated so positively by Ofsted on their provision of resources? One does not have to look very far to find evidence that this is typical of the assessment of environments for learning, a process which appears to be an anachronistic task in many cases. For example, a popular rating scale used in England to measure the quality of the teaching and learning environments of early years settings is the ECERS–E scale. In 2003, Sylva *et al.* extended the US-developed Early Childhood Environmental Rating Scale–Revised (ECERS–R) (Harms, Clifford and Cryer 1998) to develop the ECERS–E, which provides an assessment tool for measuring the quality of an early years environment in four areas – literacy, mathematics, science and environment and diversity. The literacy sub-scale contains the elements outlined in Table 2.4.

This sub-scale is being used increasingly by early years settings to self-assess their provision. It is unfortunate, therefore, that the sub-scale appears to be locked into a traditional model of literacy that is not appropriate for the digital age. There is a separate ICT sub-scale, but this addresses ICT requirements and not literacy. So, for example, nowhere in ECERS–E is there an opportunity for practitioners to consider the provision of digital texts that support literacy development in their setting. Therefore practitioners can rate themselves on their provision of books but not on the provision of on-screen reading resources, such as high quality e-books. Similarly, practitioners can use the scale to assess the quality of their interaction with children in relation to reading on paper, but not reading on screen. However, it is important for early years educators to reflect critically on how well they scaffold children's understanding of on-screen reading skills, knowledge and understanding, such as navigation, directionality and the effective integration of modes. Omitting these examples from the ECERS–E scale perpetuates a model of literacy that is increasingly at odds with literacy as it is practised outside of early years settings and schools.

This brief analysis highlights the extent of the distance between the construction of reading as a social practice in homes and early years settings. I have summarised elsewhere (Marsh in press) what I feel are the key differences between literacy as it is experienced by children in these two domains. These characteristics are reproduced in Table 2.5.

Table 2.4 Elements of the ECERS–E (literacy sub-scale) (Sylva *et al.* 2003)

- Letters and words (labels, names, environmental print);
- Books and literacy areas (accessibility, variety);
- Adults reading with children (support for developing concepts of print and comprehension);
- Sounds in words (rhymes, syllabification, phoneme–grapheme correspondence);
- Emergent writing/mark-making (provision of pencils, felt-tips, paper);
- Talking and listening.

Table 2.5 Literacy in homes and early years settings/schools

Literacy as experienced in many homes	Literacy as experienced in many early years settings and schools
• On-screen reading extensive • Multimodal • Non-linear reading pathways • Fluidity/crossing of boundaries • Multiple authorship/unknown authorship • Always linked to production • Embedded in communities of practice/affinity groups • Shaped by mediascapes • Child constituted as social reader • Reading integral part of identity construction/performance	• On-screen reading minimal • Focused on written word and image • Linear reading pathways • Limited to written page • Known, primarily single authorship • Analysis and production separate • Individualistic • Little reference to mediascapes • Child constituted as individual reader • Reading constructs school reader identities (successful or unsuccessful in relation to school practices)

Source: Marsh, J. (in press) 'New literacies, old identities: Young girls' experiences of digital literacy at home and school', in C. Jackson, C. Paechter and E. Renold (eds) *Girls and education 3–16: Continuing concerns, new agendas*. Buckingham: Open University Press. Reproduced with kind permission of Open University Press.

Some have argued that this type of analysis, which leads to the suggestion of a stark dichotomy between in- and out-of-school literacy practices, might be an over-simplification of what is a complex relationship and that indeed there may be some literacy practices that cross domains (e.g. Maybin 2007). However, I would suggest that the type of liminal practice referred to in such work is either due to the efforts of children or is encouraged by individual teachers who are keen to draw on learners' 'funds of knowledge' (Moll, Amanti, Neff, and Gonzalez 1992). A review of relevant literature, some of which is cited throughout this chapter, would suggest that it is relatively rare that this type of activity occurs because a school ethos in general welcomes open textual borders between home and school.

Conclusion: the ghost of reading future

The lack of attention paid to new technologies in some early years classrooms is a concern for all educationalists. The data outlined in this chapter contribute to a growing body of literature which indicates that, as we reach the end of the first decade in the twenty-first century, the textual landscapes of home and school still look very different for some young children (Levy 2009; O'Hara 2008; Plowman, McPake and Stephen in press). This has implications for children's understanding of reading and engagement in reading practices in both spaces. Such a textual dissonance may mean that children fail to transfer the knowledge and understanding gained in home on-screen reading practices to their school activities.

Indeed, there is evidence that on transfer to school, children begin to lose confidence in using the screen-based reading strategies they have developed in home use of technologies (Levy 2009).

There are obviously resource implications which mean that teachers may not readily have access to computers and other screen-based technologies in early years settings and classrooms. However, even when such resources are available, there is no guarantee that children will engage in the range of reading practices they encounter at home. This is not the case in all classes, of course. Increasingly, teachers are becoming more confident in their use of new technologies and certainly developments in national curricula in the UK and elsewhere have led to the inclusion of teaching objectives related to the analysis and construction of multimodal texts. In addition, there are a number of teachers forging ahead in the adoption of Web 2.0 applications in primary classrooms, some of whom I have written about previously (Marsh 2008a and b). One such teacher is Martin Waller, who teaches Year 2 children, aged six and seven, in a school in the north of England. He allows the children to use the social networking system (SNS) Twitter to log their thoughts and activities over the course of a school day. Twitter enables users to upload to the internet messages containing up to 140 characters, known as 'tweets'. Millions of people now use Twitter, including Barack Obama, who used it to communicate with supporters in his campaign for office, and Oprah Winfrey who, when she joined, created a surge of new members in her wake. Twitter enables users to log accounts of their activities over the course of a day if they so wish; some decry this seemingly trivial use of technology (Sandy and Gallagher 2009). However, others suggest that these apparently mundane exchanges have the effect of thickening offline social ties and that there are numerous examples of the way in which SNS can have a positive impact on the lives of individuals (Dowdall 2008; Ito *et al.* 2008).

In Figures 2.2 and 2.3, the 'tweets' of the six- and seven-year-olds in Martin's 'Orange class' can be seen.

Classroom Tweets

Mr W– Some of the class have been playing on 'Quiddich World Cup' (in Spain) on the Playstation 2
7.00am May 1st from web

Name Orange Class
Location United Kingdom
Bio We are a year 2 class in the United Kingdom

0 Following
7 Followers

UPDATES 22

Figure 2.2 A representation of Orange Class's Twitter Stream 1.

> **playing in spain**
> 6.43am May 1st from web
>
> **having golden time**
> 6.39am May 1st from web
>
> **we are swoping**
> 1.08am May 1st from web
>
> **Mr W – We will try to upload some pictures of our carnivorous plants!**
> 9.20am Apr 30th from web
>
> **we are about to go up to assembly after it is play time!**
> 2.14am Apr 30th from web
>
> **we have been doing comprehension work in literacy**
> 1.57am Apr 30th from web
>
> **In orange we have four divift tipse of venus fly traps. One of the fly tipse have tow bugs in it.**
> 1.18am Apr 29th from web
>
> **Now it is dinner time we are going to have lunch. I love it! CHIPS ARE GREAT!**
> 4.12am Apr 28th from web
>
> **Mrs k – I am looking forward to another busy week in orange class.**
> 1.09am Apr 28th from web

Figure 2.3 A representation of Orange Class's Twitter Stream 2.

What Martin is doing in allowing the children in his class to use this SNS is offering them opportunities for authentic engagement in literacy practices, practices which are now an integral part of the fabric of everyday life for many people. Reading in this context means not simply decoding, but involves taking part in the construction of social networks in which knowledge is co-constructed and distributed. Reading is, in this example, a social practice that extends beyond the walls of the classroom and enables children to engage in forums in which inter-generational literacy is commonplace. Adult users of Twitter respond to the Twitterstream of Orange Class by leaving positive messages, questions and suggestions. In this way, children engage with unknown interlocutors in the exchange of information and ideas, mirroring uses of technology that they will encounter in both leisure and employment in future years. Carrington and Marsh (2009), in a future-thinking report developed for the 'Beyond Current Horizons' initiative (http://www.beyondcurrenthorizons. org.uk/), suggest that communication in the decades ahead will involve a greater range of modes than are currently prevalent in text production and analysis and that as technologies continue to dissolve boundaries across space and time, the boundaries between formal and informal learning spaces, the 'real' and the 'virtual', will become even more fluid. In this context, the teaching and learning of literacy needs to ensure that children have opportunities to communicate beyond the classroom in order that they can develop the range of skills and understanding necessary for navigating this demanding terrain.

Martin Waller's practice offers an inspiring vision of what teaching and learning in the early years can be like if practitioners respond to the demands of the digital age. This is in contrast to the classrooms we encountered earlier in the chapter, in which the reading of multimedia, multimodal texts was limited. What the work of Martin and other teachers like him suggests is that in some innovative contexts, reading practices are very much located in present and future imaginaries. It is, surely, time to ensure that many other early years classrooms, places where many young children are locked into traditional models of literacy, are not persistently haunted by the ghost of reading past.

References

Appadurai, A. (1996) *Modernity at large: Cultural dimensions of globalization*, Minneapolis: University of Minnesota Press.

Aubrey, C. and Dahl, S. (2008) 'A review of the evidence on the use of ICT in the Early Years Foundation Stage', BECTA. Accessed May 2009 at: http://partners.becta. org.uk/upload-dir/downloads/page_documents/research/review_early_ years_foundation.pdf

Baker, C. and Freebody, P. (1989) *Children's first school books*, Oxford: Blackwell.

Bearne, E., Clark, C., Johnson, A., Manford, P., Mottram, M. and Wolstencroft, H. (2007) *Reading on screen*, Leicester: UKLA.

Carrington, V. and Marsh, J. (2009) 'Forms of literacy', Paper prepared for the Beyond Current Horizons Future Review Challenge area 'Knowledge, Creativity and Communication'. Accessed November 2009 at: http://www.beyondcurrenthorizons. org.uk/forms-of-literacy/

Davies, B. (1989) *Frogs and snails and feminist tales: Preschool children and gender*, Sydney: Allen & Unwin.

Dowdall, C. (2008) 'The texts of me and the texts of us: Improvisation and polished performance in social networking sites', in R. Willett, M. Robinson, and J. Marsh (eds), *Play, creativities and digital cultures*, New York: Routledge.

Gooden, A.M. and Gooden, M.A. (2001) 'Gender representation in notable children's picture books: 1995–1999', *Sex Roles: A Journal of Research*, 45, 1/2: 89–101.

Gupta, A.F. and Lee Su Yin, A. (1989) 'Gender representation in English textbooks used in Singapore primary schools', *Language and Education*, 4, 1: 29–50.

Harms, T., Clifford R. and Cryer, D. (1998) *Early childhood environment rating scale–Revised edition (ECERS–R)*, New York: Teachers College Press.

Ito, M., Horst, H.A., Bittanti, M., Boyd, D., Herr-Stephenson, B., Lange, P.G., Pascoe, C.J. and Robinson, L. (with Baumer, S., Cody, R., Mahendran, D., Martínez, K., Perkel, D., Sims, C. and Tripp, L.) (2008) *Living and learning with new media: Summary of findings from the Digital Youth Project*, The John D. and Catherine T. MacArthur Foundation Reports on Digital Media and Learning. Accessed May 2009 at: http://digitalyouth.ischool.berkeley.edu/report

Jewitt, C. (2008) 'Multimodality and literacy in school classrooms', *Review of Research in Education*, 32, 1: 241–267.

Kress, G. (2003) *Literacy in a new media age*, London: Routledge.

Levy, R. (2009) 'You have to understand words . . . but not read them': Young children becoming readers in a digital age', *Journal of Research in Reading*, 32, 1: 75–91.

Marsh, J. (2003) 'One-way traffic? Connections between literacy practices at home and in the nursery', *British Educational Research Journal*, 29, 3: 369–382.

Marsh, J. (2008a) 'Blogging as a critical literacy practice', in K. Cooper (ed.), *Critical literacy*, 171–183, Rotterdam: Sense Publishers.

Marsh, J. (2008b) 'Media literacy in the Early Years', in J. Marsh and E. Hallet (eds), *Desirable literacies: Approaches to language and literacy in the Early Years* (2nd edition), 205–222, London: Sage.

Marsh, J. (in press) 'New literacies, old identities: Young girls' experiences of digital literacy at home and school', in C. Jackson, C. Paechter and E. Renold (eds), *Girls and education 3–16: Continuing concerns, new agendas*, Buckingham: Open University Press.

Marsh, J., Brooks, G., Hughes, J., Ritchie, L. and Roberts, S. (2005) *Digital beginnings: Young children's use of popular culture, media and new technologies*, Sheffield: University of Sheffield. Accessed 11 June 2006 at: http://www.digitalbeginnings.shef.ac.uk/

Maybin, J. (2007) 'Literacy under and over the desk: Oppositions and heterogeneity', *Language and Education*, 21, 6: 515–530.

Miller, D. and Tilley, C. (1996) Editorial, *Journal of Material Culture*, 1, 1: 5–14.

Moll, L., Amanti, C., Neff, D. and Gonzalez, N. (1992) 'Funds of knowledge for teaching: Using a qualitative approach to connect homes and classrooms', *Theory into Practice*, 31: 132–141.

O'Hara, M. (2008) 'Young children, learning and ICT: A case study in the UK maintained sector', *Technology, Pedagogy and Education*, 17, 1: 29–40.

Plowman, L., McPake, J. and Stephen, C. (in press) 'The technologisation of childhood? Young children and technology in the home', *Children and Society*.

Rideout, V.J., Vandewater, E.A. and Wartella, E.A. (2003) *Zero to six: Electronic media in the lives of infants, toddlers and preschoolers*, Washington: Kaiser Foundation.

Sandy, M. and Gallagher, I. (2009) 'How boring: Celebrities sign up to Twitter to reveal the most mundane aspect of their lives', *Mail Online*, 3 January 2009. Accessed May 2009 at: http://www.dailymail.co.uk/tvshowbiz/article-1104726/How-boring-Celebrities-sign-Twitter-reveal-mundane-aspect-lives.html

Sylva, K., Siraj-Blatchford, E. and Taggart, B. (2003) *Assessing quality in the early years: Early Childhood Environment Rating Scale–Extension (ECERS–E) Four curricular subscales*, Stoke-on-Trent: Trentham Books.

Chapter 3

Reading places

Barbara Comber

Introduction

In this chapter I explore how a critical approach to reading pedagogy has evolved over time in South Australia. I start with a brief review of the ground-breaking work of Jennifer O'Brien in the early 1990s in which she adapted feminist post-structuralist approaches for early childhood classrooms. O'Brien showed that young children can and do take an analytical position with respect to reading when tasks are framed in ways that draw their attention to representation and relationships in texts. Then, drawing from a range of empirical research projects, I discuss how a semiotic approach to reading can be productive for thinking about critical and inclusive literacies. I touch briefly upon how and why we incorporated children's reading of environmental print into the *100 children go to school* project. I then outline the ways in which we have capitalised on the notion of *reading places* in several projects to work with primary school children and their teachers.

Completing a first degree in psychology, politics, history and English literature before becoming a secondary school English and History teacher, perhaps left me with a somewhat eclectic approach to reading. Alternatively it could be seen as an advantage to consider reading from multiple viewpoints. Whatever the case, as a young teacher with a passion for reading, I realised that I knew almost nothing about how people learned to read. Faced with significant numbers of students who either could not, or did not read, in my Year 8–10 English and History classes, I returned to study. At that time I learned about a psycholinguistic approach to reading (see Chapter 1 of this volume) which taught me to focus on helping students to make meaning and the value of analysing readers' miscues (Goodman 1973) and drawing on this knowledge I became what was known as a remedial reading teacher. However, despite the positive difference I was able to make with an improved understanding of the reading process there were children who still didn't read for a range of reasons. These included – amongst others – their prior school histories, gaps in pedagogies and their identities as young adolescents in a working-class regional community.

Over time, like many baby-boomer literacy teachers and teacher educators, I have continued to explore how these problems were produced, turning variously to socio-linguistic, socio-cultural, and anthropological studies, as well as sociological and other research on literacy. I am now convinced that we have much to learn from the different disciplines about how and why people read and how different people come to learn to read. I am also convinced that the teaching profession needs wide, not narrow views, of what constitutes reading in order to ensure that the most comprehensive, complex and sustaining approaches to reading pedagogy are developed (McNaughton 2002).

In this chapter I re-examine research over the past three decades which confirms the importance of a wide view of reading. I deliberately invoke the metaphorical ambiguity of the term 'reading places' to highlight that what we understand by reading alters our position in relation to texts and pedagogy and the way we approach our research. In exploring a post-structuralist and semiotic approach to reading I do not mean to discount the importance of other dimensions of reading practice, but to give space to theories perhaps less considered in relation to early reading pedagogies and reading development.

In the late 1980s a number of critical questions were raised about progressive whole language approaches to literacy teaching. The challenges to whole language emphasised the relationships between language and power and the fact that texts were neither innocent nor neutral, and nor was the talk about texts. Such critiques arose from a range of disciplines and theories, including critical language awareness, genre pedagogy, social justice, feminist post-structuralism, anti-racism and so on. I have discussed these critiques in more detail elsewhere (Comber 1994, 2003) but here I am more interested in exploring two related phenomena. First, I consider how an early childhood teacher working with feminist post-structuralist theory and informed by research on classroom discourse repositioned young readers through making conscious and deliberate changes to pedagogy. Second I explore how a critical semiotic approach to reading has led us to make particular decisions about our literacy research with teachers and students. Playing with the metaphor 'reading places', I discuss why it is important to insist on a complex theory of reading pedagogy.

A critical approach to early reading pedagogy

Many models of reading assume that in the early years of schooling teachers should focus mainly on cracking the code, making meaning and enjoying literature. Until relatively recently little emphasis was given to why young children read, or how and whether they might analyse texts. This was seen as developmentally inappropriate. However in the 1990s a number of literacy researchers theorised that reading analytically is an integral part of the reading process, not a developmental step (for example see Luke & Freebody 1999). Rather than positioning young children as innocent learners who need to climb a hierarchical ladder of reading skill development before they can actually use or question texts, teachers and researchers have demonstrated children's capacities to engage with questions concerning language and power (Dyson 1997; Luke, Comber & O'Brien, 1996; Vasquez 2004).

Jennifer O'Brien worked as an early childhood teacher in South Australia during the period when critical literacy began to be taken seriously in terms of school literacy policy. Inspired by the work of feminist post-structuralist educators and the tools provided by critical discourse analysis (Janks 1993), O'Brien set about repositioning the young learners in her classroom to interrogate texts (O'Brien 1994, 2001a, 2001b; O'Brien & Comber 2000). Across several years in different schools she invented and honed a pedagogy based around questions, tasks and texts that both altered the way in which she and the children talked about texts in their daily practices and the way she set up specific curriculum units to do particular work. For instance, even a familiar literacy event such as hearing a child read might sound just a little different in O'Brien's classroom. Her questions and prompts about the picture book *Play it Again Sam* (Duder 1987) indicate how the learner reader is positioned not simply as a decoder, who can display an oral reading, but as a reader with preferences and observations to make.

- Now would you tell me why you picked that book.
- Now can you tell me how much this is like real life. And how much might it be fantasy?
- And the person who has written this book is Tessa Duder and what has she made the piano say?
- OK. Keep going, I can see why you like this book.

Amongst the usual questions about whether the text make sense, invitations to predict and checks about whether the student can decode the text, are questions such as those above that begin to ask for commentary and analysis. The learner reader is asked to notice an author's decisions, to consider whether the book is like real life. The text is not simply taken for granted as a basal reader, a book to be performed aloud for the teacher's monitoring, but as a text in its own right and one which may appeal to a particular kind of young reader with a taste for humour and fantasy.

O'Brien also altered the pattern of classroom talk in another common literacy event – sharing a story with the whole class. Children were invited to make observations as O'Brien read rather than waiting for her to ask questions and for them to provide correct answers. In this way she sought to change the usual IRE patterns which typically restrict children to question-answering roles and also to guessing the teacher's preferred reading (Baker & Freebody 1989). This meant that children were encouraged to make their own meanings, not to simply repeat those of the teacher. As well as this shift in the participation routines, O'Brien also re-framed the activity structures, invitations and questions she did make, to encourage children to:

- work in groups to make predictions based on the title, the front cover and similar texts they may have come across;
- remember and reconsider previous readings, episodes and interpretations;
- critically review representations of particular characters;
- use prior cultural knowledge to predict story-lines and characterisation;
- use their expert knowledge of popular culture to 'read ahead' of the teacher.

These re-positionings – of who could say what and when about the story being read and the kinds of comments that were called for – are a long way from asking children to select their favourite page or even what they think is likely to happen next. O'Brien's questions position the students as knowledgeable text analysts rather than as "pre-competent" readers who must demonstrate their dependence on the teacher (Baker & Freebody 1993). Typical task sequences are exemplified below in relation to a reading of *A Lady in Smurfland* (Peyo undated), a book associated with the TV animation *The Smurfs* and brought in from home by a child. O'Brien asked the class to:

1 In groups make predictions on the basis of title, front cover, other books, or TV show.
2 Consider the questions: What will the female on the front cover do in this story? What will the writer tell you about this character? What won't you be told? What could be in the book that won't be included?
3 Report back from groups to the whole class.
4 Compare predictions and explain their rationales.

A transcript of a selected part of the whole group discussion (which followed the small group work detailed above) is provided below:

Tr:	Okay, someone said, J [male student 1] you said something about the love hearts. Would you say what you wanted to say about that, please?
Male S1:	The girl is mad because he falls in love with her.
Tr:	You think she, do you mean angry, she's angry because he falls in love. That's what she does. . . .
Female S1:	She doesn't want to.
Tr:	J, why do you say that?
Male S1:	Because I can see the love hearts around her.
Tr:	Because he's in love with her, it'll make her angry? Is that right?
Male S1:	Yes, because I can see her face.
Tr:	Ah, so you're going by the look on her face in that picture. . . . What do you think the writer won't tell you about her? K [female student 2].
Female S2:	Won't tell you how old she is.

Tr: Why do you think that? . . . [pause] A [female student 1], what do
                you think?
Female S1:   They won't tell you if she has a real name or not.
Tr: How do you mean a *real name*?
Female S1:   Because the name that she's going by in the story might not be her
                real name. 'Smurfette', it might not be her real name.

In this small segment of a lengthy shared reading of this text, we see the teacher
assisting children to articulate what they think is going on and what their
predictions and readings are based upon. After framing up their reading to ensure
an analytical position, O'Brien maintains her stance as a listener (though extremely
active), ready to be informed by the children's insights based on their wider reading
of such texts. I will not pursue it now, but this discussion went on to deal with
questions of why there is only one female character in every Smurf adventure and
why this character has no real name and can simply be called "Smurfette". My
intention here is to indicate that because the teacher takes a consistently critical
perspective on reading, classroom literacy events are so inflected. Critical readings
arose in the context of everyday literacy lessons.

In addition, O'Brien planned specific curriculum units to 'teach' specific
repertoires of text analysis and critical reading positions. Before I leave her work
I want to give a sense of key steps in her design of a critical literacy curriculum by
focusing on just one unit. Over several years with two different groups of children
O'Brien focused on Mother's Day as a cultural and consumer event. Her starting
point on the first occasion was to have children collect the junk mail that came
into their homes for several weeks prior to Mother's Day. They then pooled their
corpus of texts and began reading across them, asking questions such as: What
presents do you expect to find? What don't you expect to see? Who gets the most
out of Mother's Day? How are the catalogue mothers like/not like real mothers?
O'Brien helped the children take a research perspective and treated these texts as
data. They were able to cut up the material and re-assemble it to show the patterns
they found about the representations of mothers. Not surprisingly they found a
preponderance of young, 'wealthy-looking', beautiful, white 'mothers' often in
dressing gowns and the like. The children were invited to make new catalogues
for Mother's Day, 'full of fun things' to disrupt the dominant sexual and domestic
images of women and mothers. The following year O'Brien took this work further
and involved the community from the start about the whole cultural event of
Mother's Day. In analysing this work, Allan Luke (Luke, Comber & O'Brien
1996: 38) summarised its key elements in the following way.

> Our approach to making community texts objects of study thus proceeds in
> four interconnected moves. Their sequence can vary, but we would argue that
> all are necessary.
>
> 1 Talk about the institutional conditions of production and interpretation;
> 2 Talk about the textual ideologies and discourses, silences and absences;

3 Discourse analysis of textual and linguistic techniques in relation to (1) and (2);
4 Strategic and tactical action with and/or against the text.

O'Brien's work was significant in paving the way for many other early childhood teachers to 'have a go' at developing critical conversations about texts with young children. She shifted the kinds of:

1 texts used in classrooms, to include community, everyday and popular texts (alongside authorised reading series, library books and informational text);
2 tasks set for young children, to include survey, analysis, review, redesign;
3 talk around texts, to include questions which interrogated decisions made by authors, artists and publishers and their possible effects on readers, and also to encourage student-generated observations about how texts work.

O'Brien's work tended to start with text analysis and then move to wider issues of social and cultural injustice. Her goal was to equip young children with a critical discourse for approaching any texts they came across. Her curriculum was designed in such a way that students needed to orchestrate all four resources for reading (Luke & Freebody 1999) in order to complete assignments. Sometimes this was accomplished by students working in pairs or groups as they pooled their collective understandings about reading. Importantly, O'Brien established that young children could and did operate as text analysts and that they were able to draw on cues from print, image, context and their experiences across texts, media and modalities to take a critical position with respect to texts of various kinds. Children were positioned as knowledgeable, as having opinions and preferences, and as observant analysts who brought insights to texts from their life experiences and previous readings and viewings. Learning to read in O'Brien's classroom did not mean behaving as though they were pre-competent; indeed, these children became articulate and perceptive about how they were often underestimated by adults (see also Vasquez 2004). Rather, it meant learning to take active positions in relation to texts.

Watching students in early childhood classrooms display these repertoires of critical reading practices had implications for the way we considered literacy development in later projects and influenced the way we designed our research. Here I briefly outline how a critical semiotic approach to reading played out in three different studies which we subsequently undertook.

Researching literacy from a critical semiotic perspective

In the remainder of this chapter I outline how our belief in a critical approach to early reading affected the way we thought about, designed and collected data in three different studies of literacy – in the *100 children go to school*, the *River literacies* and the *Urban renewal from the inside-out* projects.

The aim of the *100 children go to school* project (see Comber & Hill 2000) was to investigate the connections and disconnections in literacy development in the year prior to school and the first year of school. Starting with almost 140 students in five different places around Australia (from Aboriginal communities in the western desert, to rural communities in Victoria, to inner suburban multicultural schools in South Australia) we needed to begin with assessing what these children could do in terms of literacy the year before they started school and then to analyse their learning in the first year of school. As well as using standardised measures, we were aware that we would need to find ways of accessing the range of things these very different young people could do with texts of various kinds, given their locations and access to spoken and written language. We debated at length what would constitute a valid and inclusive range of literacy assessments.

Whilst we used a range of already available approaches, we also designed several new assessments which were based on children reading environmental print and reading an everyday text, namely a toy catalogue – the kind of junk mail typically distributed in suburban households. Our rationale was twofold: these kinds of texts were more likely to be part of most children's experience, and, such texts were motivational and their purposes reasonably self-evident. Drawing on Marie Clay's notions of concepts of print (Clay 1998) we developed a series of prompts using photos of environmental print – e.g. well-known service station logos, including BP and Shell; food and drink items on the supermarket shelf with well-known logos such as Doritos and Coca-Cola; and images of the McDonald's fast food restaurant and its famous arches. The angles of the photos of the images gradually removed aspects of contextual information so that we could see what kinds of cues these young children were using to recognise various texts. We also developed a similar series of activities which allowed young children to show us what they could read in the toy catalogue and how they were able to work out what they knew about letters, numerals and words.

In designing these early assessments, taking a critical semiotic approach to reading required us to use a variety of texts and allow different young people to have opportunities to demonstrate their approaches to making meaning with somewhat familiar materials. The idea of 'reading places' is relevant here in several respects. In planning an assessment regime which was inclusive we needed literally to think about where these students were coming from and the textual landscapes (Carrington 2005) they inhabited. What were the semiotics of their everyday lives and what kinds of textual encounters had they experienced? We sought to not automatically privilege school literacies. As well as the kind of texts we selected we needed to think about the nature of the invitations we were making to these four-year-olds. Would the task make sense? Would our questions and prompts have meaning for them? Was the assessment encounter likely to allow them to demonstrate the range of understandings and strategies around texts they had already assembled? We do not claim to have met all our goals in this project but interestingly a number of aspects of our assessment portfolio have since been developed and improved in future studies (Meiers & Khoo 2006).

The second project I wish to discuss briefly is the *River literacies* project which aimed to explore approaches to environmental communication in a wide bio-region of Australia – the Murray-Darling Basin (see Note on page 42). We were invited to embark on this collaborative project with the Primary English Teaching Association because we were known for our commitment to an expanded notion of literacy which incorporated a critical approach to pedagogy. The aims of the project were to:

- critically analyse the knowledges and pedagogies related to literacy and the environment that have been developed through the *Special forever* project;
- investigate how primary teachers design curriculum and pedagogies which engage students in developing critical knowledge about the environment and the skills for communicating this knowledge in multimedia and multimodal texts.

Given the project was designed to educate young people for environmentally sustainable futures we were somewhat surprised by our initial engagement with the participating teachers who took a more celebratory and aesthetic approach to children communicating about the local environment; indeed some of the teachers seemed reluctant to consider a critical multiliteracies approach to teaching environmental communication. We raised questions such as the following:

- To what extent do texts produced in schools have consequences?
  - Are they likely to be read or viewed? By whom?
  - Which texts are children proud of/want to show others/keep/re-read and review?
  - Are children able to consider their own texts as cultural artefacts with specific local effects?
- What about everyday and media texts in and about places and the environment?
  - How do everyday and media texts work?
  - Do children have the chance to analyse and produce texts like these?

We decided that in introducing the teachers to a critical multiliteracies approach to environmental communications we needed to explicitly think about where they were coming from as teachers and as citizens – as embodied subjects living and working in particular places. Once again the idea of 'reading places' was useful to us. We invited them to collect everyday texts and images and local newspapers from their own communities to bring to the next workshop. We then modelled a critical analysis of the semiotics of texts we had collected from our own places – our own neighbourhoods – and also from different towns along the River Murray. We asked them to consider questions about billboards and signage:

- Who is telling who to do what?
- Who is telling who about which places/topics/products?
- Who is telling who about what not to do?
- Which signs welcome?
- Which signs bar?
- In what ways are meanings shaped by contexts and readers' histories?

We then invited the teachers to interrogate the texts they had brought from their communities in the light of questions such as the following:

- How are different people inserted into place (on the river, on the farm) in texts?
- How are people presented in relation to each other and in relation to the environment/places?
- What stories are told about places (and people) in tourist brochures, on Council websites, TV news and soaps, in the national and local press?
- Do certain situations, people, problems regularly appear?
- How and why might we question these?

Such questions helped the teachers problematise taken-for-granted texts of everyday life in their locales. For instance, the ways in which different ethnic groups were represented in terms of particular kinds of labour or as having particular kinds of problems, and the ways in which people were positioned as insiders and outsiders, newcomers and locals and the power relations associated with these different namings. Having taken a new look at the everyday texts from their own lives, locales and communities many teachers were then able to see the point of the deconstruction of texts as an important step in assisting young people to design and construct texts in various media. As teacher educators we began to realise just how integrally related were teachers' own places identities and their work in teaching environmental communication (Kerkham & Comber 2007). Place cannot be discounted.

The third instance in which we took a critical semiotic approach was in the context of the *Urban renewal from the inside-out* project. Here we were explicitly interested in the discourses of place in the context of urban redevelopment. We had a long-term collaboration with educators in a school in the western suburbs which was located in an area where public cheap rental housing was being demolished to be replaced with new residences built to attract the first home-buyer market. We won a small grant to work with academics and students from architecture, journalism and education and the school community to negotiate, design and document the construction of a new garden between the preschool and the school. While the project is documented in detail elsewhere (Comber *et al.* 2006; Comber & Nixon 2008), here I simply want to point to the value for literacy teachers in considering the affordances of place as the object of study and to suggest that the idea of 'spatial literacies' could be generative in meaningfully integrating learning across the curriculum in primary schools.

As literacy educators interested in the relationship between visual and verbal texts and a multiliteracies approach to pedagogy (New London Group 2000), we were interested to observe how an experienced architect, Stephen Loo, developed a pedagogy for working with children to reconsider space and place. We observed how his questions and invitations to imagine brought children into the learning environment in new ways and how the construction and deconstruction of texts and objects in different media and modes opened up new opportunities for teachers and children to represent complex ideas. Playing with the metaphor of 'building stories', Loo's first move was to ask children to think about images of unusual buildings collected from around the world (PowerPoint slides displayed on a large screen) and to imagine who might use such buildings, who might 'belong there'. He introduced the children and the educators to the idea that buildings have meanings, that the ways they are designed is important to those meanings, and that people can make those meanings rather than be passive observers. Hence before children even began to think about their garden and what they would like to see in it, he began to help them – and us – to look at the built environment anew, as if it could have been built differently. He guided the children to take note of the designs of buildings on an excursion to the capital city and to research the way the new public parks in the area were being put together. What were the elements? What was the relationship between one part or feature of a park and another (e.g. wall, path, shade structure, water feature, etc.)? He and his colleagues and students ran a workshop in the architecture studio on the concept of fenestration and small groups of architecture students and school students worked on an assignment that required them to represent the placement of doors and windows in a hypothetical building.

There is not the space here to detail Loo's pedagogies of spatial literacy, nor what the classroom teachers did to extend it back into the school site. However I include it as an example here because it indicated to us that there is great potential in explicitly attending to the reading of places as children develop their literate repertoires. These primary school children were learning to represent three-dimensional spaces, to argue for designs, to imagine the ways in which particular spaces might be inhabited and used and to examine notions of belonging at the same time as they were learning to make meaning of a range of print and electronic texts. They were positioned as powerful analysts and designers of space and were involved in actually re-making a 'belonging place' within the school environment.

Conclusion

This chapter perhaps includes some unexpected material for readers concerned with early childhood literacy pedagogy. Why is it that I have made reference to studies of environmental communication and garden design? In drawing attention in a range of ways to the notion of 'reading places' I want to suggest that we need to look beyond the basal reader and the picture book to consider how young people are learning to read the world – textual landscapes, yes – but also how they are positioned with respect to the material world. In educating young people as readers we need to remember that we are simultaneously imbuing learner dispositions, their stances to the world and their place in it. Our work with young children and their teachers suggests that often we unnecessarily limit what children do and accomplish in and through schooling. Lots of time is wasted reading forgettable texts with little meaning or satisfaction. Yet young people could be inducted into worlds of learning in school where the deconstruction and construction of texts has actual consequences – social and material.

As literacy educators and researchers we may open our minds to young people's potential by looking beyond the field of literacy studies to other disciplines, for example to the new studies of childhood, environmental psychology, communication studies or learning theory more broadly. Such disciplines remind us to think about young people's agency and competence, their deep connections with places as part of their developing psyches, the social imperative to connect and the inbuilt disposition towards learning and making sense. It may be that our own vision has been somewhat tunnelled by the continuance of unproductive debates within the field of reading. We may need to think of reading as part of wider repertoires of learning and cultural interactions. The privileging of reading as the fundamental basic skill may have meant that we have forgotten to think about what it is for and what people might do as readers.

Note

River literacies is the plain language title for 'Literacy and the environment: A situated study of multi-mediated literacy, sustainability, local knowledges and educational change', an Australian Research Council (ARC) Linkage project (No. LP0455537) between academicresearchers at the University of South Australia and Charles Sturt University, and The Primary English Teaching Association (PETA), as the Industry Partner. Chief Investigators are Barbara Comber, Phil Cormack, Bill Green, Helen Nixon and Jo-Anne Reid. The research investigated the long-running PETA program *Special forever* which facilitates primary children's writing and art about the Murray-Darling Basin environment and publishes selected works annually in an anthology. The views expressed here are those of the author.

References

Baker, C. & Freebody, P. (1989) *Children's first school books: Introductions to the culture of literacy*, Oxford: Basil Blackwell.

Baker, C. & Freebody, P. (1993) 'The crediting of literate competence in classroom talk', *The Australian Journal of Language and Literacy*, 16, 4: 279–294.

Carrington, V. (2005) 'New textual landscapes, information, new childhood', in J. Marsh (ed.) *Popular culture: Media and digital literacies in early childhood*, London: Sage.

Clay, M. (1998) *By different paths to common outcomes*, York, Maine: Stenhouse Publishers.

Comber, B. (1994) 'Critical literacy: An introduction to Australian debates and perspectives', *Journal of Curriculum Studies*, 26, 6: 655–668.

Comber, B. (2003) 'Critical Literacy: What does it look like in the early years?' in N. Hall, J. Larson & J. Marsh (eds) *Handbook of research in early childhood literacy*, 355–368, London: Sage/Paul Chapman.

Comber, B. & Hill, S. (2000) 'Socio-economic disadvantage, literacy and social justice: Learning from longitudinal case study research', *The Australian Educational Researcher*, 27, 9: 79–98.

Comber, B., Nixon, H., Ashmore, L., Loo, S. & Cook, J. (2006) 'Urban renewal from the inside out: Spatial and critical literacies in a low socioeconomic school community', *Mind, Culture and Activity*, 13, 3: 228–246.

Comber, B. & Nixon, H. (2008) 'Spatial literacies, design texts and emergent pedagogies in purposeful literacy curriculum', *Pedagogies*, 3, 2: 221–240.

Duder, T. (1987) *Play it again Sam*, Auckland, New Zealand: Shortland Publications.

Dyson, A.H. (1997) *Writing superheroes: Contemporary childhood, popular culture, and classroom literacy*, New York & London: Teachers College Press.

Goodman, K. (1973) 'Miscues: Windows on the reading process', in F. Gollasch (ed.) *Language and literacy: The selected writings of Kenneth Goodman*, 93–102, Vol. I. Boston: Routledge & Kegan Paul.

Janks, H. (ed.) (1993) *Critical Language Awareness Series*, Johannesburg: Witwatersrand University Press and Hodder & Stoughton Educational.

Kerkham, L. & Comber, B. (2007) 'Literacy, places and identity: The complexity of teaching environmental communications', *Australian Journal of Language and Literacy*, 30, 2: 134–148.

Luke, A., Comber, B. & O'Brien, J. (1996) 'Critical literacies and cultural studies', in G. Bull & M. Anstey (eds) *The literacy lexicon*, Melbourne: Prentice–Hall.

Luke, A. & Freebody, P. (1999) 'Further notes on the four resources model', *Reading online*, http//:www.readingonline.org/research/lukefreebody.html (accessed 23 October 2009).

McNaughton, S. (2002) *Meeting of minds*, Wellington: Learning Media.

Meiers, M. & Khoo, S.T. (2006) 'Literacy in the first three years of school: A longitudinal investigation', *Australian Journal of Language and Literacy*, 29, 3: 252–267.

New London Group (2000) 'A pedagogy of multiliteracies designing social futures', in B. Cope & M. Kalantzis (eds) *Multiliteracies: Literacy learning and the design of social futures*, 9–37, Melbourne: Macmillan.

O'Brien, J. (1994) 'Show mum you love her: Taking a new look at junk mail', *Reading*, 28, 1: 43–46.

O'Brien, J. (2001a) 'Children reading critically: A local history', in B. Comber & A. Simpson (eds) *Negotiating critical literacies in classrooms*, Mahwah, New Jersey & London: Lawrence Erlbaum Associates.

O'Brien, J. (2001b) "I knew that already": How children's books limit inquiry', in S. Boran & B. Comber (eds) *Critiquing whole language and classroom inquiry*, Urbana, Illinois: Whole Language Umbrella and National Council of Teachers of English.

O'Brien, J. & Comber, B. (2000) 'Negotiating critical literacies with young children', in C. Barratt-Pugh & M. Rohl (eds) *Literacy learning in the early years*, Crows Nest, New South Wales: Allen & Unwin.

Vasquez, V.M. (2004) *Negotiating critical literacies with young children*, Mahwah, New Jersey & London: Lawrence Erlbaum Associates.

Chapter 4

Young bilingual learners

A socio-cultural perspective

Rose Drury

Introduction

This chapter presents examples of the literacy practices of young bilingual children taking place at home and at school – practices which are often invisible and excluded from studies of early literacy in the early years. My starting point is the belief in the remarkable skills of children living between and within different linguistic and cultural settings. Data from an ethnographic study of three four-year-old children as they begin school in three English nursery classes reveals ways in which young bilinguals take an active role and syncretise their home and school learning. Second, the crucial role of cultural and linguistic mediators (teacher, Bilingual Teaching Assistant, sibling or peer) in early language and literacy learning is explored in relation to a new interpretation of 'scaffolding', 'guided participation' or 'synergy'. Finally, the chapter suggests the need for further work and research which can lead to new insights about early bilingualism and a deeper understanding of supporting young children's language and literacy learning. The work overall provides insights into young bilingual children's use of first languages as well as English and explores issues of identity, diversity and agency.

I begin with a snapshot of four-year-old Samia during one session in her first term of nursery. This description indicates Samia's 'route' through time and space of the nursery setting in one session. There were choices to make, areas to move to, times when playing alone was acceptable and times when participation was required, and there were instructions to understand and carry out. Throughout her first term in nursery, Samia was developing her understanding of the procedural rules (Street & Street 1993) and expectations of this new social world. For example, she knew the routine at the start of the session in which children were expected to identify 'their' picture and place it on the 'planning board' to show what area or activity they wished to choose. She knew the different areas of the nursery and what they were used for. She knew that it was acceptable to play quietly on her own at certain times but that she would be expected to join in teacher-led group activities. Haste states that 'in acquiring these rules, the child learns the basis for interactions with others, and the shared cultural framework for making sense of the world' (1987: 163). During her first term at nursery, Samia had to learn a wide range of

Samia enters nursery

Samia enters nursery holding her mother's hand. She finds her 'giraffe' picture and places it on the 'planning board'. She has planned her 'work-time' in the art and craft area and she stands watching a nursery nurse organising a hand-printing activity at the painting table. The children are individually making hand-printed cards for Mother's Day. She takes a turn at the activity in silence, except for the correct one-word response to questions about the colour of the paint and the card ('What's that colour?' 'Yellow'). Samia then moves onto the carpet where children are playing with a wooden train set, solid shapes and small construction materials. She is silent while she plays on her own. After a few minutes, another child takes one of her shapes and she protests, 'No, mine, not yours. Look.' There is no response and she continues playing. There is talk going on around her, but it is not addressed to Samia. The nursery teacher walks past the carpet and Samia attracts her attention, 'Mrs Ashley, look.' The teacher walks away and it is 'tidy up time'. Samia then sits with the teacher in a group of seven children for 'small group time'. The focus for this session is the song 'heads, shoulders, knees and toes' and playing a game to teach the parts of the body. She joins in the refrain of the song 'knees and toes', listens, watches attentively and participates predominantly non-verbally during the game. Then the teacher directs the children, 'It's time to go out in the garden.' She finds Samia sitting on her own singing to herself 'knees and toes, knees and toes', before she goes out to play.

What does her nursery teacher understand about Samia's learning? This vignette presents a picture of Samia's visible learning in the nursery context. But what are the constraints for her as she begins formal schooling in a linguistic and cultural setting which is very different from her home? What can we learn about her invisible learning and how does she make her way through nursery?

rules and routines to do with how time and space were organised in the nursery and the behaviour expected. And at the end of her first term she had gone beyond the initial stage of insecurity in a new environment. She now had the confidence to attract the teacher's attention when necessary and to object when shapes she was playing with are taken by other children ('No, mine. Not yours.'). Nevertheless, her limited understanding of English has meant that her acculturation in the setting precipitated times of stress and difficulty. The process of adaptation involved a new shaping of her identity as Samia discovered and internalised what is acceptable in the socio-cultural environment. Willett points out that learners acquire more than linguistic rules through interactional routines: 'they also appropriate identities, social relations and ideologies' (1995: 477).

The nursery setting

The nursery Samia attended was situated in a separate building adjacent to the primary school. In the large open-plan room, the main areas of learning were set out as follows; art and craft area, construction area, imaginative play area, natural area, book corner, computer area and the outside garden area. Approximately 30 children came to the morning session of nursery which Samia attended for two and a half hours a day (9.00–11.30). Nearly half the children were bilingual and the majority of these spoke Pahari. The nursery teacher worked with two nursery nurses and a part-time bilingual classroom assistant. She knew the families whose children attended her class. The structure and routines of the nursery were particularly significant as it followed a High/Scope approach to the curriculum. This encouraged the children to 'plan' their activities when they first arrived, using a planning board. Children were to 'do' the activity during 'work time' and then to 'review' or 'recall' their learning with their 'key' adult in a small group. In addition to this central 'plan, do, review' routine for the nursery session, there were focused teacher-directed small group activities based on the High/Scope 'key experiences' which covered the six areas of Learning and Development set out in the Early Years Foundation Stage Guidance (DfES 2007). The session ended with all the children outside in the garden and then back for story and singing on the carpet.

Samia's nursery: Visible learning

Samia began school a term after her fourth birthday and had two terms at nursery. When she started nursery, the nursery teacher told her mother, 'If nobody helps her now, she will find it hard to adjust to school.' Samia was viewed by her teacher as bright, confident and strong-willed. In her Early Years Record of Achievement, she had recorded the following comments at the end of Samia's first term of nursery:

> 'Samia has settled quietly into Nursery. She uses the planning board to find activities and mostly works alone at painting, jigsaws or sometimes in the imaginative area or construction area.'
> 'Samia didn't speak today – she sometimes says one or two words.'

Samia's nursery teacher commented that at times she refused to speak and was strong-willed:

> 'She is bright enough to follow what is going on. She has a definite awkward streak and at times she doesn't do what you want her to do. She can follow activities during work time and engages in a range of activities. She likes puzzles and painting. She is settled, but not chatty, because she missed a term of nursery.'

Her nursery teacher also demonstrated an understanding of Samia's language development:

'Her mother tongue is strong therefore I would expect her English to come on well too.'

Her teacher hoped that she would socialise more with her peers, develop greater confidence in English and speak it more. She reported that the Bilingual Classroom Assistant worked with Samia in the nursery and supported home–school links. Her family were viewed as supportive and 'keen for Samia to get on.'

Bilingual children starting school are obliged to face the challenges of learning the language and culture they find in the nursery context. These circumstances are predetermined by early years policy, practice and training. A bilingual child's response to the requirement to adapt to the nursery setting involves the interplay of several individual factors inherent in the child with the ways in which early formal schooling is constructed and delivered in the setting. In this sense, the decisions taken by staff are only interpretations of an existing and given context which has been socially constructed. Just as the nursery staff have absorbed what is required by the approved nursery setting so they can implement it successfully, so the children also come to understand what is acceptable and required. For bilingual children with limited English in particular, processes on the interpersonal plane (Vygotsky 1978) are more than merely an extension of those established in their prior experience in the home. They require a whole new information set to become internalised, not merely what is expected by their particular nursery, but also what is passed on through the setting of wider social, cultural and historical forces which have determined the construction and delivery of early schooling.

A socio-cultural perspective

A socio-cultural approach to the literacy learning of bilingual children helps our understanding because it emphasises the inter-relatedness of the social, cultural and linguistic aspects of children's learning. This perspective also supports our understanding of bilingual children's language and learning development within their new social environment with different cultural rules and expectations. And it can take account of the individual child's social and cultural heritage and experience from the home. This view is consistent with Vygotsky's claim 'that in order to understand the individual, it is necessary to understand the social relations in which the individual exists' (Wertsch 1991: 25–26). This view of the primary significance of social experience for children's development and learning has a particular application for children entering an English-medium schooling setting in which they have yet to learn the language. Children learning a second or additional language are dispossessed of much of their home learning and use of their first language in the new context of the nursery setting. So the social processes and how these actually develop will be of crucial importance. We will see later in this chapter, for example, how Samia utilises the play opportunities in the home as part of the process of internalising the social rules that she was learning simultaneously in the nursery.

Bakhtin's theory of dialogism reinforces the idea that language is socio-culturally situated: in producing an utterance a speaker necessarily invokes a social language, 'and this social language shapes what the individual voice can say' (Wertsch 1991: 59). What an individual says is unique but it is constructed from social languages and this process involves a type of dialogicality which Bakhtin called 'ventriloquation':

> The word in language is half someone else's. It becomes 'one's own' only when the speaker populates it with his own intention, his own accent, when he appropriates the word, adapting it to his own semantic and expressive intention. Prior to this moment of appropriation . . . it exists in other people's mouths, in other people's concrete contexts, serving other people's intentions: it is from there that one must take the word, and make it one's own.
>
> (Bakhtin 1981: 293–294)

Bakhtin envisages a process whereby one voice speaks through another voice or voice-type in a social language (Wertsch 1991). This process is an aspect of language learning and language use, which both transmits social and cultural meanings and also enables individuals to convey personal meaning and intention that relates to their specific context. Wertsch *et al.* comment: 'From the perspective of how children come to be socialised such that they can function successfully in particular socio-cultural settings, then, the issue is one of learning how to ventriloquate through new social languages' (Wertsch *et al.* 1993: 345). Although Bakhtin had in mind speakers who share the same national or regional language, his view that language is specific to social context has important implications for children learning English as an additional language since their task is not about learning a language in the abstract but about how to construct a 'voice' which accommodates the context of situation.

The child mediating their own learning

The constructs of scaffolding, guided participation, and the potential for synergy between child and a mediator help us to explore different perspectives on the ways in which 'more capable others' support learning.

Scaffolding

Central to a socio-cultural perspective is the notion of young children as novices or apprentices learning alongside more knowledgeable others. These mediators may be a teacher, adult, sibling or peer, assisting children's participation in learning contexts within the frame of Vygotsky's 'zone of proximal development' (ZPD). Wood *et al.* (1976) used 'scaffolding' to refer to the process by which an adult assists a child to carry out a task, which would otherwise be beyond the child's capability. Wood (1998) offers an interesting explanation of the underlying reason for the necessity of scaffolding learning. Uncertainty is central to human ability, argues Wood, and in unfamiliar situations, there is a high level of uncertainty so the ability to learn is greatly reduced. Assisting the child by breaking down a complex task into more manageable steps enables uncertainty to be reduced and learning to be increased.

> Children, being novices of life in general, are potentially confronted with more uncertainty than the more mature, and, hence, their abilities to select, remember and plan are limited in proportion. Without help in organising their attention and activity, children may be overwhelmed by uncertainty.
>
> (Wood 1998: 165)

This may to varying degrees describe the experience of bilingual children entering nursery and it calls into question whether adequate 'scaffolding' is provided to enable them to overcome their 'uncertainty'.

Guided participation

For Rogoff, guided participation assists the child in appropriating changed understandings. But as Gregory (2001) points out, the term 'guided participation' implies 'an *unequal* relationship between participants in that learning is uni-directional from the older or more experienced person to the younger child' (2001: 303). Moreover, the terminology used by Rogoff does not highlight the part played by the more proficient teacher, adult, sibling or peer in engaging the child in the ZPD. In her study of siblings playing and working together, Gregory suggests that the reciprocity involved stimulates the development of both children. She extends the ways in which 'scaffolding' has generally been interpreted in her use of the notion of the 'synergy' which takes place between siblings: '. . . we refer to the interaction between the children as a *synergy*, a unique reciprocity whereby siblings act as adjutants in each other's learning, i.e. older children 'teach' younger siblings and at the same time develop their own learning' (2001: 309). Indeed, she suggests that it is, in Vygotskyian terms, a mediational means for transforming social engagement on an interpersonal plane into knowledge internalised on an intrapersonal plane. Drawing on Cole's (1985) understanding of the process of 'internalisation', she argues that 'synergy is the key mediator through which knowledge . . . is internalised' (2001: 311).

Using the notion of synergy emphasises Gregory's interest in how learning involves processes of coming together both within and between people. She views the process of blending different cultural, linguistic and literacy experiences as a form of syncretism which arises from the synergy produced by the child's engagement with mediators and which ultimately influences the shaping of identity. Thus, in describing the literacy experience of Bangladeshi women, she and Williams comment:

> When Ros explains how her Bengali classes enriched her knowledge about literacy in the English school, she highlights the syncretism of different literacies and different ways of becoming literate in all the women's lives. Reading fairy-tales, comics and reading schemes in English opens new worlds which blend with and transform the traditional worlds of the Bengali and Qur'anic classes and vice versa. But literacy only symbolises a wider syncretism between languages and identities taking place in the women's lives.
>
> (Gregory and Williams 2000: 140)

Gregory also points to the importance of understanding the role of the mediator (2000: 11) from a socio-cultural perspective. The mediator provides the means for 'scaffolding' learning (in Bruner's terms), or engages in 'guided participation' which enables appropriation of new understanding (in Rogoff's terms), or contributes to the synergy which assists the syncretism that leads to new knowledge (in Gregory's terms). For Gregory, the mediator is not just the teacher but may equally be a sibling, a peer or another adult. The mediator assists the child not only to take on new learning but more particularly to take on a new culture and language alongside the existing one. The role of the mediator is likely to be highly influential in most contexts, but nowhere more so than in the case of a bilingual classroom assistant. For bilingual children entering the nursery the presence of such a 'mediator' of language, culture and learning may be crucial to how a child is enabled to 'appropriate' all that is expected in the new setting.

Taking the highly constrained situation of a beginner bilingual child entering the nursery as a starting point, the construct of agency is illuminated by the ways in which the children make their own choices and exercise some control. As Pollard (2000: 127) states:

> the child must make sense of new experiences, and in so doing will also contribute to the experiences of others. It is only when the socially created 'planned intervention' of curriculum and schooling is introduced that the child is repositioned as 'pupil' and becomes viewed, in terms of the education system as deficient. We may conclude that children have their own integrity and agency. . . .

This has resonances for young bilingual children starting school whose starting points may be viewed as deficit because, unless their teachers have a language and cultural match, the literacy learning that is taking place will be far less visible than for English-speaking children. The following study provides the basis for a consideration of Samia's agency in this chapter.

Using ethnographic approaches, I studied three Pahari-speaking girls in three different multi-ethnic nursery classes in Watford, near London, over the period of one school year. The children were randomly selected in consultation with bilingual outreach assistants who work in the homes of the focus families, the

Table 4.1 Methodological approach

Child	Mother tongue	Family position	Nursery	Age starting nursery class	Community language	Recordings in nursery	Recordings at home	Interviews
Nazma	Pahari	Youngest of 6 Grandmother lives at home	Nursery A; Watford	3:6 at April 1996 4 terms in nursery	no	15 hrs total	6 hrs total	2 with teacher 2 with mother
Maria	Pahari	Eldest of 2 Grandparents (4), cousins, aunts, uncles live at home	Nursery B; Watford	4:0 at September 1996 3 terms in nursery	no	15 hrs total	6 hrs total	2 with teacher 2 with mother
Samia	Pahari	Middle child of 3 Grandmother lives at home	Nursery C; Watford	4:4 at January 1997 2 terms in nursery	Attends local Qur'anic/ Urdu class	15 hrs total	6 hrs total	2 with teacher 2 with mother

nursery staff and the children's parents. The largest minority ethnic group in the community originated from Azad Kashmir in north-east Pakistan and the mother tongue spoken by the majority of these families at home was Pahari, a Punjabi dialect. The nursery staff in the schools were monolingual English speakers who did not share the first languages of their bilingual pupils.

My data came from three sources. First, audio-recordings were made of the three children using radio-transmitter microphones in the home and nursery contexts. I recorded the two-and-a-half-hour nursery session six times; first when the child started nursery and subsequently once every half term until she entered the Reception class for four- to five-year-olds. I conducted six tapings of between 30 minutes and one hour in each home. In both settings 'naturally occurring' interactions were recorded, when the children were engaged in normal activities. The tapes are transcribed by working with a bilingual informant who was a native speaker of Pahari and a respected member of the community. Second, observations of the children in the nursery and at home were carried out while the audio recordings were being made. Third, I conducted two interviews each with the nursery teacher and the child's parents in addition to informal conversations. This chapter reports selected aspects of the study: the interviews with the children's nursery teachers, interviews with the mothers of the children and the transcribed tapes.

The data I present in this chapter demonstrates how Samia responds as an individual to the nursery situation, finds her own way through early schooling and makes choices. How she does so reveals the particular strategy she discovers and adopts in order to deal with the situation in which she finds herself. Samia responds to the flow of experience with all the resources at her disposal, displayed through her individual personal characteristics and personality. The strategies highlight her ability to manage the situation and set about learning the language and culture of early schooling. When we follow this interpretation, we can see aspects of Samia's learning which remain invisible to her teachers and which demonstrate her individuality and developing control over her learning.

Samia at home: invisible learning

Samia's family originated from Azad Kashmir, which borders north-east Pakistan. She was the middle child of three. She lived with her mother, grandmother and brothers. Her father, a Pahari speaker and a shopkeeper, also shared their home, although he now had a new family in Watford. Samia's father came to Watford when he was nine years old. He had some schooling in England and some in Pakistan, but no qualifications. He spoke, read and wrote in Urdu and English. Samia's mother had attended primary school in Pakistan, but never completed her schooling. She married in Azad Kashmir and came to Watford with her husband. She spoke Pahari, but very little English or Urdu. Samia's older brother was also born in Azad Kashmir, but Samia and her younger brother, Sadaqat, were both born in Watford.

Samia spoke Pahari to her younger brother, mother and grandmother, while her elder brother spoke some English at home. The recognised community language is Urdu and Samia had started to attend Qur'anic classes after school, where she would learn the Arabic required for reading and reciting the holy text. Her mother was keen to teach her Pahari at home, and tried to nurture the home culture. Samia had no formal pre-school experience in the UK but she had taken a six-month holiday in Azad Kashmir with her grandmother before she started school. Her grandmother reported that what Samia had valued most was the space there for free play. Samia had followed the animals around and played intensively with her cousins and other children in the village. Back in England, she had frequently said 'Let's go back.'

Samia's mother and grandmother, both present at the interview, were particularly vocal and clear in their views on the education of children and the differing roles of schools and families. Her mother's view was that there is a clear separation between the roles of the home and the school. Only the home can teach the mother tongue, and that is what it should do. It was only when children went to school that they needed to learn English – to teach was the school's role. The home could provide the cultural – and, by implication, linguistic – nurturing the child needs in her early years. That this excluded English need not be a problem, as English could easily be acquired later. Samia's mother believed she was doing well at school, 'Samia is an intelligent girl. She is learning very quickly. I hope she will do well, providing she gets enough help, because I cannot help her.'

Samia's grandmother's shared these views. She saw herself as an uneducated woman, yet she fully understood the importance of education. She tried to help her grandchildren by staying with them and supporting them morally. She and her daughter missed Pakistan, but appreciated the advantages of a UK education. Nonetheless, she saw how the children missed the open spaces and freedom that Azad Kashmir was able to offer.

The data presented in this chapter shows how a young bilingual child responds to her ongoing experience, both at home and in nursery. I argue that Samia exercised considerable control over her learning in the nursery and home context, both with children and with adults. This was identified in the strategies she uses in response to her situation as a key player in her own learning. Although she spent long periods of time on her own, making minimal engagement within the setting and not speaking as she acclimatised to her new environment, she responded to her situations as a key player and agent of her own learning. Starting nursery as a bilingual learner was a difficult and crucial time for Samia. This was highlighted in the spoken evidence collected in the data – in both English and mother tongue – which indicated her response to the early days in nursery and added up to a revealing picture of her experience.

Two examples of data from my study reveal ways in which synergy and scaffolding begin from a very early age amongst bilingual children in spite of a very limited command of the new or 'school' language – they both take place in Samia's home. In this transcript all talk in Pahari is translated into English and presented in italics, and the spoken English is in roman script.

Samia and Sadaqat play school

[Samia: 4 years old, Sadaqat: 2 years old]

1	Samia:	*Sadaqat, stand up*
		we're not having group time now
		group time
		you can play, Sadaqat
5		*shall we play something?*
		you want to do painting?
		[noise from Sadaqat]
		O.K. get your water
		let's get a water
10		let's get a water
		let's get a paper
		baby didn't cry
		hurry up [whispering]
		you want paper
15		and put in the painting
		do that and what are you choose colour
		black
	Sadaqat:	back
20	Samia:	no, there's a black
		did you finish it?
		painting
		you make it
		Sadaqat, do it with this finger
25		*do it like this, do it like that*
		wash
		which colour *are you going to choose*
		next thing
		don't do it, Sadaqat
30		*orange satsuma*
		I'm doing it satsuma colour
		[clapping, knocking]
		you are having your . . .
		[crying]
35		like it?
	Sadaqat	*mummy* [calling to mother]

(Drury 2007: 27–28)

Samia's home play with her brother reveals the extent to which she has absorbed the everyday language used by adults in the nursery. This displays her remarkable but invisible capacity to use linguistic skills within a role play, a situation entirely managed on her own terms, satisfying her need to practise or rehearse English, and in effect vicariously taking on and completing the routine school tasks. This contrasts sharply with the language she learns through social interaction with her peers at nursery. It also shows how successfully she has absorbed school routines and, for her, the demanding expectations in the nursery setting. Cultural learning of this kind is very important for her confidence in learning what to do and how to behave, and is closely interwoven with her language learning.

Her use of the language of adults in the nursery in her role play illustrates how her language learning and her developing socio-cultural positioning is related to taking on the 'voice' of influential others. In lines 18–20 in this excerpt, we see the synergy or unique reciprocity whereby an older child 'teaches' her younger sibling while at the same time developing her own learning. This is also demonstrated by how she code-switches to include Sadaqat in her role play (see lines 4–6 for example). Throughout her school game with her younger brother Samia is scaffolding her own learning and demonstrating an understanding of early schooling that has previously been invisible to educators of young bilingual children.

A key insight into young bilingual children's learning is shown in her play at home with a younger brother; it reveals not only how school learning flows over into play at home but also how Samia takes control of her learning herself. She becomes the key player in the learning process. She 'manages' the play with her brother in such a way so as to engage him and to reinforce her language learning in addition to learning acquired through the nursery curriculum. Again, much of the developmental process which Samia demonstrates is not visible to the nursery teacher. The skills she shows in play with her brother, her use of English, her facility with code-switching, her ability to engage, sustain and direct her younger brother's involvement, her manipulation of 'school knowledge' (for example, colours), are manifest, but their invisibility means they are not known to, or understood by, her nursery teacher.

Nursery rhymes

A further powerful cultural script in Samia's literacy learning at home is her use of nursery rhymes and songs. The following transcript occurred during the first taping session in her home. Samia has a conversation with her mother, grandmother and little brother, Sadaqat. In this transcript Pahari is shown in italics and English in roman script:

Nursery rhymes transcript during the first term

1	Samia	Baa baa black sheep
		Yes sir yes

		One two
		Twinkle twinkle
5		Baa baa
		Twinkle twinkle
		Twinkle twinkle
		I got pencils [to Grandmother]
		Twinkle twinkle
10	Grandmother:	*don't touch that*
	Samia	*I'm not going to talk*
		Mum, Sadaqat's got a sweet
		Head shoulders knees and toes [Sadaqat imitates her]
		No, head shoulders knees and toes
15		Eyes and nose and nose and eyes and mouth
		Touch your forehead, touch your hair, shoulder
		Knees and toes

(Drury 2007: 82)

Here Samia is singing, practising her English through the familiar nursery songs. She again involves her brother Sadaqat in her play. There are echoes of her teacher when she corrects his version of 'Heads shoulders knees and toes' (line 14). She skilfully code-switches from her nursery songs in English, to Pahari when she speaks to her Grandmother or gives her brother important instructions.

The importance of learning English nursery rhymes and songs from nursery is highlighted through the data. However, it is the skills of Samia in her use of English, her facility with code-switching, her ability to engage and sustain her younger brother's involvement and her manipulation of school literacy knowledge which are remarkable – and invisible to the nursery teacher.

Concluding thoughts

In this chapter I have presented a detailed account of Samia's literacy learning at home and at school during her first term at nursery. I have highlighted the constraints for young bilingual children as they set about the task of learning in a new culture and language. Her visible learning is articulated by the nursery teacher and described in the vignette at the beginning of the chapter. Thus it is for the bilingual learner to make the necessary adaptation to the language and culture of the nursery. A socio-cultural framework is used to understand Samia's invisible learning and exemplified through two transcripts of Samia and her little brother playing school at home and practising and rehearsing English nursery rhymes. Through this lens, Samia is viewed as taking control of her learning. The key player in the learning process is the child herself.

References

Bakhtin, M.M. (1981) *The dialogic imagination: Four essays by M. M. Bakhtin* (M. Holquist, ed.; C. Emerson and M. Holquist, trans.), Austin, TX: University of Texas Press.

Cole, M. (1985) 'The zone of proximal development where culture and cognition create each other', in J.V. Wertsch (ed.) *Culture, communication and cognition: Vygotskian perspectives*, Cambridge: Cambridge University Press.

Department for Education and Skills (2007) *Practice guidance for the Early Years Foundation Stage*, Nottingham: DfES.

Drury, R. (2007) *Young Bilingual Learners at home and at school: Researching multilingual voices*, Stoke-on-Trent: Trentham.

Gregory, E. and Williams, A. (2000) *City literacies: Learning to read across generations and cultures*, London: Routledge.

Gregory, E. (2001) 'Sisters and brothers as language and literacy teachers: Synergy between siblings playing and working together', *Journal of Early Childhood Literacy*, 1, 3: 301–322.

Haste, H. (1987) 'Growing into rules', in J. Bruner, and H. Haste (eds) *Making sense: The child's construction of the world*, London: Methuen.

Pollard, A. (2000) 'Child agency and primary schooling', in M. Boushel, M. Fawcett and J. Selwyn (eds) *Focus on early childhood principles and realities*, Oxford: Blackwell Science.

Street, C. and Street, B. (1993) 'The schooling of literacy', in P. Murphy, M. Selinger, J. Bourne, and M. Briggs (eds) *Subject learning in the primary curriculum: Issues in English, science and mathematics*, London & New York: Routledge in association with the OU.

Vygotsky, L.S. (1978) *Mind in society: The development of higher psychological processes* (M. Cole, V. John-Steiner, S. Scribner, and E. Souberman, eds), Cambridge, MA: Harvard University Press.

Wertsch, J.V. (1991) *Voices of the mind: A sociocultural approach to mediated action*, Hemel Hempstead: Harvester Wheatsheaf.

Wertsch, J.V., Tulviste, P. and Hagstrom, F. (1993) 'A sociocultural approach to agency', in E. Forman, N. Mimick and C. Addison Stone (eds) *Contexts for learning sociocultural dynamics in children's development*, Oxford: Oxford University Press.

Willett, J. (1995) 'Becoming first graders in an L2 classroom: An ethnographic study of L2 socialisation', *TESOL Quarterly*, 29: 473–503.

Wood, D., Bruner, J.S. and Ross, G. (1976) 'The role of tutoring in problem solving', *Journal of Child Psychology and Psychiatry*, 17: 89–100.

Wood, D. (1998) 'Aspects of teaching and learning', in M. Woodhead, D. Faulkner and K. Littleton (eds) *Cultural worlds of early childhood*, London: Routledge.

Part II

Comprehension

Chapter 5

Comprehension as a social act

Texts, contexts and readers

Vivienne Smith

This chapter attempts to position comprehension as a complex social act – a habit of situated mind. Drawing on insights into reading from literary theory and critical literacy it makes two claims. First, it claims that text is never a neutral depository of extractable meaning. It is always a product of the circumstance of writing and of the intentions and ideologies of the writer. Second, it claims that meaning is never 'fixed' in text, but emerges temporarily in readers' minds as a result of the interactions they make with that text, and that those interactions are influenced and moderated, not just by the experiences and interests of the individual, but also by the social, intellectual and cultural communities to which those readers belong.

The chapter argues that positioning comprehension in this way presents a significant challenge to much current practice in the teaching and testing of reading. It explores the implications of this challenge and asks: What might be the consequences of this for teaching?

Literacy and social practice

The understanding that literacy is a social practice was established by the mid-1980s and is now widely accepted. When Heath (1983) demonstrated that different communities in the same geographical area had different 'ways with words' and Scribner and Cole (1978) showed how the Vai people used different literacies for quite different purposes in their daily lives, it was easy to agree with Street (1984) that literacy was ideological, rather than autonomous: that it stemmed from the practices and purposes of the people who used it, and had no universal, automatic application or benefits to its users.

At roughly the same time, Vygotsky's work became available to the West (Cole *et al.* 1978). His understanding that language and language learning was a social phenomenon, and that the society in which learning took place was as important as the mind of the learner, was revolutionary. Like the work of Heath and Street, it repositioned literacy, placing its locus in the community of use, rather than in the head of the individual.

Together these ideas caused a major shift in thinking about literacy learning, especially in education. Whereas previously, literacy learning could be conceptualised as a set of relatively stable and neutral skills which, once taught and acquired, would set a person up for life, now, it needed to be seen as a complex social act, reliant on custom, purpose and expectation in the various shifting communities to which learners belonged. In schools this challenged thinking considerably. Some researchers followed Heath (1983) in asking 'How do we do reading and writing in this particular context?' (Weinberger 1996; Moss 2005) and explored the sometimes very different expectations of reading and writing at home and in school (Minns 1990; Marsh and Millard 2000). In attempts to make literacy teaching more effective, the importance of the classroom as a community of readers and writers was highlighted. Chambers (1985, 1993) showed how the physical and intellectual environment of the classroom could be manipulated in order to create communities where literacy can and does thrive, and more recently, there has been a steady increase in the understanding that collaborative writing (Cliff-Hodges 2002), group and paired reading (Calkins 2000), literature circles (Ellis *et al.* 2005) and other community activities can have lasting benefits both in the way that children see themselves as readers and writers and in their motivation and performance.

So persuasive are these ideas on the social nature of literacy learning that they have radically influenced thinking about literacy provision for children in the UK outside as well as within the school system. The Book Trust's *Bookstart* initiative – part funded by government – for example, provides free packs of books for babies, toddlers and three-year-olds and instructions for parents about what to do with them. The idea, clearly, is that children who interact with books at home during infancy learn practices that will ease them into reading at school. Another government-funded project, *Reading Champions*, encourages sporting heroes to talk to children about their own love of books. The hope is that the glamour of associated stardom will make young people who might otherwise be reluctant to read think that reading will make them cool. The social dynamic of aspiration is key to this idea: what makes it work is the possibility of gains in social status. The books themselves, and what children might get from these books is secondary to the argument. It is not what the reader reads that counts, but who that reading makes the reader become.

The aims of both *Bookstart* and *Reading Champions* are entirely laudable. Everybody who is interested in reading wants to see children read widely and read for pleasure and Stanovich's work on the 'Matthew Effect' (1986) provides the evidence that it is important that they do so. But there are some who feel that building a pedagogy for reading on the social dynamic alone is not enough. Meek (1988), for example, has argued that *texts* matter, that *what* one reads is as important in developing reading competence as *how much* one reads, because some texts offer better reading lessons than others. Others (for example, Smith 2008) worry that relying on the social dynamic alone for progress in reading leaves too much to chance. Teachers need to know which texts provide the lessons in reading that children especially need to learn. Perhaps because of concerns such as these, a cognitive model of reading, which continues to place the locus of reading in the individual's head rather than in society, has always prevailed in some quarters.

The cognitive approach

Phonics is an obvious example of a pocket of thinking about literacy that has been unaffected by the social practice tsunami. Its proponents would argue that phonics is a set of fixed, non-negotiable, cognitive skills that a reader must acquire in order to decode text. These are skills that must be explicitly and systematically taught, because relying on social models of reading, such as an apprenticeship approach (Smith 1978; Waterland 1988) is inefficient and ineffective. The basic supposition is that reading is essentially decoding, and that decoding is an individual, atomistic, cognitive function. Until and unless that function is in place, the argument goes, social practice is as nothing.

Reading comprehension is very often positioned alongside phonics as another example of a cognitive reading activity that bypasses the social. In this understanding, value is placed on the neutral and transferable skills that are thought to be necessary in uncovering meaning in text, for example: the ability to retrieve facts, to retell stories accurately or to make deductions from inferences provided. This emphasis on skills puts the locus of thinking about what comprehension is firmly in the head of the individual reader, rather than in the practices of making meaning that are prevalent in the communities in which he or she reads. Given the predominance of the socio-cultural model in so much of twenty-first century Western thinking about reading, the tenacity of these ideas in reading comprehension is strange.

There are however, reasons to explain it. One is the relative paucity of thinking about comprehension at all: it is the least researched area of the reading curriculum. Those who have studied it generally fit into one of two camps – the cognitive psychologists, or those with a pragmatic interest in how comprehension is already tackled in schools. Neither of these parties would naturally look towards a social practice model.

The cognitive psychologists, reasonably enough, have considered comprehension as a function of individual mind. In their overview of the research into the development of children's reading comprehension skills, Oakhill and Cain (2003) note the lack of any developmental model to describe how children might acquire these skills. In the absence of such a model, they outline a number of processes (e.g. the speed and efficiency of decoding; vocabulary development; syntactic development; learning to make inferences) which, in no particular order, and probably in parallel, enable children to comprehend what they read: that is, to achieve 'a representation of the state of affairs the text describes' (Oakhill and Cain 2003: 155). They write of children who are 'good comprehenders' and 'poor comprehenders', and by doing so firmly place comprehension as an attribute of the individual intelligence. In this view of comprehension, it is not the text or the context that makes the difference in how well a text is understood, but the ability of the reader to apply the necessary skills.

Those writing from an educational perspective have mostly followed the psychologists in seeing comprehension as a series of skills and strategies. Thus

Pressley (2001) can present the components of successful teaching that lead to 'an increase in comprehension skills', and while his ideas are measured, validated by research and make some concession to cultural perspectives on reading, those who apply those ideas are not always so careful. In their analysis of comprehension strategy instruction in American core reading programmes, Dewitz, Jones and Leahy (2009) find a confusing plethora of skills and strategies put forward for teachers to get their pupils to learn and practise. They find no differentiation between skills and strategies and little clear help for teachers in understanding how to teach, rather than test, the skills and strategies recommended. Dewitz, Jones and Leahy present the sort of muddle in thinking about comprehension that I suggest is common in the UK too, and is partly a result of the overuse of the cognitive approach in thinking about children's reading comprehension.

Why the cognitive approach is of limited use to teachers

There are a number of difficulties that arise when a cognitive approach to understanding comprehension is imported wholesale into reading pedagogy. Many of these problems are caused by the scientific paradigm that psychologists very often use to frame their work. In order to make a fair experiment in which cognitive functions can be isolated, they find it necessary to reduce the variables that might affect results. In practice this means three things: using artificial texts that isolate features that need to be tested, adopting a position on text that assumes it carries stable, retrievable meaning, and taking a view of readers that ignores their moods, motivation and histories. Social and cultural theorists find these texts and the assumptions unacceptable.

Texts first: Comprehension test passages have to be short, especially for inexperienced readers. There are two reasons for this. One is that a lengthy test would be daunting, and the other is that the longer a passage is, the more room there is for variety in interpretation. This, in a controlled test, is to be avoided. As well as being short, passages need to include the salient features or skills that are to be tested (for example, information to be retrieved; inferences to uncover). In most real texts, such features are embedded in rich contexts, and rarely occur in the quick succession that testers would prefer. Because of this, test passages need to be written specially. This in itself distances them from other texts that readers encounter: most texts are constructed because a writer has something to communicate, not to see what the reader can do. Added to this, and also to improve reliability, vocabulary is often restricted in these passages and sentences kept short. This might well make decoding simple and lessen syntactic complication, but often the result is passages of stilted, unnatural prose that ignores the rhythms and cadences of familiar language. Given that comprehension tests differ in structure, content and language from most other texts that children are likely to encounter, questions can be asked about the validity of their results. Do they show which children comprehend genuine texts in real life, or just those that can do comprehension tests?

Perhaps even more seriously, the understanding that text carries stable meaning that can be retrieved by any reader with competence has long been questioned. Rosenblatt (1978) showed how different readers take and make quite different meanings from the poems she presented them with. Even though the words of the poems she used remained constant, what readers did with those words to make them meaningful depended on the stance they took and the experiences and attitudes they brought with them to the text. Meaning, she explained, was in the transaction between the text and the reader, not the text alone. Iser (1980) took the idea further. His idea was that the words of texts set up points of reference for readers, like stars in constellations or dot-to-dot games for children. The reader's job, he explained was to join up the dots to make a meaningful pattern. To do this, the reader had to supply the thinking in between the dots. Without the reader's input the text would be as nothing. Fish (1980) developed the idea on to a social plane. He was interested in the similarities and differences in readers' readings of Milton's sonnets. His contribution was to suggest that readers belonged to 'communities of interpretation', which, because of similarities of outlook, resulted in similar understandings from otherwise diverse readers. What these (and other) reader response theorists show is that it is difficult to understand meaning in text as stable. If it depends on the reader, and what the reader brings to it, how can we be sure that the results of a comprehension test show cognitive function rather than general knowledge, or membership of the right hermeneutic circle?

Then there is the matter of differences in the readers themselves. As Catt (2009) makes clear, the background knowledge that readers bring with them to a text makes all the difference in how much or how little they understand. So-called 'good comprehenders' can struggle with a text outwith their experience, while 'poor comprehenders' presented with a difficult text on a subject they are know-ledgeable about will do well. Mood, attitude and expectation make a difference too. Readers are affected by how they feel about a text, the reason they are reading it and what they think they need to do with whatever it is they have read. *What* they understand and *how* they understand it will change according to purpose. It is one thing to browse through a gardening book dreaming of planting schemes; it is quite another to consult it in order to find out why a favourite shrub is dying. There are social considerations too. Readers who belong to book clubs will know that talking about a text is a delicate matter. There are decisions to be made about how much or how little of one's thinking can safely be revealed, and what other people will think if a certain idea or position is expressed. In classrooms, where teachers are powerful and status matters enormously, admitting or not admitting to understanding can be even more risky. Trying to measure comprehension without taking into account these social and emotional factors seems at best limited and at worst, unhelpful.

Perhaps most worrying of all is an unintended consequence of the cognitive approach, rather than the approach itself. As Cain and Oakhill (2003) note, as yet, no model of reading comprehension development in children exists. This means that although it is possible to describe *what* children must have done to make a text meaningful, it is hard to say *how* they learned to do it. It is not surprising therefore, that many teachers find teaching comprehension hard. When the achievement is easier to see than the process, the temptation is to ignore the process altogether. So comprehension is tested rather than taught, and good comprehension is seen as an automatic facet of the intelligence of the child, and something that teachers can do relatively little about. What teachers need then, is a better model of comprehension: one which helps them understand the process by which readers come to understand text and one which enables them to see what might be taught.

How else might comprehension be conceptualised?

The purpose of this chapter is to position comprehension as social practice, and to show how the habits of thinking that experienced readers employ to make reading meaningful can be demonstrated and encouraged in classrooms in order to help children understand more from the texts they read. There are two steps to this process. The first is to establish comprehension as thinking – that is a dynamic and continuous process of thought, rather than as a series of pre-packaged skills to be taken off a shelf and applied. The second is to demonstrate that the ways of thinking readers employ are learned habits – moderated and sustained by the communities of practice, and to suggest that because of this, differences in community will result in different habits of comprehension. Finally, the implications of this understanding for teachers will be explored.

I. Comprehension as a dynamic process

This understanding of comprehension (from Smith 2000, 2005) makes two assumptions. It accepts with Iser (1980) that text is indeterminate and malleable, and it assumes the reader to be a social being who is involved in an active process of shaping the indeterminacies of that text into something that is personally meaningful.

The reader does this, I suggest, by importing the unread text into the projected imaginative space in his or her mind where thinking takes place. This space has much in common with Winnicott's (1971) 'third area' and I will call it the interpretative framework. Because readers are social beings and live lives, this framework is never blank. It is busy with all the things that people think about: their feelings and emotions, the things they have seen and done in their lives and the texts they have read, watched, heard or created. The framework can be represented as shown in Figure 5.1.

For the sake of clarity, here the contents of the reader's framework have been organised into 'layers of resonance'. First there is an emotive layer, which represents the reader's most personal concerns: emotions, moods, worries, gut

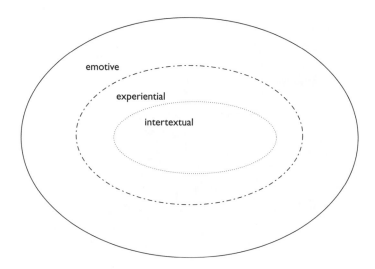

Figure 5.1 The interpretative framework.

reactions – those responses to life that are most irrational and stem from the person of the reader rather than from any logical thought. Then comes an experiential layer, made up of ideas and memories that the reader has experienced through living. These are not independent of the first layer: to a great extent, what one does in life stems from the emotive, that is, who one is and what one feels. Third there is an intertextual layer consisting of ideas and memories from all the texts the reader has ever found significant. Again, this is dependent on the other layers. The texts a reader encounters and remembers will vary according to what he or she likes and what he or she knows already. My suggestion is that readers import new texts into this framework as they read. What they do with the text when it is there is the process of comprehension.

Imagine the text as a lump of newly mixed bread dough. It is sticky and sloppy at first. The reader kneads it by thinking within the framework. The more ideas from the text that can be pulled and pushed towards ideas in the layers of resonance, the better the dough is kneaded and the more shape and firmness the text takes on. Ideas and difficulties are tested against similar or contrasting memories in the framework, and thinking is adapted or adopted as is appropriate. Readers who find plenty in their interpretative frameworks against which to push and pull the new text, comprehend it well. Those who find little to work with, or who forget to work the text as they explore their own memories, are less successful. This idea is represented in Figure 5.2.

In this model then, comprehension rests on two variants. The first is the amount of 'baggage' in the interpretative framework that the reader can call into use, and the second is the reader's ability to 'think within the framework', that is, to

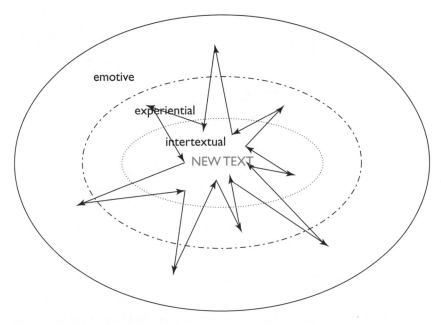

Figure 5.2 The new text pushed, pulled and integrated into the interpretative framework.

manipulate that baggage to make the new text meaningful. If this is what comprehension is, then the way forward is clear to those who want to help readers get better at it. They can do two things: they can help readers populate their interpretative frameworks with texts and experiences that will fuel their thinking, and they can teach them the habits of mind that will enable them to use those experiences well.

2. Habits of mind as social practice

What I want to argue here is that the habits of mind that readers use to pull and push text into meaningful shape are neither natural, instinctive nor automatic facets of intelligence; rather, they are socially learned behaviour. How readers think about books, talk about books and what they do with books in their head depends on what they have seen others do, been encouraged to do and are expected to do by the communities they move in. Heath's work (1982, 1983) shows this clearly. While the mainstream children she studied had bedtime stories read to them and were encouraged to speculate and respond to their content, Roadville children mostly had alphabet books. Their interaction was factual. They learned to name the things represented in the pictures, but they were not encouraged to play with the ideas, to imagine, to connect, to respond. In terms of the model presented above, they used only the experiential layer of their interpretative frameworks to understand the texts they read. They did not connect what they read to their emotive, personal feelings, nor did they imagine what other books might have done with the apples and balls and cats they saw in the pictures. With these habits of mind in place, the children were perfectly successful at home and in their communities and in the early years of school. It was only when the school began to expect habits of thinking in reading and writing that went beyond home practice that these children began to flounder, and then, it was not that they *couldn't* understand the texts they were expected to read or create, rather that they had *learned to understand* in a way that was unhelpful in the context they found themselves in.

Of course, it is not only at home that children learn to think about text. The practices and expectations of school too will influence what children accept as normal in the way they interact with texts and therefore how they comprehend what they read. In classrooms where texts are broadly discussed and children are encouraged to use all areas of their interpretative frameworks to understand them, they will develop habits of thinking that make that behaviour automatic. In classrooms where, conversely, texts are used mainly for retelling, or for information retrieval, or to monitor surface understandings, children will learn that that is what they have to do, and will be successful at doing it. I think of a small boy I knew once who had learned to read in a school where reading accuracy mattered above all else. He read to me eagerly, attacking each word with determination and vigour. But when I asked him what he'd thought about the story, he looked at me blankly. Think? His job was to read the words, not think about them. This anecdote demonstrates two important points. First is the potency of social expectation in determining practice: the boy was doing exactly what he thought was expected of him. Second is the essential and situated nature of comprehension in reading: even at this early stage in his reading life, the practice he had been taught was affecting how he thought about what he read. Far from being a discrete part of the curriculum that can be isolated and taught as separate skills, comprehension is part of what reading is. Because of this, the habits that govern it need to be fostered from the beginning. Bad habits, in reading like everything else, are never easy to break.

Teachers who understand comprehension as socially learned behaviour are empowered to do something about it. They can adopt in their classrooms practices which help children understand the patterns of thinking which they value and which will afford the children success in the educational system. They can examine the habits of thinking about text the children bring with them and they can help children develop new patterns of thought that will serve them better. They can, in fact, teach comprehension, rather than merely test it.

What might this socially constructed approach to comprehension look like in the classroom?

A socially constructed approach to comprehension in the classroom is likely to differ from more traditional approaches in a number of ways. It will take more account of the texts that children read, the personalities and interests of the children in the class, the role of the teacher as model and the place of interaction.

The texts

In this model of reading, the texts themselves become very important. Because they are seen as the products of writers and illustrators who have meanings to communicate and purposes to fulfil, rather than neutral depositories of information for the children to mine, they become part of the social interaction of the classroom. Children will be encouraged to engage with the ideas and personalities they find in texts just as if the writers or, sometimes, the characters were guests in the classroom. The obligation for the children is not to 'get it right', but to listen to and think about what the writer has to say.

The thinking is especially important, because different texts encourage thinking in different ways. A traditional narrative, for example, might make demands on a reader's ability to understand linear plot development, maintain interest in characters, and anticipate plot complication and resolution. A postmodern picture book, such as Lauren Child's *My Uncle is a Hunkle*, necessitates something quite different. Here the reader's thoughts need to make sense of fractured narrative, take on discourses from other media and understand the dynamic of words and pictures working together. Learning to make sense of different books sets up different patterns of thinking in a reader's interpretative framework that can be used again. It is easier to comprehend a fairy-tale, or a postmodern novel, or even a research report, when one's mind has developed the habits of thinking to deal with them efficiently.

Therefore, in a classroom where comprehension is seen as social practice there will be a variety of books and lots of reading will be happening. The role of the texts in encouraging and achieving all sorts of comprehension will be highlighted. What will matter will not be that the book has been completed, but the lessons in reading from that book which have been achieved.

The children

In a model of reading where the readers matter more than skills, there needs to be an awareness of who the readers are and what they are likely to be interested in. Children, of course differ in personality, in experience and in levels of motivation. To deal with this, teachers need to be responsive to individual need and interest. This means that for some teachers, the class novel or the reading scheme will assume a less significant place in their teaching of reading. Books will be targeted to particular children who are likely to enjoy them and learn from them. The onus will be on the teacher therefore to know the children well and to be well read in children's literature and other texts.

The role of the teacher

The teacher who takes on the idea that comprehension is socially learned will have a clearer idea of what comprehension is. She will understand what it is that she wants children to do as they read and will therefore be able to teach it explicitly. She will do this by modelling her own thinking about texts to the children, showing she makes use of the whole interpretative framework; by encouraging children to think out loud as they make meaning, so that she can monitor the effectiveness of their thinking, and put in place measures to help them think more widely or more fully when necessary; and by encouraging the children to make meaning together. This will mean arranging for children to talk about texts in pairs and groups and sometimes as a whole class so that understandings can be shared and interpretative frameworks strengthened.

The place of interaction

Interaction around text is at the heart of any social practice model of literacy. Here it is vital in that it is only through interaction that children can learn the habits of mind that make comprehension possible. There will be interaction with text and interaction with other readers: both children and adults. This community of readers will be important in forming the hermeneutic circle that Fish (1980) describes. It will set expectations, moderate interpretation and extend the possibilities of thinking for individual readers. The soundness and strength of the community of readers in a classroom will be the measure of the comprehension that can take place. Where good habits of thinking become the norm, more children will be able to make more meaning from more and more texts.

Conclusion

Positioning comprehension as a social act is valuable for a number of reasons. It is useful in that it demystifies comprehension itself because it shows how readers use the communities of practice to hone how they think about texts. A clear and practical outcome of this is that it gives teachers something useful to work with. If they can see what comprehending a text might look and feel like to a reader, then they can build a pedagogy around that understanding. Teaching comprehension in a way that is situated, that takes account of the reader, the texts and the contexts in which reading takes place will surely be more fruitful than relying on the off-the-shelf programmes that Dewitz, Jones and Leahy (2009) criticise and which are popular in America.

A further advantage of positioning comprehension in this way is that it extends the way social practice is sometimes understood. In projects such as *Bookstart* and *Reading Champions*, where reading engagement is the main concern, the social dynamic of belonging to the reading community overshadows the important cognitive gains that reading is usually claimed to ensure. In this approach to comprehension, the cognitive gains are contextualised and the role of the community in developing them is explored more fully. In effect, it shows not just that reading is a social process, but how that process actually works in forming readers who are in control of the meaning they make from texts.

References

Bookstart: http://www.bookstart.org.uk/Home   Reading   Champions: http://www.literacytrust.org.uk/campaign/champions/research.html

Calkins, L. (2000) *The Art of Teaching Reading*, Needham Heights, MA: Allyn & Bacon.

Catt, H.W. (2009) 'The narrow view of reading promotes a broad view of comprehension', *Language, Speech and Hearing Services in Schools*, 40: 178–183.

Chambers, A. (1985) *Booktalk: Occasional Writing on Literature and Children*, London: Bodley Head.

Chambers, A. (1993) *Tell Me: Children, Reading and Talk*, Stroud: Thimble Press.

Child, L. (2000) *My Uncle is a Hunkle Says Clarice Bean*, London: Orchard Books.

Cliff-Hodges, G. (2002) 'Learning though collaborative writing', *Reading, Language and Literacy*, 31, 1: 4–10.

Cole, M., John-Steiner, V., Scribner, S. and Souberman, E. (eds) (1978) *L.S. Vygotsky: Mind in Society*, Cambridge, MA: Harvard University Press.

Dewitz, P., Jones, J. and Leahy, S. (2009) 'Comprehension strategy instruction in core reading programmes', *Reading Research Quarterly*, 42, 2: 102–126.

Ellis, S., Pearson, C. and Allan, J. (2005) *Literature Circles, Gender and Reading for Enjoyment*, http://www.scotland.gov.uk/Resource/Doc/930/0021345.pdf (accessed 26/10/2009).

Fish, S. (1980) *Is There A Text In This Class? The Authority Of Interpretive Communities*, Cambridge, MA: Harvard University Press.

Heath, S.B. (1982) 'What no bedtime story means: narrative skills at home and school', *Language and Society*, 11: 49–76.

Heath, S.B. (1983) *Ways With Words*, Cambridge: Cambridge University Press.

Iser, W. (1980) 'The reading process: a phenomenological approach to criticism', in J.P. Tompkins (ed.) *Reader-Response Criticism: From Formalism to Post-structuralism*, Baltimore, MD: The Johns Hopkins Press.

Marsh, J. and Millard, E. (2000) *Literacy and Popular Culture: Using Children's Culture in the Classroom*, London: Paul Chapman.

Meek, M. (1988) *How Texts Teach What Readers Learn*, Stroud: Thimble Press.

Minns, H. (1990) *Read It To Me Now: Learning At Home and School*, London: Virago Press.

Moss, G. (2005) *Literacy and Gender: Researching Texts, Contexts and Readers*, London: Routledge.

Oakhill, J.V. and Cain, K. (2003) 'The development of comprehension skills', in T. Nunes and P. Bryant (eds) *Handbook of Children's Literacy*, Dordrecht: Kluwer Academic Publishers 155–180.

Pressley, M. (2001) 'Comprehension instruction: what makes sense now, what might make sense soon?', http://www.readingonline.org/articles/handbook/pressley/index.html (accessed 26/10/2009).

Rosenblatt, L. (1978) *The Reader, the Text, the Poem*, Champaign, IL: South Illinois University Press.

Scribner, S. and Cole, M. (1978) 'Literacy without schooling: testing for intellectual effects', *Harvard Educational Review*, 48, 4: 448–461.

Smith, F. (1978) *Reading*, Cambridge: Cambridge University Press.

Smith, V. (2000) *Developing Critical Reading: How Interactions Between Children, Teachers and Texts Support the Process of Becoming a Reader*. Unpublished thesis, University of Coventry.

Smith, V. (2005) *Making Reading Mean*, Royston: UKLA.

Smith, V. (2008) 'Learning to be a reader: promoting good textual health', in P. Goodwin (ed.) *Understanding Children's Books*, London: Sage.

Stanovich, K. (1986) 'Matthew effects in reading: some consequences of individual differences in the acquisition of literacy', *Reading Research Quarterly*, 21, 4: 360–407.

Street, B. (1984) *Literacy in Theory and Practice*, Cambridge: Cambridge University Press.

Waterland, L. (1988) *Read With Me*, Stroud: Thimble Press.

Weinberger, J. (1996) *Literacy Goes to School*, London: Paul Chapman.

Winnicott, D.W. (1971) *Playing and Reality*, London: Routledge.

Chapter 6

Reading for meaning

The skills that support reading comprehension and its development

Kate Cain

Successful understanding of written text (and spoken discourse) enables the individual to learn and apply new knowledge, to experience other (fictional) worlds, to communicate successfully, and to achieve academically. This chapter explores the skills and knowledge that help readers to read for meaning and support the development of reading comprehension. I draw on research from the psychological study of reading, focusing on the mental processes and knowledge that influence the development of a child's ability to understand text.

First, I consider what we mean when we talk about comprehension and the product of comprehension, then I review the relation between reading and listening comprehension and the influence of word reading on our ability to understand what we read. Key skills that aid the construction of meaning are considered and longitudinal research that demonstrates their influence on comprehension development will be discussed. I end with some final thoughts on the implications of this research for the teaching and assessment of reading.

What is comprehension?

Adequate comprehension of a written text requires the reader to retrieve the sense of individual words and combine them into phrases and sentences. However, good comprehension involves more than simply processing single words or sentences. To understand text in a meaningful way, skilled comprehenders build a representation of the meaning of a text that is accurate and coherent.

Local and global coherence in text comprehension

Readers establish *local coherence* by integrating the meanings of successive sentences in a text and they establish *global coherence* by ensuring that the information in the text fits together as a whole (Long and Chong 2001). For both local and global coherence, readers need to incorporate background knowledge and ideas (retrieved from long-term memory) to make sense of details that are only implicitly mentioned.

The importance of local and global coherence and the role of background knowledge in comprehension are illustrated by this short text:

Arthur wanted to send his girlfriend some flowers.
He surfed some sites on the Internet.
Everything was too expensive.
Arthur decided to go to the florist's, instead.

Local coherence involves linking the meanings of adjacent phrases and sentences. One way to establish local coherence is through pronoun resolution. In the above text, the pronoun "he" in sentence two refers back to the protagonist "Arthur", who was introduced in the first sentence. The pronoun links the two sentences and enables their meanings to be integrated.

Local coherence alone is often not sufficient to understand the overall meaning of the text. Why did Arthur decide to go to the florist's? This sentence is anomalous unless the reader makes the causal inference that he might purchase some flowers more cheaply at a flower shop than through an Internet site. (And perhaps he is prepared to deliver the flowers in person to reduce the costs further). The role of general knowledge in successful comprehension is demonstrated by consideration of sentences two and four: our knowledge about the use of the Internet, and where to purchase flowers (websites and flower shops) is required to make sense of these two sentences. This analysis illustrates that, even for very short texts, readers engage in meaning-making processes in addition to word identification and sentence processing.

How does a reader represent the meaning of a text?

The product of successful comprehension is a representation of the state of affairs described in the text. This representation is multidimensional. It includes causal relations between events, the goals of protagonists, and spatial and temporal information that is relevant to the story line (Zwaan and Radvansky 1998). Models of skilled comprehension refer to this representation as a mental model (Johnson-Laird 1983) or situation model (Kintsch 1998).

A reader's situation model of a text's meaning goes beyond the sense of the individual words and sentences and is a representation of the situation described by the text. This feature of a situation model is well illustrated by a classic experiment by Bransford, Barclay and Franks (1972). They presented adult listeners with sentences such as:

1a) 'Three turtles rested *on* a floating log, and a fish swam beneath *them*.'
and
1b) 'Three turtles rested *beside* a floating log, and a fish swam beneath *them*.'

After a short interval, the participants completed a recognition test: they heard sentences and had to state whether or not the sentence was one that they had heard previously. Some of the new sentences differed in wording but described the same situation as an original sentence. For example:

2a) 'Three turtles rested *on* a floating log, and a fish swam beneath *it*.'

describes the same state of affairs as sentence 1a. Other test sentences also differed by only a single word but described new situations. The sentence:

2b) 'Three turtles rested *beside* a floating log, and a fish swam beneath *it*.'

describes a different situation to sentence 1b, above. The adult listeners often falsely recognised sentences that described the same situation and they were much better able to 'reject' sentences that described a different situation. This study supports the notion that readers and listeners remember the state of affairs described by the text, rather than the specific words used to describe it.

In summary, readers construct a representation of a text's meaning that encodes the situation described by the text, rather than the precise wording or syntax. When constructing this representation, successful comprehenders ensure that sentence meanings are integrated and that missing details are filled in, often through a process of inference-making with reference to general knowledge. These meaning-based representations are not unique to reading comprehension: successful comprehension of spoken discourse also results in an accurate and coherent situation model. Comprehension and the construction of a coherent situation model of a particular text is a dynamic process: it involves an interaction between the information provided by the author in the text, the reader's linguistic, pragmatic and world knowledge, and their current memory for the text, i.e., the representation of the text constructed so far (Kintsch 1998).

As a psychologist, I seek to identify the mental processes, skills and knowledge that underpin a child's ability to comprehend text and the skill weaknesses that can lead to comprehension failure. In the remainder of this chapter, I discuss work that has investigated the language and cognitive skills and knowledge that support good reading and listening comprehension and the reasons why some children fail to develop adequate comprehension skills.

The relation between word reading, reading comprehension, and listening comprehension

Word reading skills are essential for successful reading comprehension. Indeed, reading comprehension cannot take place if word reading fails. Word reading draws on a child's awareness of the sounds in spoken words, which develops before reading instruction begins (Goswami and Bryant 1990). In a similar way, reading comprehension draws on skills and knowledge that are developing before children are taught to read. Many of the skills that support successful reading comprehension are important for successful comprehension of other media: a listener needs to establish local and global coherence to understand a spoken discourse, and the ability to comprehend the essence of static or moving cartoon sequences is highly correlated with listening comprehension in children and adults (Gernsbacher *et al.* 1990; Kendeou *et al.* 2008). In this way, comprehension of stories in the preschool years before literacy instruction can serve as an important foundation for reading comprehension.

The importance of these two broad skill sets, word reading and listening comprehension, is recognised in the Simple View of Reading (Gough and Tunmer 1986). The Simple View of Reading is a useful framework in which to consider reading development. Within the Simple View, reading comprehension is the product of readers' ability to read the words on the page and their listening comprehension skill.

The Simple View stresses the importance of both word recognition skills and language comprehension skills. If young children cannot decode a word or do not decode words accurately, they will not be able to comprehend that word. Poor word recognition skills will compromise readers' ability to extract the meaning of individual sentences and more extended text, particularly if the word is essential to the meaning of the text. Consider the difference in meaning between '*He thought the girl was pretty*' and '*He thought the girl was petty*', two sentences that differ by only a single letter. Accurate decoding of words enables access to their meanings if the words are known by the reader, that is if they have an entry in their store of spoken or written word meanings. A wealth of studies has demonstrated the close relationship between young readers' ability to read the words on the page and their ability to understand what they read (see Kirby and Savage 2008; Stuart *et al.* 2008).

Young readers can often understand longer and more advanced texts if spoken than if written, because in the early stages of reading development their word reading abilities are still developing and use up a substantial proportion of their processing resources (Perfetti 1985), although differences between the form and register of written and spoken text also make different demands on knowledge and memory skills (Garton and Pratt 1998). As word reading develops and becomes more efficient and automatic, the impact of word reading on reading comprehension decreases and the relations between an individual's ability to comprehend written and spoken texts increases (Gough *et al.* 1996; Vellutino *et al.* 2007).

Children with reading comprehension difficulties

If we consider these two sets of component skills and their relationship with each other, it is clear that just as language comprehension will not ensure adequate word reading skills, learning to read words will not ensure adequate comprehension. There is empirical support for this claim. In addition to children who experience problems with both word reading and reading comprehension, "poor readers" who have difficulties with one particular skill set have been identified. Children with developmental dyslexia tend to have particular difficulties with word reading; their language comprehension is often intact (Snowling 2000). In contrast, children with specific comprehension difficulties have particularly poor reading (and listening) comprehension, but acquire age-appropriate word reading skills (Cain and Oakhill 2007). These children might be considered *unexpectedly poor comprehenders*, because they have acquired word reading skills that are commensurate with their chronological age but, for whatever reason, their comprehension lags behind. Table 6.1 illustrates the typical characteristics of poor comprehenders.

An examination of the language skills of children with poor reading comprehension highlights some skills and aspects of knowledge that appear crucial to good reading comprehension. Children with unexpectedly poor comprehension do not typically demonstrate pronounced difficulties at word or sentence level (but see Nation 2005, for evidence of subtle word reading and semantic deficits). Poor comprehenders consistently experience difficulties with several skills that influence the construction of the situation model of a text's meaning. They are poor at integrating meanings across sentences, combining information in the text with general knowledge to generate inferences, monitoring their comprehension, and imposing a coherent structure on narratives. They also do more poorly than same-age typically developing readers on assessments of memory and general listening comprehension (Cain and Oakhill 2007). These skills all make an important contribution to the construction of a coherent meaning-based representation.

Integration and inference making are crucial skills that map conceptually onto local and global coherence. Integration involves relating the ideas in successive clauses and sentences by establishing meaning overlap and co-reference of pronouns (see example above). Poor comprehenders' difficulties with text integration were first demonstrated by Oakhill (1982). She presented seven- to eight-year-old good and poor comprehenders with three-line texts and later gave them a sentence recognition text. Some of the sentences were originals presented earlier, some of the recognition sentences combined the meaning from two original sentences, and some of the recognition sentences conflicted with the meaning of the original text. An example of a text and recognition sentences is provided in

Table 6.1 Characteristics of good and poor comprehenders aged 9–10 years (After Cain *et al.* 2005)

	Poor comprehenders (N=14)	Good comprehenders (N=14)	t(26)
Variables commonly used to select and match groups			
chronological age	9,08 (4.15)	9,08 (3.83)	< 1.0, ns
Gates-MacGinitie sight vocabulary	34.00 (2.04)	34.20 (2.75)	< 1.0, ns
word reading accuracy in context	10, 07 (6.97)	10, 06 (7.05)	< 1.0, ns
reading comprehension	7, 11 (5.33)	10, 07 (9.60)	=10.71***
number of stories	6.00 (0.00)	6.00 (0.00)	< 1.0, ns

Note
Where appropriate, ages are given as years, months (with standard deviations in months). Maximum score for Gates-MacGinitie sight vocabulary is 45 (MacGinitie *et al.* 2000). The word reading accuracy and reading comprehension scores are the age-equivalent scores from the Neale Analysis of Reading Ability (Neale 1997); the number of stories refers to the stories completed in this assessment.

Table 6.2. In the later recognition test, the good comprehenders were more likely to falsely recognise a sentence that integrated the meaning of two of the presentation sentences, but which had not been heard previously. This finding suggests that poor comprehenders do not routinely integrate the meanings of successive sentences in the same way as good comprehenders.

Inference involves going beyond the explicit details included by the author of a text and filling in details to make full sense of events. In the example given earlier, the causal inference that Arthur might purchase flowers more cheaply at a flower shop than through an Internet site is needed to make sense of his actions. Inference generation is an early developing skill that aids the language comprehension of preschoolers (Akhtar 2006; Kendeou *et al.* 2008). Poor comprehenders are less likely to answer questions correctly when the response requires an inference, generated by linking information in the text with general knowledge (Cain and Oakhill 1999). An inference can only be made if the requisite knowledge is available, so one possibility is that poor comprehenders have impoverished knowledge from which to draw inferences. Knowledge availability does not appear to be the source of their difficulties (Cain *et al.* 2001). However, it may be that poor comprehenders are less able to readily access relevant information when reading, an issue that requires further research attention.

The research findings on integration and inference making strongly suggest that some children struggle with two processes that are crucial for the construction of coherent representations of meaning. These difficulties will compromise their ability to fully understand written and spoken texts.

Good readers appear to monitor their understanding of the text. We have all experienced the situation of turning over two pages of a book resulting in a disruption to our understanding. When skilled readers detect a comprehension failure they can engage in remedial actions: checking the page number, looking up the meanings of unknown words, re-reading, and generating inferences. The ability to monitor comprehension – or to be alerted to comprehension failures – may be crucial for successful comprehension. Researchers often talk about comprehension monitoring as if successful readers engage in deliberate strategic meaning checks. It may actually be that the process we tap in tasks designed to

Table 6.2 Materials used by Oakhill (1982) to study integration

Presentation text:

The mouse ate the food.
The food was bread.
The mouse looked for some cheese.

Recognition sentences:

The mouse ate the food (original)
The mouse ate the bread (meaning combined by integrating two sentences)
The food was some cheese (incorrect)

assess this skill is the ability to detect when something is wrong (Harris *et al.* 1981; Ruffman 1996), i.e. when the meaning of a new sentence cannot be integrated with the situation model constructed thus far.

Children appear to monitor their understanding from an early age. When the material is familiar, such as a well-known storybook, children as young as 30 months demonstrate awareness that something is 'wrong', for example they express surprise, i.e., detect, when an actor or the temporal order of events is changed during a narration (Skarakis-Doyle 2002). Readers with poor comprehension are less likely than their typically developing peers to spot anomalies in short texts (Ehrlich *et al.* 1999; Oakhill *et al.* 2005). Poor comprehenders are particularly poor at two types of anomaly: conflicts between information in different parts of the text, which may lead to integration errors, and conflicts between information in the text and general knowledge. Examples of these types of anomaly are provided in Table 6.3.

Detection of comprehension failures aids comprehension, enabling the reader to engage in remedial strategies that may result in a more coherent representation of a text's meaning. However, readers cannot monitor their understanding if they have not constructed a rudimentary situation model of the text's meaning. Thus, comprehension monitoring and the construction of a situation model appear to be intimately related.

The final factor influencing the construction of situation models, which I consider in detail, is knowledge about text structure. Texts from the same genre share some broad structural features. For example, narrative text structure typically consists of a sequence of causally related events (Stein and Trabasso 1982). This underlying structure is typically encoded into a reader's situation model: the reasons (causes) for events are included in a coherent situation model.

Knowledge about text structure may help young children's comprehension when reading, by providing a framework or guide to the identification and integration of important information. Comprehension of narratives involves the identification of the individual character's goals, e.g., a knight's quest to rescue the princess, inference of goal plans, and interpretation of actions in relation to

Table 6.3 Examples of text with anomalies used to assess children's ability to monitor comprehension

---

Once there was a rabbit named Albert. He had dark brown fur that was as soft as could be.[a] He was very fluffy and had a beautiful tail. All the other rabbits wished they had his snow-white fur.[a] Albert liked to eat in Farmer Smith's garden. Lots of good things grew in the garden. But Albert especially liked the ice cream that grew there.[b] Farmer Smith did not like rabbits to eat his food. Albert was lucky he never got caught.

---

[a] Sentences contain information that is internally inconsistent
[b] Sentence contains a prior knowledge violation

Note
Passage adapted from one published in Baker (1984).

that plan, e.g., attempts to find the princess, fight the dragon, etc. Goals are central to narrative: they provide the reasons for a character's actions. They enable the interpretation of both the temporal and causal sequence of events within a goal plan, and the evaluation of the outcome of those attempts to reach the goal as successful or not (Trabasso and Nickels 1992).

Poor comprehenders demonstrate weaknesses in many tasks that tap knowledge of text structure (in fact, most of this work has focused on narrative, because this is the genre with which most children are familiar). For example, poor comprehenders produce narratives with less coherent structures than typically developing readers (Cain and Oakhill 1996; Cain 2003): they are more likely to 'tell a story' that consists of a string of unrelated events. Poor comprehenders are also poorer than good comprehenders at selecting the main point of a short narrative, either presented aurally or as a sequence of pictures (Yuill and Oakhill 1991). Poor comprehenders appear to be less knowledgeable about the information provided by particular features of stories, such as titles, beginnings and endings (Cain 1996). Such features can help readers to appreciate the structure of a text and to activate relevant knowledge structures.

These three broad skills: integration and inference, comprehension monitoring, and knowledge and use of text structure, are all correlated with young children's reading comprehension. Between the ages of seven to eight (UK Year 3) and ten to eleven (UK Year 6), measures of these skills predict variance in reading comprehension over and above word reading, verbal IQ, and vocabulary knowledge ability (Oakhill *et al.* 2003; Cain *et al.* 2004). Thus, it seems that good reading comprehension and its development depend on more than simply learning to decode print: other cognitive skills are important.

Which skills drive the development of reading comprehension?

When we look at the skills that explain the development of reading ability across time, we find evidence for a degree of independence between the development of word reading and reading comprehension. This work supports the idea that reading development depends on both skills important for word reading and skills important for comprehension. Several studies have demonstrated that different skills are related to the development of word reading and reading comprehension. In the first few years of reading instruction, the former is associated with phonological awareness; the latter is associated with meaning-related skills such as vocabulary, sentence comprehension, and listening comprehension (de Jong and van der Leij 2002; Muter *et al.* 2004).

With colleagues, I have explored how the skills that are linked to the construction of situation models influence comprehension development in young readers. Here I present an overview of our study and its findings (see Oakhill and Cain, under review, for a more detailed account). Two questions addressed by this research were:

1   Do different skills predict the development of word reading and reading comprehension?
2   Do discourse-skills and knowledge make independent contributions to the prediction of reading comprehension over and above verbal IQ, vocabulary, and word reading?

To examine these (and other issues) we monitored the progress of approximately 100 children from the year of their eighth birthday until the year of their eleventh birthday. Each child completed a range of assessments including: general ability (verbal and non-verbal IQ), vocabulary knowledge, grammatical knowledge, memory, word reading, reading comprehension, and measures of integration and inference, comprehension monitoring, and knowledge and use of story structure. These assessments were completed when children were aged seven to eight, eight to nine, and ten to eleven.

We found that different skills explained variance in word reading and reading comprehension. For example, word reading accuracy at Time One and Time Two was explained by children's verbal IQ, vocabulary knowledge, and phonological awareness. IQ and vocabulary also explained reading comprehension, but performance on other measures that aid the construction of meaning explained additional variance. These measures were memory, integration and inference, comprehension monitoring, and knowledge and use of story structure (Oakhill *et al.* 2003). These results strongly suggest that over and above general cognitive ability (e.g., IQ) and vocabulary (a good indicator of verbal ability), different skills contribute to word recognition and reading comprehension: phonological awareness skills are related to a child's ability to read words and the skills that aid the construction of meaning are related to a child's ability to understand text. Further, these data show children's reading comprehension level is not fully determined by their word reading ability: key comprehension-fostering skills explained additional variance in this outcome measure.

A similar pattern was found when we considered the development of word reading and reading comprehension over time. For word reading ability, we found that phonological awareness measured when children were aged seven to eight and eight to nine helped to explain their word reading skills when aged ten to eleven. In contrast, specific comprehension skills explained reading comprehension outcomes. A diagram of the skills that made significant contributions to the determination of reading comprehension level is presented in Figure 6.1. A particularly interesting finding was that the three specific comprehension skills made a unique contribution to the prediction of the final comprehension score. Thus, similar to the within-time analyses, different skills help to explain word reading and reading comprehension development across time.

The empirical study of children's reading comprehension development by psychologists has identified several separable skills and sources of knowledge that are important for successful comprehension. There is converging evidence that weaknesses in these may result in poor comprehension for individual children. The

7 to 8 years   8 to 9 years   10 to 11 years

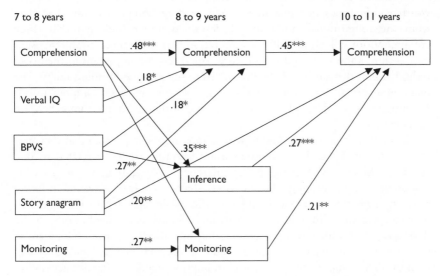

Figure 6.1 Diagram to illustrate the longitudinal prediction of reading comprehension.

Note

The value associated with each significant relation is the standardised beta weight from the final model, which indicates the strength of the contribution of that skill. * = p < .05; ** = p < .01; *** = p <.001.

identification of these specific skills can inform both the teaching and assessment of comprehension, which I consider next.

Implications for teaching and assessment

The research reviewed in this chapter demonstrates that learning to read is dependent on a broad range of language comprehension skills in addition to the ability to read the written word. Further, there is evidence that specific skills that enable the reader to construct coherent representations of meaning are weak in some readers. However, although poor comprehenders make up approximately 10 per cent of young readers (Yuill and Oakhill 1991), they often go unnoticed in the classroom. This is because they develop accurate word reading skills and often read with apparent intonation. When asked questions about what the content of what they have been reading ('What happened in that story?' 'Why did Arthur go to the flower shop?' 'Why did the village cheer when the prince slew the dragon?') poor comprehenders' difficulties with text comprehension become apparent.

Word reading skills are essential for reading comprehension to take place and weak word reading will limit comprehension for some children. However, the identification of unexpectedly poor comprehenders demonstrates that good word reading does not guarantee good reading comprehension. The data from the longitudinal study that I described above indicated that three comprehension-fostering skills – integration and inference, comprehension monitoring, knowledge and use of story structure – are important in their own right. It seems that a broad skill set is needed to support good reading ability. The main educational implication of this body of work is these comprehension-fostering skills could usefully be taught to help foster children's comprehension development.

The implications of these findings are a little more complicated that they may at first appear. First, these comprehension-fostering skills are related to one another: children who are good at inference making tend to be good at comprehension monitoring. One question, which can only be answered by future research, is whether or not we should teach these skills separately or as a combined package. Second, although these skills make individual contributions to the development of reading comprehension, they may also foster the development of each other. For example, teaching a child to reflect on their understanding and monitor their comprehension may lead to improvements in inference generation because their awareness of when an inference is required will be reinforced. These skills develop before literacy instruction begins, providing ways to nurture these skills in pre-readers and also poor word readers.

The research reviewed in this chapter highlights the fact that teachers, researchers, and those involved in the development of assessment tools should be aware that comprehension can be limited not just by word reading proficiency, but by other skills that aid the extraction of meaning and enable the reader to build a complete and coherent representation of the text's meaning. Thus, psychological research into reading comprehension can inform both the teaching and testing of reading comprehension.

References

Akhtar, N. (2006) 'Contexts of early word learning', in G. D. Hall & S. R. Waxman (eds) *Weaving a lexicon*, Cambridge, MA: MIT Press.

Baker, L. (1984) 'Spontaneous versus instructed use of multiple standards for evaluating comprehension: Effects of age, reading proficiency, and type of standard', *Journal of Experimental Child Psychology*, 38: 289–311.

Bransford, J. D., Barclay, J. R. & Franks, J. J. (1972) 'Sentence memory: A constructive versus interpretive approach', *Cognitive Psychology*, 3: 193–209.

Cain, K. (1996) 'Story knowledge and comprehension skill', in C. Cornoldi & J. Oakhill (eds) *Reading comprehension difficulties: processes and remediation*, Mahwah, NJ: LEA.

Cain, K. (2003) 'Text comprehension and its relation to coherence and cohesion in children's fictional narratives', *British Journal of Developmental Psychology*, 21: 335–351.

Cain, K. & Oakhill, J. (1996) 'The nature of the relationship between comprehension skill and the ability to tell a story', *British Journal of Developmental Psychology*, 14: 187–201.

Cain, K. & Oakhill, J. (2007) 'Reading comprehension difficulties: Correlates, causes, and consequences', In K. Cain & J. Oakhill (eds) *Children's comprehension problems in oral and written language: A cognitive perspective*, New York: Guilford Press.

Cain, K., Oakhill, J. & Lemmon, K. (2005) 'The relation between children's reading comprehension level and their comprehension of idioms', *Journal of Experimental Child Psychology*, 90: 65–87.

Cain, K. & Oakhill, J. V. (1999) 'Inference making and its relation to comprehension failure', *Reading and Writing: An Interdisciplinary Journal*, 11: 489–503.

Cain, K., Oakhill, J. V., Barnes, M. A. & Bryant, P. E. (2001) 'Comprehension skill, inference-making ability and their relation to knowledge', *Memory and Cognition*, 29: 850–859.

Cain, K., Oakhill, J. V. & Bryant, P. E. (2004) 'Children's reading comprehension ability: Concurrent prediction by working memory, verbal ability, and component skill', *Journal of Educational Psychology*, 96: 671–681.

De Jong, P. F. & Van Der Leij, A. (2002) 'Effects of phonological abilities and linguistic comprehension on the development of reading', *Scientific Studies of Reading*, 6, 51: 51–77.

Ehrlich, M. F., Remond, M. & Tardieu, H. (1999) 'Processing of anaphoric devices in young skilled and less skilled comprehenders: Differences in metacognitive monitoring', *Reading and Writing*, 11: 29–63.

Garton, A. & Pratt, C. (1998) *Learning to be literate: The development of spoken and written language*, Oxford: Blackwell Publishers.

Gernsbacher, M. A., Varner, K. R. & Faust, M. (1990) 'Investigating differences in general comprehension skill', *Journal of Experimental Psychology: Learning, Memory and Cognition*, 16: 430–445.

Goswami, U. & Bryant, P. E. (1990) *Phonological skills and learning to read*, Hove: Erlbaum.

Gough, P. B., Hoover, W. A. & Peterson, C. L. (1996) 'Some observations on a simple view of reading', in C. Cornoldi & J. Oakhill (eds) *Reading comprehension difficulties: Processes and interventions*, Mahwah, NJ: Erlbaum.

Gough, P. B. & Tunmer, W. E. (1986) 'Decoding, reading and reading disability', *Remedial and Special Education*, 7: 6–10.

Harris, P. L., Kruithof, A., Terwogt, M. M. & Visser, T. (1981) 'Children's detection and awareness of textual anomaly', *Journal of Experimental Child Psychology*, 31: 212–230.

Johnson-Laird, P. N. (1983) *Mental models: Towards a cognitive science of language, inference, and consciousness*, Cambridge: Cambridge University Press.

Kendeou, P., Bohn-Gettler, C., White, M. & Van Den Broek, P. (2008) 'Children's inference generation across different media', *Journal of Research in Reading*, 31: 259–272.

Kintsch, W. (1998) *Comprehension: A paradigm for cognition*, New York: Cambridge University Press.

Kirby, J. & Savage, R. (2008) 'Can the simple view deal with the complexities of reading?', *Literacy*, 42: 75–82.

Long, D. L. & Chong, J. L. (2001) 'Comprehension skill and global coherence: A paradoxical picture of poor comprehenders' abilities', *Journal of Experimental Psychology: Learning, Memory, and Cognition*, 27: 1424–1429.

MacGinitie, W. H., MacGinitie, R. K., Maria, K. & Dreyer, L. G. (2000) *Gates-MacGinitie Reading Tests*, Itasca, IL: Illinois Riverside Publishing.

Muter, V., Hulme, C., Snowling, M. & Stevenson, J. (2004) 'Phonemes, rimes, vocabulary and grammatical skills as foundations of early reading development: Evidence from a longitudinal study', *Developmental Psychology*, 40: 665–681.

Nation, K. (2005) 'Children's reading comprehension difficulties', in M. J. Snowling & C. Hulme (eds) *The science of reading: A handbook*, Malden, MA: Blackwell Publishing.

Neale, M. D. (1997) *The Neale Analysis of Reading Ability – Revised (NARA–II)*, Windsor: NFER–Nelson.

Oakhill, J. V. (1982) 'Constructive processes in skilled and less-skilled comprehenders' memory for sentences', *British Journal of Psychology*, 73: 13–20.

Oakhill, J. V. & Cain, K. (under review) 'The precursors of reading ability in young readers: Evidence from a four-year longitudinal study', *Scientific Studies of Reading*.

Oakhill, J. V., Cain, K. & Bryant, P. E. (2003) 'The dissociation of word reading and text comprehension: Evidence from component skills', *Language and Cognitive Processes*, 18: 443–468.

Oakhill, J. V., Hartt, J. & Samols, D. (2005) 'Levels of comprehension monitoring and working memory in good and poor comprehenders', *Reading and Writing*, 18: 657–713.

Perfetti, C. A. (1985) *Reading Ability*, New York: Oxford University Press.

Ruffman, T. (1996) 'Reassessing children's comprehension-monitoring skills', in C. Cornoldi & J. V. Oakhill (eds) *Reading comprehension difficulties: Processes and intervention*. Mahwah, NJ: Lawrence Erlbaum Associates.

Skarakis-Doyle, E. (2002) 'Young children's detection of violations in familiar stories and emerging comprehension monitoring', *Discourse Processes*, 33: 175–197.

Snowling, M. J. (2000) *Dyslexia*, Oxford: Blackwell Publishing.

Stein, N. L. & Trabasso, T. (1982) 'What's in a story: An approach to comprehension and instruction', in R. Glaser (ed.) *Advances in the psychology of instruction*, Hillsdale, NJ: Lawrence Erlbaum Associates.

Stuart, M., Stainthorp, R. & Snowling, M. (2008) 'Literacy as a complex activity: Deconstructing the simple view of reading', *Literacy*, 42: 59–74.

Trabasso, T. & Nickels, M. (1992) 'The development of goal plans of action in the narration of a picture story', *Discourse Processes*, 15: 249–275.

Vellutino, F. R., Tunmer, W. E., Jaccard, J. J. & Chen, R. (2007) 'Components of reading ability: Multivariate evidence for a convergent skill model of reading development', *Scientific Studies of Reading*, 11: 3–32.

Yuill, N. M. & Oakhill, J. V. (1991) *Children's problems in text comprehension: An experimental investigation*, Cambridge: Cambridge University Press.

Zwaan, R. A. & Radvansky, G. A. (1998) 'Situation models in language comprehension and memory', *Psychological Bulletin*, 123: 162–185.

Chapter 7

New literacies in the elementary classroom

The instructional dynamics of visual-texts

Dawnene D. Hassett

This chapter examines the hypertextual, interactive, and visual elements of contemporary children's texts, and proposes a pedagogy of multiliteracies that draws on social semiotics and sociocultural theories. As an organizational framework, the discussion employs a widely accepted heuristic for reading comprehension, which defines reading as the interaction among four elements: the *reader*, the *text*, the *activity*, and the *sociocultural context*. This model of reading comprehension was developed with a traditional print-based notion of "text" in mind, and thus contains particular expectations about what the reader is to "do" with the text (e.g., decode the graphophonic cueing system). However, basic print literacy alone, while remaining ever-important, is no longer enough to meet the demands of new forms of texts and new literacies. Thus, this chapter updates the terrain of early literacy pedagogy to include highly interactive visual-texts, and outlines roles for the reader/writer when producing and consuming these texts, as well as roles for the teacher/facilitator for designing interactive-visual activities. The chapter closes with a discussion of the instructional dynamics necessary for a pedagogy of multiliteracies.

Introduction

This chapter is situated within a larger evaluation of the ways in which new literacies affect the teaching of reading. Kress (2003) notes that "the world of communication is not standing still" (p. 16), and as literacy educators working to find our balance on this shifting terrain of communication, we must begin by looking at the changing nature of reading itself. Studies in new literacies have pointed to two important shifts in the nature of reading, involving 1) ontological changes to texts; and 2) paradigmatic changes to our instructional mindsets (Lankshear & Knobel, 2003).

First, in a very real and ontological sense, texts have changed, because they look, feel, and sound completely different from traditional print-based texts where graphemes are the primary carrier of meaning. Visual, interactive and hypertextual modes of communication have become more prevalent with the advent of new technologies, and texts today combine alphabetic print and images in ways that rival the printed word (Kress, 1998, p. 57). In the chapter, I define "text" as the cohesive whole of a document, including words, images, design, and their relations; and I use the term "print" to refer specifically to the units of writing. This expanded definition of "text" includes innovative approaches to communication (nonlinear, interactive, dynamic, multimodal, visual, imaginative, interpretive, and mobile). These texts challenge notions of representation and interpretation commonly associated with traditional print – and traditional literacy instruction.

Second, alongside ontological changes to texts, sociocultural theories and the idea of "multiliteracies" have become important tools for re-thinking our paradigms about the reading process. Sociocultural forms of "new literacies" involve an understanding that specific codes (like an alphabetic sign system) don't mean anything outside the context of the text (including its images) or the social and cultural practices that the children bring to a reading. The social contexts and purposes for making sense of any text are (of course) shaped by the reader's experiences, background knowledge, and social/cultural identities. But beyond this, the social context for making sense of text is also shaped by the makeup of the text itself, and what the reader is to "do" with it. To read, interpret, and create meaning through various forms of communication and representation requires a new role for the reader/writer – as well as a new role for the teacher in designing learning spaces and activities that highlight the multiple literacies of the children in our classrooms.

These two shifts to the nature of reading (one ontological and one paradigmatic) indicate the need for an updated reading pedagogy for classroom use. In this chapter, I examine the hypertextual, interactive, and visual elements of contemporary children's literature as a starting point for rethinking what it means to read and write with new forms of text. The first section ('Updating models of reading comprehension') outlines a traditional heuristic of reading comprehension, and argues that this model needs to be renovated for new texts and new times using social semiotics and sociocultural theories of literacy learning. The second section ('Visual-texts') examines specific characteristics of highly interactive, hypertextual, and visual children's literature, and employs the updated model of reading comprehension to discuss the implications of using these texts in the classroom for early reading and writing instruction. Finally, in the third section ('Reader/writer/teacher/designer'), I discuss the classroom contexts and instructional dynamics necessary for a pedagogy of multiliteracies. Taken together, this chapter argues for the inclusion of highly interactive visual-texts in the classroom, and outlines roles for the reader/writer when producing and consuming these texts, as well as roles for the teacher/facilitator for designing interactive-visual activities.

Updating models of reading comprehension: social semiotics and visual-texts

In this highly visual and interactive world of communication, "the basics" of traditional literacy education may not be enough for students to know how to read and write new forms of text. Yet in schools, literacy instruction continues to be dominated by traditional texts and alphabetic print (Hassett, 2006b). In this section, I describe a traditional heuristic for reading comprehension as a starting point for understanding the process of reading, and then I discuss how social semiotics and multidynamic literacy theories can help us update that model for new texts and new times.

Traditional heuristic for reading comprehension

As an organizational framework, I draw upon four components of the reading process that are widely accepted by reading researchers, and depicted by the RAND Reading Study Group (2002) in the heuristic below (Figure 7.1).

This model defines *reading comprehension* as the process of getting meaning from written language, and it consists of four interrelating elements: the *reader*, the *text*, the *activity* (or purpose) of reading, and the larger *sociocultural context* in which the reading occurs. In this model, the reader brings something to the text (e.g., knowledge and skills); the text has particular characteristics and codes; and the activity defines what we are to do with the text – the purpose of the reading or the outcome of a lesson. All of this occurs within a sociocultural context, such as defined by the social and cultural plane of the classroom, including the students' *and* the teachers' backgrounds, identities, expectations and ways of being in the classroom as a learning environment (Hammerberg [Hassett], 2004a).

This model of reading comprehension was developed with a traditional print-based notion of "text" in mind. When learning to read, the print on the page is primary, as we teach children to move from left to right and top to bottom. While readers can bring their own background knowledge to the reading, comprehension of the printed word involves being able to decipher the code to find the author's meaning. While graphics may speckle the printed page, educationally speaking

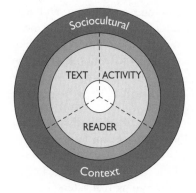

Figure 7.1 Traditional heuristic view of reading comprehension showing four components of the reading process depicted by the RAND Reading Study Group (2002).

(e.g., notions of reading development; literacy assessment) the images and pictures are primarily there to support the printed text (Hassett, 2006a). Thus, the traditional model for reading comprehension contains particular expectations about what the reader is to "do" with the text (e.g., decode the graphophonic cuing system; decipher the author's meaning), as well as particular kinds of "good reading behaviors" we look for as children engage with the texts and activities in our classrooms. These "good reading behaviors" are seen in our educational activities, standards and assessments, and are tightly tied to the printed word (Hassett, 2006b).

Of course, definitions of *text, reading, writing,* and *literacy* should not be understood as absolute. One look across the changes that have occurred educationally over time shows how the knowledge used to make decisions about best practice is not a matter of "given" knowledge, but more a matter of histories, practical techniques, and social forms of reasoning (Graff, 1979, 1986; Hassett, 2006b; Myers, 1996).

In this moment of our history, the history that makes up our present, we are living with a variety of communication techniques, which clearly indicate that basic print literacy skills alone, while remaining ever-important, are no longer enough to meet the demands of new forms of texts and multiple literacies. As the New London Group (2000a) points out, literacy pedagogy must account for "text forms associated with information and multimedia technologies" (p. 9). Beyond this, changes to our working lives, our public lives, and our personal lives demand that individuals be flexible, multi-skilled negotiators across languages, discourses, and cultures (New London Group, 2000a, pp. 14–18). Thus, the notion of a singular form of literacy as the reading and writing of print has been transformed into the notion of "multiliteracies" (Anstey, 2006; Kalantzis & Cope, 1997; Kress, 2000; New London Group, 2000b). This is not just a matter of reading the word, but rather, a matter of interpreting and representing meaning across various contexts and audiences with multiple sign systems.

Educationally, then, our social forms of reasoning about basic and best practice, as well as our practical techniques for teaching reading and writing, need to "catch up." In order to modify and update the traditional model of reading comprehension, I turn to sociocultural theories and social semiotics, described in the next section.

Social semiotics and sociocultural theories

In an updated model of reading comprehension, we can begin by thinking of "text" as involving more that the printed word, as many sociocultural theorists already have (see e.g., Gee, 1991; Hammerberg [Hassett], 2004b; Pérez, 1998). The texts children encounter today embody cues for reading that extend beyond the letters and words on the page, requiring readers to (inter)actively focus on textual elements beyond the decoding of print. To further understand the textual elements that extend, yet often embrace, printed text, I offer semiotic and sociocultural definitions of *mode, multimodal,* and *visual-texts* to help us update our model of reading comprehension.

Mode

Bezemer and Kress (2008) define a mode as a "socially and culturally shaped resource for meaning making" (p. 171). Beyond the printed word, there are numerous other socially and culturally shaped modes of communication and representation that can be counted as a part of the "text" to be "read," including, but not limited to, images, talk, directional lines, gestures, utterances, or icons. Although this definition is broad, Bezemer and Kress's characterization of "mode" helps us educationally to note that children have numerous resources to draw upon as they engage in literacy learning. When we help children to focus on print, itself a socially and culturally shaped mode to interpret, we can also utilize additional resources (modes) that children have available to them, be it simple gestures and pointing at words and print, or conversations around the text at hand, or interactive whiteboards that help us to create meaning in new ways. In the end, it is our job, as educators, to get the most out of the signs children are attuned to; but it is also our job to provide them with, and demonstrate for them, the multiple resources (modes) we have available for making meaning.

Multimodal

With a changing definition of "text" that includes multiple modes for making sense, the role of the reader/interpreter changes to one who can construct meaning from the multiple resources available. Siegel (2006) notes that children have always been multimodal; their resources for making meaning include talk, gesture, drama, drawing, and ways of incorporating, integrating, and extending linguistic signs (pp. 65–66). In a digital and technological culture, though, actual texts have become multimodal as well, containing multiple forms of symbolic representations (diSessa, 2000).

Hassett and Schieble (2007) point out that the use of computerized type design and photomechanical printing technologies create multimodal texts with various levels of meaning, as evidenced in some children's literature. Rather than having simple, static images paired with standardized alphabetic print, multimodal texts take on dynamically interactive elements. Thus, being able to navigate the Internet, use digital media, or even read a children's book involves being able to decode and comprehend alphabetic print in conjunction with other socially and culturally shaped forms of representation, that is, in conjunction with multiple modes.

Visual-text

I use the term "visual-text" to refer to the network of semiotic systems available within texts that contain and combine images and print. In semiotic terms, print itself can take on multiple modes of meaning through visual design and synergy with images (Dresang, 1999; Hammerberg [Hassett], 2001; Hassett, 2006a; Sipe, 1998). Unless the print is literally "pushed off the page" (Kress, 1998, p. 57), font itself can be a mode, because the way the word looks and "feels" on the page contains more meaning than the word itself.

Heuristic of reading comprehension updated

In an updated model of reading comprehension (see Figure 7.2), the text to be understood is a visual-text with a variety of modes for making sense. With this change to "text," the reader becomes one who uses the multimodal resources available to negotiate the text and interactively write/construct new meaning. Thus, the activity of reading/writing visual-texts involves meaning construction through a reflective recombination of the signs available (Siegel & Carey, 1989). In this sense, the signs available become the "semiotic scaffolds" that the reader/writer can use to create new meaning.

In the updated model of reading/writing with visual texts, the sociocultural context in which a reading takes place is informed by all three elements within the inner model. The visual-text itself sets up a sociocultural context for negotiating the multiple modes available; the reader/writer brings sociocultural backgrounds (both knowledge and skills) to the reading; and the activity of constructing meaning necessarily relies on the social and cultural resources available (semiotic modes) both in the text and in the classroom. In this way, the activities designed by teachers in the classroom around visual-texts become the scaffolding support for the instructional use of multimodal resources.

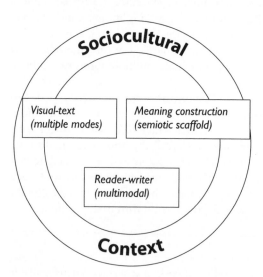

Figure 7.2 Model of reading/writing with visual-texts.

Visual-texts: Relationships between images and print in books for children

So, the text always has certain "real" (ontological) signs to interpret; the reader always has certain "real" sociocultural backgrounds (both knowledge and skills) to use with the text; and the activity of interpretation always takes place within a sociocultural field. In this section, I will use the updated model of reading/writing to explore specific characteristics of interactive visual-texts. Examples of contemporary children's literature will highlight the ways in which visual-texts contain: 1) words that express meaning through typesetting; 2) interactive narration; 3) images that expand meaning; and 4) multiple perspectives.

Words express meaning through typesetting: The text

In *Charlie Parker played be bop* by Christopher Raschka (1992), the *ways* in which various repetitive, melodious, and nonsense words are printed on the page – their typeface and graphical placement – lend themselves to a musical reading, with some words jumping around the page, some pounding, some rocking, and some rolling. One way to approach this reading might be to repeat the phrases over and over, in pairs and in groups, letting the words wash over you in all of their nonsensical sensibilities until you realize that . . . maybe you sound like jazz.

In *Froggy gets dressed* by Jonathan London (1994), images show mom yelling Froggy's name throughout the book: "Frrrroooooggggy!!" The print informs young readers to stretch out Froggy's name in terms of decoding, but additionally, the font changes color from a cool purple/blue on p. 7, to burnt orange on p. 10, and to fire red on p. 14. As a mode, the color changes show the mother's progressive anger with Froggy, and illustrates how, in this instance, more meaning is carried visually through color than decoding itself allows.

In Jules Feiffer's (1997) book *Meanwhile*, the word "RAYMOND!" is printed in huge capital letters, in a megaphone shape, with "noise lines" running through it. There is no need for quotation marks or a signifying trailer like: [comma, close quote] Mom yelled. We know mom is yelling by the way the word is placed on the page, and through our own cultural knowledge of mothers yelling, comic-book forms, and image–text relations.

In these and many other instances available in visual-texts, graphics represent more meaning than the word alone. The reader is required to decode not only the word, but also the way the word is printed and placed on the page, in what color, with what other designs (e.g., noise lines), in what shape (e.g., megaphone). Here, the visual-text itself sets up a social context for using our own backgrounds to interpret the modes available (e.g., *Froggy's mom is getting more mad*). Thus, the visual-text affords multiple ways to make sense of the elements in front of us in terms of our own lives.

Interactive narration: The reader

A key characteristic of interactive visual-texts is the way in which the reader is necessarily involved, not only as a consumer of the text and not only as a producer of meaning, but also as intrinsically mixed up in the plot and unfolding of the story itself. In *Don't let the pigeon drive the bus* (Willems, 2003), the narrator, a bus driver, directly addresses the reader, via a speech balloon in the very beginning prior to the title page, to watch over things while he goes away for a bit, and under no circumstances to let the pigeon drive his bus. As the story goes on, though, the little blue pigeon jumps through hoops and circles to try to get us to allow him to drive the bus. He begs us sweetly; he invents bus-driving games to play together; he cries; he screams . . . and so the story goes. But to read or hear this story is not merely to passively accept what is written. To read or hear this story is to respond back: often loudly, often with gusto! In the telling and viewing of this story, the reader/writer takes up dialogue with the pigeon, simultaneously in an object–subject position; and the reader/writer is, as a matter of fact, the only other "character" the pigeon speaks to.

In *Follow the line through the house* (Ljungkvist, 2007), the reader does not take the position of a character who moves through the story dialoguing with the other characters. Instead, the reader takes the position of moving through the *house* to explore, answer questions, and play hide-and-seek with small images of robots or mice. On the cover of this book, the title words are formed by means of a thin line that can be followed throughout the entire book. We enter the coat room, then the kitchen . . . and we realize that all of the major visual lines throughout the house are connected as one long line to follow. As we go from room to room, we follow the line into something else. For example, in the kitchen, we enter the refrigerator, where the line marks out milk containers, melons, pitchers, cheese. Within each "smaller space" of a room (e.g., refrigerator, closet, bathroom cabinet), there are questions and problems posed to the reader. In the refrigerator, readers are asked, through print scattered over the page, how many pickles are in the jar, or whether they can find all of the cherries that fell out of the bag. These types of questions require the reader to search and actively seek both the images and the text in concert. Additionally, many of the questions posed compel readers to draw on their own personal interests: What would *you* use from this refrigerator to make a sandwich? The images and signs in the text, then, serve as a scaffold for further thinking as new texts and stories are produced through interactive conversations.

In the cases where visual-texts directly address the reader and/or require an interactive form of story-telling, we can clearly see how the reader's role has changed. Beyond reading to decipher a particular (singular) meaning, highly interactive visual-texts require that young readers are a part of a larger milieu where they can respond altogether in a group and/or openly dialogue with their little colleagues who are experiencing the same thing. But make no mistake: these visual-texts themselves set up the context that calls for readers who can use the multimodal resources available to them in interactive ways. In order to negotiate and play with the text, and in order to interactively write/construct new meanings, the text and the social context (expectations) of the classroom are primary.

Images expand meaning: the activity

Another characteristic of visual-texts involves the heavy use of visuals to carry more meaning than the printed word alone. In Christopher Bing's (2000) artistic depiction of Ernest Lawrence Thayer's traditional poem, *Casey at the bat*, a traditional ballad is opened up into a new form of historical fiction. Graphics weave real and fictitious artifacts from the nineteenth century into the poem, such as newspaper clippings, ticket stubs, and photographs. Thus, images carry information about things outside the poem and add to the poem's meaning.

The activity of reading/writing visual-texts involves constructing meaning via a continual recombination of the signs available. Many texts for children combine print and images in such a way that the image *is made of* the print. Known as "synergy" (Dresang, 1999; Sipe, 1998, 2001), printed words and images blend together on the page and can no longer be separated. For example, in Peter Sis's (1996) *Starry messenger*, a book about Galileo, there is an image where printed words in script font are shaped in an "eyeball image" (n.p.). The image itself – the eyeball made up of Galileo's words – conveys meaning about Galileo's science and vision, yet the words cannot be disconnected from the image since they *are* (a part of) the image. To read this visual-text, the reader has to combine both the text and the image as one because the words themselves don't contain the overall larger meaning: that Galileo was a visionary; that Galileo observed the world; that Galileo used his eyeball to see into the skies. These meanings are not "in" the text; instead, they are "in" the interpretation and recombination of the signs available.

A similar form of image–text relations occurs in *Meow Ruff* (Sidman, 2006), a children's book in which *all* of the images are made up of words: the grass, the table, the tree, the rain. The clouds are the words; the words are the clouds. All actions, animals, places, and things are depicted in complete synergy between words and images. Additionally, the words used to form the objects in this book change from page to page depending upon the context of the story, even when the same object is being described in poetic form. For example, early on in the book, the picnic table is formed out of the words: "platform for picnics and crumbs and ants" (n.p.). Later, after it starts raining, the picnic table reads: "platform that's spotting and splatting and dripping" (n.p.). As the cat and the dog cuddle beneath the table, the activity of reading this visual-text requires the reader to constantly recombine the signs available and notice the nuances of meaning available everywhere on the page.

Siegel and Carey (1989) suggest that "sense-making involves the creation of new ideas" (p. 19). With visual-texts, the network of signs available for making sense becomes a scaffold for further thinking, questioning, and idea-creation. The new ideas created through the activity of reading visual-texts are not always "in" the text itself, but instead, are a part of a "dynamic and non-linear process" (Siegel & Carey, 1989) of critical and reflective thinking about the signs available.

Multiple perspectives: the sociocultural context

In the book *Loki & Alex* (Smith, 2001), Loki is the dog, and Alex is the boy, and each has his own perspective about what is happening at the moment. For example, a clear, full-color, photograph of Loki eating out of a trash bag has a superimposed image of Alex's face, saying how naughty Loki can be. On the opposite page, a distorted black-and-white photo of Alex grasping his cheeks with his mouth wide open reads from Loki's perspective, about how he thinks Alex just loves it when he digs for his own treats. The images show how Alex sees in color, as a human might, and Loki sees in black and white, as dogs are thought to do. But beyond the mode of color to convey meaning about seeing the world differently, the multiple perspectives on the same event are carried in the words and actions of each character. The book itself sets up a sociocultural context of living and being like Loki and Alex, each with his own perspective. The act of reading this book means living within their sociocultural push-and-pull world, but the reader is also living within the sociocultural contexts he or she brings to the reading as students share and laugh about these ideas with friends in the classroom.

Likewise, *Throw your tooth on the roof* (Beeler, 1998) describes what various cultures do when children lose a tooth. These tooth traditions are told in encyclopedic format: not to be read front-to-back, but instead, to be picked and chosen as the reader desires. This suggests a new way of reading books to and with children. Instead of reading a book out loud from front to back and cover to cover, adults and children necessarily have to communicate with each other about various elements and stories within the story. The social and cultural act of reading interactive visual-texts with multiple narratives sets up a space *outside* of the book to produce new knowledge around the book at hand.

Multiple perspectives and multiple narratives in interactive visual-texts require the reader to interpret across many social and cultural realms, as well as across many different story lines. For instance, *Black and white* by David Macaulay (1990) is a non-linear text that contains multiple narratives for the reader to interconnect and think about. Four distinct stories happen on the page at the same time, and while one *could* read each story individually, that would be missing the point. Links and connections among panels hold this book together: for example, the main character in the text is a robber, but he is never written about in the print: he only appears in images that connect the panels. This book does not have a singular meaning to interpret in the end, but instead, sets up a context for talking with each other about the many possible meanings. With each new reading a new meaning may be produced.

Reader/writer/teacher/designer: classroom contexts and a multidynamic pedagogy

Using a theoretical frame that combines sociocultural theories of language and literacy with semiotic theories that explore the changing nature of text enables us to understand the act of reading as always embedded within a social context and purpose for meaning-making, while also understanding the ways in which new forms of text set up different social contexts. Burbules (1998) notes that this is not a matter of whether a "new" form of reading will displace an "old" form of reading, because the practice of reading takes place "within contexts and social relations . . . [and] significant differences in those contexts and relations alter the practice" (p. 102).

As we have seen, highly interactive visual-texts are significantly different from traditional linear texts on several levels. From the look of the print on the page to the synergy of images and words, interactive visual-texts create "transactive spaces" (Dwight & Garrison, 2003) where the reader/writer can engage with multiple modes in an interplay, informing and reinventing meaning in multiple and innovative ways. For Smagorinsky (2001), this space is an "experiential space" rather than just a "social space" because the tools for reading (signs, symbols, texts, images) exist within a social space (accepted genre conventions, the pragmatics of the activity), which in turn exists in reciprocal relation to the human reader's "head" (cognition, skills, knowledge, identity, and abilities) (Hammerberg [Hassett], 2004b; Shaffer & Clinton, n.d.).

In this frame of mind, the socio-cognitive processes of reading involve not only the tools of the text (the modes of representation), but also the social practices that allow us to recognize and interpret various signs and modal genres *as meaningful* in the first place. Thus, reading, as an interaction between a reader and a text, involves the social use of these representational modes as part and parcel of conceptual thinking. This understanding of reading as a socio-cognitive process is meant to highlight the ways in which complex cognitive actions and various social resources are reciprocally and inextricably coupled.

It is important to note, then, that the design of activities and lessons around visual-texts encompasses more than the text itself. With visual-texts, reading is not always a matter of "getting" the author's meaning; instead, reading is about constructing sense out of the mass of cultural artifacts, tools, signs, and symbols at hand. In the classroom, the social (instructional, conversational) practices at work within the learning environment form a part of the "experiential space" in which meaning is produced. Thus, teachers as facilitators of visual-text experiences *design* their learning spaces and activities in order to highlight the multiple literacies of the children in our classrooms (New London Group, 2000a), and in order to highlight the multiple modes available in any text.

Elsewhere, I have proposed a multidynamic literacy pedagogy (Hassett, 2008) where literacy is viewed as multifaceted, socially constructed, and inextricably linked to the real lives and thoughts of children. In the case of highly interactive visual-texts, a multidynamic literacy pedagogy allows teachers the flexibility to add semiotic toolkits to their instructional repertoires. As teachers/facilitators design experiential spaces for their young readers/writers, there is a "letting go" of some of the dogma around traditional reading instruction. For example, our reading strategies and cuing systems can be updated to include graphics, textual placement, synergy, and images that represent more than the printed word alone. We can include the possibility of mixed genres and dialect cues, and a purpose for reading beyond deciphering an author's singular meaning. If we truly value "children's powers of imagination and generativity" (Siegel, 2006), then we must accept that, in the end, there is no singular meaning to take away, no one "right" answer. Rather, there are multiple story-lines and modes to integrate together as readers/writers create a larger meaning for themselves. Thus, a pedagogy of multiliteracies continually reinvents the story of what's "new" about "new literacies" in the elementary classroom using visual-texts as a starting point.

References

Anstey, M. (2006). *Teaching and learning multiliteracies: Changing times, changing literacies.* Newark, DE: International Reading Association.

Beeler, S. B. (1998). *Throw your tooth on the roof: Tooth traditions from around the world.* Boston: Houghton Mifflin.

Bezemer, J., & Kress, G. (2008). Writing in multimodal texts: A social semiotic account of designs for learning. *Written Communication, 25*(2), 166.

Bing, C. H. (2000). *Ernest L. Thayer's Casey at the Bat: A ballad of the republic sung in the year 1888* (1st ed.). Brooklyn, NY: Handprint Books.

Burbules, N. C. (1998). Rhetorics of the web: hyperreading and critical literacy. In I. Snyder (ed.), *Page to screen: Taking literacy into the electronic era* (pp. 102–122). New York: Routledge.

diSessa, A. A. (2000). *Changing minds: Computers, learning, and literacy.* Cambridge, Mass.: MIT Press.

Dresang, E. T. (1999). *Radical change: Books for youth in a digital age.* New York: H.W. Wilson Co.

Dwight, J. & Garrison, J. (2003). A manifesto for instructional technology: Hyperpedagogy. *Teachers College Record, 105*(5), 699–728. doi: 10.1111/1467–9620.00265.

Feiffer, J. (1997). *Meanwhile—.* New York: HarperCollins Publishers.

Gee, J. (1991). Socio-cultural approaches to literacy (literacies). *Annual Review of Applied Linguistics, 12,* 31.

Graff, H. J. (1979). *The literacy myth: Literacy and social structure in the nineteenth-century city.* New York: Academic Press.

Graff, H. J. (1986). *The labyrinths of literacy: Reflections of literacy past and present.* London; Philadelphia, Penn.: Falmer Press.

Hammerberg [Hassett], D. D. (2001). Reading and writing 'hypertextually': Children's literature, technology, and early writing instruction. *Language Arts, 78*(3), 207–216.

Hammerberg [Hassett], D. D. (2004a). Technologies of the self in classrooms designed as "learning environments": (Im)possible ways of being in early literacy instruction. In

Dangerous coagulations? The uses of Foucault in the study of education (pp. 359–382). New York: Peter Lang.

Hammerberg [Hassett], D. D. (2004b). Comprehension instruction for socioculturally diverse classrooms: A review of what we know. *Reading Teacher, 57*(7), 648–658.

Hassett, D. D. (2006a). Signs of the times: The governance of alphabetic print over 'appropriate' and 'natural' reading development. *Journal of Early Childhood Literacy, 6*(1), 77–103.

Hassett, D. D. (2006b). Technological difficulties: A theoretical frame for understanding the non-relativistic permanence of traditional print literacy in elementary education. *Journal of Curriculum Studies, 38*(2), 135–159.

Hassett, D. D. (2008). Teacher flexibility and judgment: A multidynamic theory for early childhood literacy instruction. *Journal of Early Childhood Literacy, 8*(3), 297–330.

Hassett, D. D. & Schieble, M. B. (2007). Finding space and time for the visual in K–12 literacy instruction. *English Journal, 97*(1), 62–68.

Kalantzis, M. & Cope, B. (1997). *Multiliteracies: Rethinking what we mean by literacy and what we teach as literacy in the context of global cultural diversity and new communications technologies.* Haymarket, NSW: Centre for Workplace Communication and Culture.

Kress, G. (1998). Visual and verbal modes of representation in electronically mediated communication: The potentials of new forms of text. In *Page to screen: Taking literacy into the electronic era* (pp. 53–79). New York: Routledge.

Kress, G. R. (2000). Design and transformation: New theories of meaning. In *Multiliteracies: Literacy learning and the design of social futures,* (pp. 153–161). London: Routledge.

Kress, G. R. (2003). *Literacy in the new media age.* London: Routledge.

Lankshear, C., & Knobel, M. (2003). *New literacies: Changing knowledge and classroom learning.* Open University Press.

Ljungkvist, L. (2007). *Follow the line through the house.* New York: Viking, Penguin.

London, J. (1994). *Froggy gets dressed.* New York: Puffin.

Macaulay, D. (1990). *Black and white.* Boston: Houghton Mifflin.

Myers, M. (1996). *Changing our minds: Negotiating English and literacy.* Urbana, Ill.: National Council of Teachers of English.

New London Group. (2000a). A pedagogy of multiliteracies: Designing social futures. In *Multiliteracies: Literacy learning and the design of social futures,* (pp. 9–42). London: Routledge.

New London Group. (2000b). *Multiliteracies: Literacy learning and the design of social futures.* London: Routledge.

Pérez, B. (1998). *Sociocultural contexts of language and literacy.* Mahwah, NJ: Lawrence Erlbaum Associates.

RAND Reading Study Group. (2002). Reading for understanding: Toward an R&D program in reading comprehension. Retrieved November 14, 2008, from http://www.rand.org/multi/achievementforall/reading/readreport.html.

Raschka, C. (1992). *Charlie Parker played be bop.* New York: Orchard Books.

Shaffer, D. W. & Clinton, K. A. (n.d.). Toolsforthought: Re-examining thinking in the digital age. *WCER Working Paper 2005–2006.* University of Wisconsin–Madison.

Sidman, J. (2006). *Meow ruff.* Boston: Houghton Mifflin.

Siegel, M. (2006). Rereading the signs: Multimodal transformations in the field of literacy education. *Language Arts, 84*(1), 65–77.

Siegel, M. G. & Carey, R. F. (1989). *Critical thinking: A semiotic perspective.* Monographs on teaching critical thinking. Bloomington, Ind.: ERIC Clearinghouse on Reading and Communication Skills, Smith Research Center, Indiana University.

Sis, P. (1996). *Starry messenger: a book depicting the life of a famous scientist, mathematician, astronomer, philosopher, physicist, Galileo Galilei.* New York: Farrar Straus Giroux.

Sipe, L. R. (1998). How picture books work: A semiotically framed theory of text–picture relationships. *Children's Literature in Education, 29*(2), 97–108.

Sipe, L. R. (2001). Picturebooks as aesthetic objects. *Literacy Teaching and Learning, 6*(1), 23–42.

Smagorinsky, P. (2001). If meaning is constructed, what is it made from? Toward a cultural theory of reading. *Review of Educational Research, 71*(1), 133.

Smith, C. R. (2001). *Loki & Alex: The adventures of a dog and his best friend* (1st ed.). New York: Dutton Children's Books.

Willems, M. (2003). *Don't let the pigeon drive the bus!* New York: Hyperion Books for Children.

Part III

Beginning to read print

Chapter 8

Phonology, reading and reading difficulties

Usha Goswami

Language development and literacy are intimately related. In particular, the way in which the brain represents the sound-structure of spoken language – phonology – is critical for the future development of literacy. The brain develops phonological 'representations' in response to spoken language exposure and learning to speak, and the quality of these phonological representations determines literacy acquisition. Both perceptual and articulatory processes are important in developing a child's phonological representations. In infancy and early childhood, the representation of phonology relies on prosodic or rhythmic features of language and on perceptual units like syllables. As an alphabet is acquired and visual codes become associated with these pre-existing phonological representations, the brain restructures its language-based representations into so-called 'phonemic phonology'. However, individual differences in the acquisition of phonemic phonology depend on individual differences in the quality of the phonological representations that were acquired prior to literacy. A specific problem with phonology suggests that a child will have specific learning difficulties with respect to literacy, irrespective of IQ.

Introduction

Our life-long experience with the alphabet biases our perceptual experience of speech. As literate adults, 'when we hear someone say "tomato", we seem to hear . . . a sequence of consonant and vowel sound units . . . [yet] there is virtually no evidence that supports the traditional view of linguistic representation' (Port 2007: 143–4). Babies do not appear to experience speech in the form of the letter-like symbolic units experienced by adults, and neither do pre-reading children. A literate adult will be slow to decide that words like 'sign' and 'wine' rhyme, because the word-specific visual sequences that have been learned for these words are different (the spelling of the rhyming part of the words is 'inconsistent', namely —ign and —ine; see Ziegler, Ferrand & Montant 2004). A preliterate child will show no speed impairment in deciding that 'wine' and 'sign' rhyme. This is because the word-specific visual learning that is necessary to become a reader has not yet taken place (Goswami, Ziegler & Richardson 2005). For the preliterate child, phonology is based on auditory experiences and not on visual experiences.

Rather than learning spoken words as sequences of 'phonemes' or individual sound elements, infants and young children appear to learn language-specific phonotactic templates based on their specific experiences of adult input and their own babbling practices (Vihman & Croft 2007). A phonotactic template is essentially an auditory pattern. When learning spoken language, children are learning complex acoustic structures that are linked to unique meanings. Spoken words vary in terms of auditory cues like loudness, duration, pitch and rhythm, and the brain appears to learn the specific combinations of these auditory parameters that represent individual words very rapidly (Saffran 2001). These auditory patterns are the first 'phonological representations', indeed, the first phonological representation that is acquired is the baby's own name (at around four months of age, see Bortfeld *et al.* 2005). According to recent linguistic theories (Pierrehumbert 2003; Port 2007), speech processing is initially auditory rather than specifically linguistic. Lower levels of the auditory pathways in the brain respond to the pitch, duration and intensity of any sounds, linguistic or not. With experience, higher levels then respond to whether the sounds are from conspecifics (other humans) and whether they carry linguistic meaning. For example, if you speak a 'click' language (some African languages such as Zulu use clicks as elements of words), you will show an advantage for processing 'click' stimuli with the left-hemisphere language areas of your brain. If you do not speak a click language, these same identical click stimuli will be processed as clicks rather than as linguistic elements, and will not show a left-hemisphere advantage (Best & Avery 2002). The special auditory patterns that comprise words in a particular language have to be learned.

Early word learning by babies

Infant work in the area of language acquisition, just like current work in the area of literacy acquisition, used to assume that learning depended on the 'phoneme'. *Phoneme* was the short-hand term that linguists used to refer to the individual sound elements that appeared to literate adults to make up words in languages. For example, words like *bat* and *bit* appear to differ by one sound element, the middle element. *Bat* and *pat* also appear to differ by one element, the initial element, and *bat* and *back* appear to differ by one element, the final element. These differences in acoustics were described as differences in phonemes. Phonemes are an abstraction from the physical stimulus, as (for example) the vowel phoneme in *bat* and *back* is not exactly the same sound, and neither is the /p/ phoneme in *spoon* and *pat*. However, to the literate linguists who invented the international phonetic inventory, phonemes were clearly discernible in the speech signal (Port 2007). It was therefore believed that all languages were created from a universal pool of phonemes, and that babies began learning language by learning to discriminate these phonemes. Phonemes were assumed to correspond to acoustic cues such as spectral energy peaks (formants), which correspond to rapid changes in frequency and intensity (Blumstein & Stevens 1981).

Babies could indeed learn differences in speech sounds that corresponded to phonemic differences, such as the difference between 'ba' and 'pa' (this difference depends on their ability to detect differences in voicing, or in the degree of vibration of the vocal cords; Eimas, Siqueland, Jusczyk & Vigorito 1971). However, so could other animals, including chinchillas, budgerigars and dolphins (Dooling, Okanoya & Brown 1989). This suggested that the acoustic cues to which the babies were responding were not linked to the identity of phonemes as the basic elements of human speech. Perplexingly, it was then demonstrated that adults could recognize and interpret speech even when no formant structure was present (Remez, Rubin, Pisoni & Carrell 1981). Further research with adults suggested that the slower (syllable-level) modulations in the auditory signal were more critical for speech intelligibility than formant structure (Shannon *et al.* 1995). These slower (amplitude) modulations are most easily conceptualised as corresponding to the rhythmic patterning or prosodic structure of spoken language. When we make syllables with our articulators, we produce variations in acoustic energy which are perceived as rhythmic or intonational patterning. Each individual syllable is also perceived as comprising particular sound elements, such as 'ba' versus 'pa', or 'ba' versus 'wa'. Deaf babies who are given cochlear implants only hear the syllable-level modulations in speech (as the rapid fine structure is not transmitted by the implant). Yet deaf children with cochlear implants can develop reasonable spoken language skills and awareness of phonology (James *et al.* 2005).

As well as accurate acoustic perception, social interaction is fundamental to natural language learning (Kuhl 2007). Infants learn language because of social communication with partners, not because of passive exposure to sequences of sounds. Kuhl argues that the importance of making shared meaning probably explains why a computational system that can learn language has been so difficult to develop (Kuhl 2004). Infants also benefit from the fact that those communicating with them use a special intonational register called 'Motherese' or infant-directed speech (IDS). Even other children will adopt IDS patterns when speaking to infants. IDS is an exaggerated prosodic register that emphasises word and phrase boundaries via utilising heightened pitch and increased rhythm, stress and durational cues. IDS appears to make the segmentation of the speech stream easier for the infant (Echols 1996).

Thus at least two aspects of language acquisition are critical for the eventual acquisition of literacy. One is learning the sounds and combinations of sounds that are permissible in a particular language, so that your brain can develop high-quality phonological representations of the sound structure of individual words. The second is to learn to produce these words yourself, by learning how to articulate the required sounds correctly. Both types of learning undergo protracted development. Word learning usually takes off between 12 and 15 months of age. The earliest age for producing your first word is around nine months. By

16 months of age, median spoken vocabulary size is 55 words (Fenson, Dale, Reznick, Bates, Thal & Pethick 1994). By 23 months, it is 225 words. By 30 months, median vocabulary size is 573 words, reflecting a tenfold increase in 14 months. By age six, the average child has a spoken vocabulary of around 6,000 words and a comprehension vocabulary of around 14,000 words (Dollaghan 1994). Each of these words is represented by the brain as a distinct phonological representation, a unique auditory pattern comprising a particular combination of local changes in pitch, intensity and duration corresponding to a unique meaning. In order to learn how the alphabet (or another orthographic code) can systematically represent these complex patterns in visual form, the child needs to develop 'phonological awareness'.

The development of phonological awareness

When we teach literacy, we are teaching children to hear sounds ('phonemes') that we ourselves perceive to be fundamental to spoken words, but which are not in fact fundamental to spoken words. As already discussed, although literate adults automatically hear spoken language as sequences of consonant and vowel sound units, children hear acoustically complex patterns that are linked to meanings. However, through language acquisition itself the child's brain is acquiring some knowledge of phonological similarities and differences between words. Phonological awareness, the awareness of the component sounds in words, undergoes an apparently universal cross-language developmental sequence from larger to smaller units (see Ziegler & Goswami 2005). Prior to learning to read, children are aware of relatively large units of phonology such as syllables. If they are taught to read an alphabetic script, they eventually become aware of 'small' units of phonology – phonemes. Frith (1998) pointed out that the acquisition of the alphabetic code was like catching a virus: 'This virus infects all speech processing, as now whole word sounds are automatically broken up into sound constituents. Language is never the same again'. In other words, once the brain has learned phonology–orthography connections, spoken language processing is changed forever. Spoken words are now automatically experienced in terms of orthography as well as phonology, even during oral language processing. Therefore, it takes an adult longer to decide that 'sign' rhymes with 'wine' than to decide that 'mine' rhymes with 'wine'. Orthographic knowledge affects phonological judgements.

For English-speaking children, this universal developmental sequence means that they first become aware of syllables in words, and then of sub-syllabic units called 'onset' and 'rime' (see Ziegler & Goswami 2005 for a detailed review). To divide any syllable into onset-rime units, we segment the syllable at the vowel. Because of the phonological structure of English, English onsets and rimes do not usually correspond to alphabetic letters. For many other European languages however (e.g. Finnish, Spanish, Italian, Greek), the onset-rime division of the syllable results in a single-phoneme onset, and a single-phoneme rime. This is because for the majority of the world's languages, syllable structure is simple or CV (consonant–vowel). Syllables in languages like Spanish and Italian are like the English words 'see' or 'go'. Division at the vowel results in two phonological units, as in /s/ and /E/, which are also the two phonemes making up the syllable. For these languages, therefore, onset-rime segmentation also corresponds to the sounds or phonemes made by the letters used to write the syllable down.

In contrast, the English language has primarily complex syllables. The dominant syllable structure in English is CVC. For single-syllable words (of which English has more than most languages), this structure accounts for 43 per cent of monosyllables (e.g. 'cat', 'dog', 'soap' and 'look'; see De Cara & Goswami 2002). English also has many CCVC syllables (15 per cent of monosyllables, e.g. 'trip', 'plan' and 'spin'), CVCC syllables (21 per cent of monosyllables, e.g. 'fast', 'pant' and 'jump'), and some CCVCC syllables (6 per cent, e.g. 'crust'). Only 5 per cent of monosyllabic words follow the CV pattern ('sea', 'go', 'do') that is dominant in so many other languages.

As might be expected, it is perceptually more challenging for a child to segment a complex syllable like 'pant' into four discrete elements than to segment a simple syllable like 'go' into two discrete elements. Other linguistic factors also play a role in segmentation, such as the relative difficulty of perceiving nasal sounds like /n/, which is why children often omit sounds like the penultimate consonant phoneme when they learn to spell (e.g., writing PAT for 'pant', Treiman 1998). Further, the dominant phonological CVC template in English does not necessarily correspond to a CVC spelling pattern. Words like 'coat', 'book', 'make' and 'time' all have a CVC phonological pattern, but not a CVC spelling. Indeed, when a child spells these words using a CVC orthographic pattern (for example, TIM), the spelling is counted as wrong. Children's 'invented spellings' are actually a rich source for understanding their preliterate intuitions about phonological similarity. For example, preliterate children hear the same sound at the beginning of TRAY and CHICKEN, and accordingly invent spellings such as CHRAC (truck), ASCHRAY (ashtray) and CHRIBLS (troubles; for systematic analyses see Read 1986; Treiman 1993).

Both the phonological complexity of English syllables and the inconsistency of English spelling patterns make it difficult to become aware of phonemes in English. This can be illustrated by considering the development of phonological awareness in young children across languages. Whereas young children across languages are aware of syllables, onsets and rimes prior to being taught to read, awareness of phonemes develops at very different rates depending on orthographic consistency (see Ziegler & Goswami 2005, for detail). This is because phonemes need to be learned from letters. As letters are learned, however, orthographic learning quickly begins to affect children's phonological judgements. This was shown clearly in the study by Goswami *et al.* (2005), who compared phonological judgements in English and German pre-readers and beginning readers. Prior to learning to read, phonological awareness should depend on spoken language factors only. As the phonological structure of English and German words is essentially the same, pre-readers should therefore show equivalent performance in phonological awareness tasks. However, children learning to read should begin to show divergent performance, since German is an orthographically consistent orthography and English is not. English children will be learning inconsistent letter–sound correspondences at both the rime level (e.g. *chair, pear, stare, where*) and the phoneme level (e.g. *talk, form, dawn*). German children will not. As the brain incorporates orthographic information into its phonological representations, visual learning should begin to affect phonological judgements.

To test this hypothesis, Goswami *et al.* (2005) gave their participants an oddity task at both rime and phoneme level, and predicted similar cross-language performance by pre-readers but not by readers. At the rime level, word triples differed by rime (e.g. *house, mouse, **kiss***), and at the phoneme level by vowel phoneme (e.g. *house, loud, **path***). For half of the triples, the orthographic representations were inconsistent (e.g. *boat, note, **root**, dawn, fork, **rice***). As predicted, the pre-reading children performed at the same overall level across the two languages, for both rime and phoneme judgements. The children who were beginning to read, however, showed marked effects of orthographic consistency. For the English children, rime consistency improved performance in the rime oddity task by 19.5 per cent (comparable rime consistency effect for German, 0.7 per cent). For the German children, phoneme consistency improved performance in the phoneme oddity task by 14.2 per cent (comparable phoneme consistency effect for English, 2.3 per cent). The fact that consistency effects were found only for *readers* in both languages suggests that orthographic knowledge very quickly started having an effect on phonological judgements. The German children also showed significantly higher levels of phoneme awareness than the English children, presumably because of the greater overall consistency with which letters represent phonemes in German (see Goswami *et al.* 2005, for a fuller discussion).

Letters and phonemes

The development of phonemic awareness by children clearly depends on learning about letters. As outlined above, phonemes are not discrete acoustic units in the speech stream that correspond to particular auditory cues like formants. Phonemes are learned via their visual representation as letters, and so orthographic consistency (i.e. consistent, 1:1 mappings between letters and phonemes) facilitates the development of phonemic awareness. Preliterate children have not learned words as sequences of consonant and vowel phonemes. Rather, they have learned complex acoustic patterns that they now need to match to sequences of letters. To make these matches successfully, some aspects of phonological similarity (such as the shared sounds that begin the words TRAY and CHICKEN) have to be ignored, and some aspects of phonological difference (such as the difference in the actual sound that is represented by the letter P in PIT and SPOON) have to be ignored as well. This is essentially why individual differences in preliterate phonological sensitivity determine how well an individual child will be able to learn to use the alphabet efficiently for reading and spelling (Anthony *et al.* 2002).

For many children, phonemic learning as the alphabet is taught is rapid. This is particularly true for children who are learning to read very consistent or transparent orthographies, such as Finnish, Italian and Spanish. For other children, phonemic learning is not rapid. The children who will struggle with learning to read are those children who come to the task of reading with less well-developed phonological representations. New research is suggesting that the origin of these individual differences in phonological representations lies in basic auditory processing skills. Children with less well-developed phonological representations have difficulties with auditory cues to the syllable structure of speech.

Auditory processing and phonological awareness

As noted earlier, speech is a very complex acoustic signal. One way to model this signal is to factor it mathematically into the product of a slowly varying envelope (also called amplitude modulation) and a rapidly varying fine time structure (see Smith, Oxenham & Delgutte 2002). Experiments that have created 'chimeric' sentences using the envelope of one sentence and the fine time structure of another have shown that the brain relies primarily on envelope cues for understanding speech (Smith *et al.* 2002). Related experiments have suggested that speech intelligibility relies on the slower amplitude modulations in the lower frequency regions (1–16 Hz) of the speech signal (Drullman, Festen & Plomp 1994). These slower modulations are essentially the acoustic consequences of the relatively slow movements made by our vocal tracts (Nittrouer 2006). These movements of the vocal tract are exaggerated by Motherese (IDS), which appears to be important for language-learning in infancy. Therefore, it seems likely that the accurate perception of the slowly varying amplitude envelope information in speech will be central to setting up a phonological lexicon in infancy (see Corriveau, Pasquini & Goswami 2007 for detail).

Perception of the amplitude envelope of any sound, speech or non-speech, depends on basic auditory processing of the rates of change in amplitude as the envelope varies, and on basic auditory processing of duration, intensity and frequency. A simplified and schematic example is shown as Figure 8.1. Recently, we have been exploring whether individual differences in children's ability to hear changes in auditory cues like rise time (rate of change of amplitude), duration, intensity and frequency are associated with individual differences in phonological awareness. We have been finding very strong associations, with knock-on effects for literacy. In particular, children who have a diagnosis of developmental dyslexia, and who have very poor phonological awareness, show consistent impairments in rise time discrimination in our studies (Goswami *et al.* 2002; Richardson *et al.* 2004; Thomson & Goswami 2008). Children with specific language impairments who have phonological difficulties also show rise time impairments (Corriveau, Pasquini & Goswami 2007; Corriveau & Goswami 2009). Adults who had dyslexia as

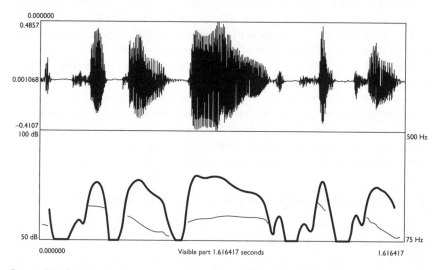

Figure 8.1 Schematic representation of a speech utterance ('The kettle boiled quickly') illustrating local changes in features like pitch (thin lines), duration (area) and rise and fall times (dark lines).

children continue to show rise time processing difficulties (Thomson, Fryer, Maltby & Goswami 2006; Pasquini, Corriveau & Goswami 2007). Finally, rise time processing difficulties are found in developmental dyslexia across languages (see Muneaux *et al.* 2004; Hämäläinen, Leppänen, Torppa, Muller & Lyytinen 2005; Hämäläinen, Salminen & Leppänen in press). In their cross-language survey of auditory processing studies of developmental dyslexia, Hämäläinen *et al.* (in press) found that rise time was associated with dyslexia in 100 per cent of studies, and showed large effect sizes (median Cohen's d = 1.00, this means that the impairment in perceiving rise time is relatively large). Frequency and duration detection are also impaired in some auditory processing studies. However, the dominant auditory cue to amplitude envelope structure that is impaired is rise time.

If rise time perception is important for the development of well-specified phonological representations, then children who have exceptional phonological awareness would be expected to show superior rise time discrimination. This is in fact the case (Goswami *et al.* 2002). Goswami *et al.* (2002) compared rise time perception in 11-year-olds who had taught themselves to read when they were four years old (see Stainthorp & Hughes 1998) and in typically developing control 11-year-olds from the same longitudinal study. The precocious readers had significantly superior rise time perception and superior phonological awareness. Similarly, if rise time perception is important for phonological awareness and consequently for literacy, then rise time impairments should lead to poor literacy skills across the IQ range. There has been a lot of debate about the role of IQ in diagnosing developmental dyslexia, which has been misleading with respect to the issue of causality (see Stanovich 1988). If poor phonological development has its roots in a less efficient auditory sensory system, then any child who has relatively inefficient auditory processing is likely to show later problems with reading, irrespective of their IQ. Similarly, any child who has efficient auditory processing is unlikely to show later problems with reading, other factors being equal. These other factors would include the richness of initial language input and linguistic environment, parental investment in literacy, and access to the curriculum.

Recently, we have begun to explore the role of basic auditory processing in the reading abilities of so-called 'garden variety' poor readers (Killing & Goswami 2008; Kuppen, Huss, Fosker, Mead & Goswami in press). Garden-variety poor readers traditionally have been distinguished from dyslexic poor readers because they have lower IQs. Therefore (it had been argued), their reading impairments were not unexpected given their overall intellectual abilities. However, if auditory sensory processing is at the roots of poor phonology and poor reading, then children with lower IQs who have very good auditory sensory processing should acquire phonological awareness and reading along a typical developmental trajectory, at least for initial reading decoding skills (other factors being equal; reading comprehension skills are *a priori* more likely to vary with IQ). To test this hypothesis, we have compared two groups of children, children with lower IQ (mean IQ 76) whose reading is age-appropriate or ahead of their chronological age (LIQ readers), and children with lower IQ (mean IQ 73) who show significant delays in reading (these are the garden variety poor readers, or GV poor readers). We have found that auditory processing and phonological awareness are both preserved in the LIQ group, that is, that auditory processing skills and phono-logical development are equivalent to age-matched controls with normal IQ. In contrast, auditory processing and phonological awareness are significantly impaired in the GV group compared to the same group of age-matched controls. Although preliminary, these data support the view that phonological development, and therefore reading development, depend at least in part on very basic sensory processing mechanisms which differ between children. According to such data, IQ is irrelevant in terms of causing poor reading for these children. Rather, a basic aspect of brain function – namely, auditory processing – is causing poorer phonological development, which consequently leads to poorer acquisition of reading. Children who have poor auditory processing skills should thus receive extra support and tuition in phonology and literacy, whatever their IQ.

Reading development and reading difficulties

As discussed above, the child's brain develops phonological 'representations' of words in response to spoken language exposure and learning to speak. The quality of these phonological representations then determines literacy acquisition (relevant studies have not been discussed here, but there is ample evidence for a causal connection, see Goswami & Bryant 1990; Ziegler & Goswami 2005). Developmental research has shown that both perceptual and articulatory processes are important for developing a child's phonological representations. So far in this chapter, we have focused on perceptual processes. However, brain imaging studies also tell us that children who have phonological difficulties rely *more* on articulatory networks when developing phonological representations than other children. Imaging studies of both dyslexic and deaf readers show that the areas of the brain that control the motor output of speech (i.e., articulatory processes) are very active during phonological tasks. It seems plausible that this is because brains with inherently poorer auditory perceptual systems are recruiting articulatory systems in compensation (see Goswami 2008a, for a simple overview of the brain imaging data).

In terms of supporting reading development and remediating reading difficulties, these insights are important. First, on the perceptual side, we have seen that the ability to discriminate cues to the rhythmic structure of speech are implicated in phonological difficulties (rise time is a cue to which syllables in the speech stream are stressed and which are unstressed, and it is also important for deliberately producing speech rhythmically, as in counting to a rhythm). As noted earlier, early phonological representations can be seen as 'phonotactic templates' or 'prosodic templates', namely auditory patterns varying in intensity, duration, pitch and rhythm (Vihman & Croft 2007; Pierrehumbert 2003). The dominant prosodic template in early language acquisition in English is bisyllabic, with stronger stress on the first syllable (e.g. 'mummy', 'daddy', 'baby'). This template is so strong that we amend the words we use with babies to fit the strong–weak pattern, as in 'milkie' and 'doggie'. This is also the first template that young children produce (e.g., 'nana' for 'banana'). It therefore seems likely that word play with words longer than one syllable, exaggerating stress patterns or playing around with internal rhythms, would be helpful in fostering the development of high-quality phonological representations. Second, on the production side, learning to articulate longer words, and in particular matching articulation with an external rhythm or beat (e.g., clapping to stressed syllables, which is natural for many nursery rhymes, as in 'Pat-a-cake' or 'Humpty Dumpty') is also likely to be helpful for phonological development.

In terms of identifying reading difficulties, it would be very helpful to have a robust test that could identify the auditory processing difficulties discussed above early in development. This would enable language enrichment for children with less efficient auditory processing systems to begin as early as possible. Unfortunately, the current state-of-the-art has not reached this point. The auditory rise time studies discussed above relied on determining psycho-acoustic thresholds for individual children (i.e., using repeated trials to determine exactly when the child stopped being able to distinguish between two different sounds). Such methods are not amenable for use in widespread screening, as they take a long time to administer, are susceptible to distraction and require highly specialized equipment. Perhaps more promising for the early identification of learning difficulties are attempts to find the 'neural signature' or neural marker of impaired rise time processing (Thomson, Baldeweg & Goswami 2009). As neural markers can be measured without attention, and do not rely on IQ, the direct measurement of the auditory neural networks that process sounds in the child's brain offers a useful way of identifying those at risk for learning difficulties (Szücs & Goswami 2007; Friedrich 2008). Again, however, the required technology and reliability at the level of the individual child is not here yet. Therefore, the most efficient way to intervene early in potential learning difficulties is to enrich the linguistic and phonological environments experienced by all children, not just those children at risk (Goswami 2008b). The rise time research suggests that preschool activities based around rhythm and language (including music and singing) could be particularly beneficial (Goswami in press).

Conclusion

In this chapter, I have tried to provide an overview of some of the different factors that affect the development of phonological representations of spoken language by children, and to show how these link with reading and reading difficulties. Literacy acquisition is dependent on good phonological foundations, and phonology is best described in terms of syllables and prosody (rhythm and intonation) prior to the acquisition of an alphabetic orthography. Spoken language processing abilities at the levels of rhythm, syllable and rhyme help determine these phonological foundations. 'Phonemic phonology', or the experience of spoken words as sequences of consonant and vowel phonemes, depends on learning to read and to spell. The effects on phonological development of becoming literate in an alphabetic language are profound. Pre-reading phonological awareness is important because it is the best predictor we have of how easily a child will be able to learn about how letters correspond to phonemes. Recent studies suggest that phonological awareness depends on intact auditory processing of rise time. A child who has poor phonological awareness is likely to have relatively poor auditory processing skills, irrespective of their IQ. Similarly, children who have good auditory processing skills appear to develop good phonological awareness and good reading (decoding) abilities, irrespective of IQ. Hence improving the basic rhythmic sensory processing skills of all children, via enriched linguistic and musical activities in infancy and early childhood, is likely to benefit phonological and language development and consequently to benefit reading development.

References

Anthony, J.L., Lonigan, C.J., Burgess, S.R., Driscoll, K., Phillips, B.M., & Cantor, B.G. (2002) 'Structure of preschool phonological sensitivity: Overlapping sensitivity to rhyme, words, syllables, and phonemes', *Journal of Experimental Child Psychology*, 82: 65–92.

Best, C.T. & Avery, R.A. (2002) 'Left-hemisphere advantage for click consonants is determined by linguistic significance and experience', *Psychological Science*, 10: 65–70.

Blumstein, S.E. & Stevens, K.N. (1981) 'Phonetic features and acoustic invariance in speech', *Cognition*, 10: 25–32.

Bortfeld, H., Morgan, J., Golinkoff, R., & Rathbun, K. (2005) 'Mommy and me: Familiar names help launch babies into speech stream segmentation', *Psychological Science*, 16: 298–304.

Corriveau, K. & Goswami, U. (2009) 'Rhythmic motor entrainment in children with speech and language impairment: Tapping to the beat', *Cortex*, 45: 119–130.

Corriveau, K., Pasquini, E., & Goswami, U. (2007) 'Basic auditory processing skills and specific language impairment: A new look at an old hypothesis', *Journal of Speech, Language and Hearing Research*, 50: 1–20.

De Cara, B. & Goswami, U. (2002) 'Statistical analysis of similarity relations among spoken words: Evidence for the special status of rimes in English', *Behavioural Research Methods and Instrumentation*, 34, 3: 416–423.

Dollaghan, C.A. (1994) 'Children's phonological neighbourhoods: Half empty or half full?', *Journal of Child Language*, 21, 2: 257–271.

Dooling, R.J., Okanoya, K., & Brown, S.D. (1989) 'Speech perception by budgerigars (Melopsittacus undulates): The voiced–voiceless distinction', *Perception and Psychophysics*, 46: 65–71.

Drullman, R., Festen, J.M., & Plomp, R. (1994) 'Effect of temporal envelope smearing on speech perception', *Journal of the Acoustical Society of America*, 95: 1053–1064.

Echols, C.H. (1996) 'A role for stress in early speech segmentation', in J.L. Morgan & K. Demuth (eds), *Signal to Syntax: Bootstrapping from speech to grammar in early acquisition*, 151–170, Mahwah, NJ: Lawrence Erlbaum Associates.

Eimas, P.D., Siqueland, E.R., Jusczyk, P., & Vigorito, J. (1971) 'Speech perception in infants', *Science*, 171: 303–306.

Fenson, L., Dale, P.S., Reznick, J.S., Bates, E., Thal, D., & Pethick, S. (1994) 'Variability in early communicative development', *Monographs of the Society for Research in Child Development*, 59, 5, Serial no. 242.

Friedrich, M. (2008). *Mental capital and wellbeing: Making the most of ourselves in the 21st century*, Foresight Report SR-D14, London: The Government Office for Science.

Frith, U. (1998) Editorial: Literally changing the brain, *Brain*, 121: 1051–1052.

Goswami, U. (2008a) 'Reading, dyslexia and the brain', *Educational Research*, 50, 2: 135–148.

Goswami, U. (2008b) *Learning difficulties: Future challenges*, Foresight Mental Capital and Wellbeing Project, London: The Government Office for Science.

Goswami, U. (in press) 'Language, music and children's brains: A rhythmic timing perspective on language and music as cognitive systems', in P. Rebuschat (ed.) *Language and Music as Cognitive Systems*, Cambridge: Cambridge University Press.

Goswami, U. & Bryant, P.E. (1990) *Phonological Skills and Learning to Read*. Part of the series 'Developmental Essays in Psychology', London: Lawrence Erlbaum.

Goswami, U., Thomson, J., Richardson, U., Stainthorp, R., Hughes, D., Rosen, S., & Scott, S.K. (2002) 'Amplitude envelope onsets and developmental dyslexia: A new hypothesis', *Proceedings of the National Academy of Sciences of the United States of America*, 99, 16: 10911–10916.

Goswami, U., Ziegler, J., & Richardson, U. (2005) 'The effects of spelling consistency on phonological awareness: A comparison of English and German', *Journal of Experimental Child Psychology*, 92: 345–365.

Hämäläinen, J., Leppänen, P.H.T., Torppa, M., Muller, K., & Lyytinen, H. (2005) 'Detection of sound rise time by adults with dyslexia', *Brain and Language*, 94: 32–42.

Hämäläinen, J.A., Salminen, H.K., & Leppänen, P.H.T. (in press) 'Basic auditory processing deficits in dyslexia: Review of the behavioural, event-related potential and magnetoencephalographic evidence', *Journal of Learning Disabilities.*

James, D., Rajput, K., Brown, T., Sirimanna, T., Brinton, J., & Goswami, U. (2005) 'Phonological awareness in deaf children who use cochlear implants', *Journal of Speech, Language and Hearing Research*, 48: 1511–1528.

Killing, S. & Goswami, U. (2008) 'Auditory processing and phonological representations in garden-variety poor readers', 7th International Conference of the British Dyslexia Association, Harrogate, UK, 27–29 March.

Kuhl, P. (2004) 'Early language acquisition: Cracking the speech code', *Nature Reviews Neuroscience*, 5: 831–843.

Kuhl, P. (2007) 'Is speech learning "gated" by the social brain?', *Developmental Science*, 10: 110–120.

Kuppen, S., Huss, M., Fosker, T., Mead, N., & Goswami, U. (in press) 'Basic auditory processing skills and phonological awareness in low IQ readers and typically developing controls', *Scientific Studies of Reading.*

Muneaux, M., Ziegler, J., Truc, C., Thomson, J., & Goswami, U. (2004) 'Deficits in beat perception and dyslexia: Evidence from French', *Neuroreport*, 15: 1255–1259.

Nittrouer, S. (2006) 'Children hear the forest', *Journal of the Acoustical Society of America*, 120: 1799–1802.

Pasquini, E., Corriveau, K., & Goswami, U. (2007) 'Auditory processing of amplitude envelope rise time in adults diagnosed with developmental dyslexia', *Scientific Studies in Reading*, 11: 259–286.

Pierrehumbert, J. (2003) 'Phonetic diversity, statistical learning and acquisition of phonology', *Language and Speech*, 46: 115–154.

Port, R. (2007) ' "How are words stored in memory?" Beyond phones and phonemes', *New Ideas in Psychology*, 25: 143–170.

Read, C. (1986) *Children's Creative Spelling*, London: Routledge.

Remez, R.E., Rubin, P.E., Pisoni, D.B., & Carrell, T.D. (1981) 'Speech perception without traditional speech cues', *Science*, 212: 947–949.

Richardson, U., Thomson, J., Scott, S.K., & Goswami, U. (2004) 'Supra-segmental auditory processing skills and phonological representation in dyslexic children', *Dyslexia*, 10, 3: 215–233.

Saffran, J.R. (2001) 'Words in a sea of sounds: The output of infant statistical learning', *Cognition*, 81: 149–169.

Shannon, R.V., Zeng, F-G., Kamath, V., Wygonski, J., & Ekelid, M. (1995) 'Speech recognition with primarily temporal cues', *Science*, 270: 303–304.

Smith, Z.M., Delgutte, B., & Oxenham, A.J. (2002) 'Chimaeric sounds reveal dichotomies in auditory perception', *Nature*, 416: 87–90.

Stainthorp, R. & Hughes, D. (1998) 'Phonological sensitivity and reading: Evidence from precocious readers', *Journal of Research in Reading*, 21: 53–68.

Stanovich, K.E. (1988) 'Explaining the differences between the dyslexic and the garden-variety poor reader: The phonological-core variable-difference model', *Journal of Experimental Child Psychology*, 38: 175–190.

Szücs, D. & Goswami, U. (2007) 'Educational neuroscience: Defining a new discipline for the study of mental representations', *Mind, Brain and Education*, 1, 3: 114–127.

Thomson, J.M. & Goswami, U. (2008) 'Rhythmic processing in children with developmental dyslexia: Auditory and motor rhythms link to reading and spelling', *Journal of Physiology, Paris*, 102: 120–129.

Thomson, J., Baldeweg, T., & Goswami, U. (2009) 'The ERP signature of sound rise time changes', *Brain Research*, 1254: 74–83.

Thomson, J.M., Fryer, B., Maltby, J., & Goswami, U. (2006) 'Auditory and motor rhythm awareness in adults with dyslexia', *Journal of Research in Reading*, 29, 3: 334–348.

Treiman, R. (1993) *Beginning to Spell: A Study of First-grade Children*, New York: Oxford University Press.

Treiman, R. (1998) 'Beginning to spell in English', in C. Hulme & R.M. Joshi (eds), *Reading and Spelling: Development and Disorders*, 371–393, Mahwah, NJ: Lawrence Erlbaum Associates.

Vihman. M. & Croft, W. (2007) 'Phonological development: Towards a "radical" templatic phonology', *Linguistics*, 45, 4: 683–725.

Ziegler, J.C. & Goswami, U. (2005) 'Reading acquisition, developmental dyslexia and skilled reading across languages: A psycholinguistic grain size theory', *Psychological Bulletin*, 131, 1: 3–29.

Ziegler, J.C., Ferrand, L., & Montant, M. (2004) 'Visual phonology: The effects of orthographic consistency on different auditory word recognition tasks', *Memory & Cognition*, 32: 732–741.

Chapter 9

English is a difficult writing system for children to learn

Evidence from children learning to read in Wales

J. Richard Hanley

A number of studies have shown that the word recognition skills of children learning to read English develop much more slowly during the first years of formal reading instruction than in other countries that use alphabetic writing systems. This chapter discusses the results of a research programme that investigated the word recognition skills of children living in Wales in order to understand this discrepancy more fully. Even though the children were matched for age, teaching methods, and the syllabic structure of their native language, children learning to read Welsh (a transparent orthography) progressed much more quickly than children learning to read English (an opaque orthography). There was also evidence of an underachieving tail of English readers that did not exist in children learning to read Welsh. These findings indicate that English is a particularly difficult writing system for children to learn. Consequently more extensive phonics training of letter–sound relationships together with training at larger *grain sizes* (Ziegler & Goswami 2005) may be required if all English children are to develop adequate literacy skills.

Introduction

In 2003, Seymour, Aro and Erskine reported the results of a comprehensive investigation of written word recognition skills at the end of first grade in 14 different European countries. Results showed that children who were learning to read English performed far worse than the children of any other nationality at reading both real words and non-words with a similar structure to real words. Whereas children from most of the 14 countries read over 90 per cent of real words accurately, the children learning to read English were correct on only 34 per cent. The next lowest score was 71 per cent of words read correctly by children from Denmark.

Following Wimmer and Hummer (1990), this is just one of many studies published in the last 20 years to show that the word recognition skills of children learning to read English take longer to develop than those of children from countries such as Austria, Croatia, Greece, Germany, the Netherlands, Italy, Turkey, Serbia and Spain. Although the reading speed of children from these countries increases as they get older, the accuracy of their decoding skills is at a very high level by the end of their first year of formal instruction.

Why do children from the UK consistently perform so much worse in these cross-cultural comparisons? Seymour *et al.* (2003) highlighted two important differences between the English language and European languages where children's word recognition skills develop particularly quickly. The first is the opaque nature of the English writing system (or "orthography"). The second is the complex nature of the syllabic structure of spoken English. The reasons why both the spoken and written form of English might be associated with relatively slow development of reading skills are discussed below.

The English writing system

In common with all European and American languages, English employs an alphabetic writing system in which letters (or *graphemes*) represent the spoken sounds of words (*phonemes*). A phoneme is the smallest unit of sound that can affect the meaning of a word, and a grapheme is the representation of a phoneme in written form. The problem with English is that there is less consistency in grapheme–phoneme relationships than in almost any other alphabetic writing system. Graphemes for vowels in particular can represent a large number of different phonemes in different words. Hence English is said to have a *deep* or *opaque* orthography in contrast with languages that are written in *shallow* or *transparent* orthographies where each grapheme represents the same phoneme in every word in which it appears.

There are two obvious reasons why English is not transparent. First, although the pronunciation of many words has changed over the centuries, their spelling remains frozen in its earlier form. For example the now silent *k* at the start of the word *knight* was sounded out at the time when its written form was established. Second, when foreign words are imported into English, we generally keep the written form of the word in the language from which it originated. For example, the spelling of the word *café* was retained when it entered English from French instead of being changed to *caffay*. In languages with transparent orthographies such as Spanish or Welsh, spelling reform ensures that the written form of a word is congruent with its current spoken form. Consequently, frozen spellings and spellings of imported words are altered to ensure that they are consistent with the letter–sound rules of the transparent orthography.

There are some advantages for English in not having a completely regular orthography. For example, skilled readers of English can distinguish the meanings of homophones such as *colonel* and *kernel* directly from their written form. In a transparent orthography, they would be spelled the same way. The disadvantage of an opaque orthography is the existence of many irregular words whose pronunciation cannot be predicted from their spelling. Moreover, many frequent and early-acquired English words are irregular.

The existence of irregular words means that a child learning to read English faces two potential problems that are not encountered by most of his or her counterparts in Continental Europe. When children read a word in a transparent orthography that is part of their speech vocabulary, they can reliably generate its spoken form and hence access its meaning even if they have never encountered the word in print before. Such a strategy will not be successful for many words in English because letter–sound rules will not produce the correct pronunciation. The second problem is that the existence of exceptions means that the letter–sound correspondences that apply in regular English words are likely to be more difficult for children to learn. Decoding skills may therefore take longer to develop in opaque writing systems.

The syllabic structure of English

In many languages, including Italian and Spanish, words typically contain simple syllabic structures in which a vowel is preceded by a single consonant. English is more complex because clusters containing two or more consonants can occur either at the start or end of syllables. According to Ziegler and Goswami (2005), the preponderance of consonant clusters in English affects the acquisition of literacy by making it more difficult for children to learn grapheme–phoneme consistencies.

Before they start to read, many children become aware that spoken languages have smaller units than words and can count the number of syllables that spoken words contain (Liberman, Shankweiler, Fischer & Carter 1974). Later, awareness of the sub-syllabic units of onset and rime develops in pre-literate children, particularly in the UK where nursery rhymes are part of the culture (e.g. Bradley & Bryant 1983). However, alphabetic writing systems do not contain visual symbols for onsets, rimes or syllables. Instead they represent phonemes. As Usha Goswami's chapter in this volume makes clear, phonemes are not natural units of speech and cannot be produced or perceived in isolation. Furthermore, sounds that are physically different in words or syllables (e.g. the /p/ sound in *spoon* and *pit*) must be mapped onto the same phoneme. As a consequence, awareness of phonemes does not develop automatically. It is totally absent in illiterate adults (Morais, Cary, Alegria & Bertelson 1979), pre-literate children (Bruce 1964) and in Chinese people who can read only a logographic script (Reid, Zhang, Nie & Ding 1986). It therefore appears that speakers do not know about the existence of phonemes until they learn an alphabet.

Children whose languages have a simple syllabic structure may find the transition from representations based on onset and rime to representations based on phonemes easier to master. This is because onsets and rimes will frequently be single phonemes in languages where there are relatively few consonant clusters. Consequently, splitting an Italian or Spanish word into its onset and rime will often automatically produce two phonemes. It may therefore be relatively easy for Italian or Spanish children to learn the relationship between the letter sounds that they are taught in school and the words that these letters represent when the words are written down. However, only 5 per cent of English phonemes have a CV structure (De Cara & Goswami 2002), which means that English onsets and rimes will both typically contain more than one phoneme. English children may therefore need much more explicit training before awareness of phonemes develops.

If the development of phoneme awareness takes much longer for English children than those in Italy or Spain, it is worth asking whether it would be easier if English orthographic symbols represented larger auditory units than phonemes. In the Japanese script *Kana*, written symbols represent syllables. In the Taiwanese script, *zhu-yin-fu-ha*, there are distinct written symbols for each possible Mandarin onset or rime. The problem is that, unlike Japanese and Chinese, English contains too many syllables for such systems to work. There are so many syllables, onsets and rimes in English that children would be required to learn thousands of different visual symbols during the course of reading development.

Other reasons for slow development of written word recognition skills in English

There are two other possible factors that might explain why cross-cultural studies show that children learn to read English relatively slowly. The first is that children are younger when starting formal reading instruction in English than in Continental Europe. In the UK, children start to learn to read in school when they are approximately four to five years old. Conversely, teaching children of this age to read is actively discouraged in Austria, for example, where formal reading instruction does not begin until the children are at least six years old. The fact that children from Continental Europe are typically at least a year older than the participants from the UK in cross-cultural comparisons raises a series of questions. Would these comparisons show the same pattern of results if the children learning English were matched for chronological age with children from Continental Europe? If not, at what age do the reading skills of children learning English catch up with those from Europe? Does formal instruction commence too early in the UK, at a point when children are not ready to learn to read?

A second possibility is that poor word recognition ability is a consequence of the way in which reading has been taught in some UK schools in the years when these studies were carried out. In the USA, the National Institute of Child Health and Human Development (2000) published a review of the effectiveness of different methods of teaching reading. The UK Government has been so concerned about high levels of illiteracy that it implemented the National Literacy strategy and commissioned the Rose Report (2006) in what it saw an attempt to improve and standardize early reading teaching methods in the UK. As Kathy Hall's chapter in this volume makes clear, there has been a great deal of controversy in English-speaking countries for many years concerning the best way to teach early reading skills. Some of the methods that are described in Hall's chapter, such as those associated with *the psycholinguistic tradition*, are unlikely to produce fluent single word reading skills in young children.

Research study of learning to read in Wales

Between 1996 and 2004, my colleagues and I conducted a research programme that investigated some of the reasons why early reading skills develop relatively slowly in children learning English. In this investigation, the ease of learning to read English was compared with learning to read Welsh (Hanley 2010; Hanley, Masterson, Spencer & Evans 2004; Spencer & Hanley 2003, 2004). The research was conducted in Denbighshire in North Wales, where 27 per cent of the population described themselves as Welsh speakers in the 1991 Office of Population Censuses and Surveys. Some towns in this county contain both English- and Welsh-speaking Primary schools, and parents can choose which school their child will attend. It was not always thus, because use of the Welsh language was banned in schools during the nineteenth century. At that time, even in the playground, children heard speaking Welsh could be made to wear a piece of wood around their neck known as the *Welsh Not*. Unless the bearer of the *Welsh Not* could pass it on to another child who was heard to speak Welsh before the end of the day, there was a good chance they might end the day with a beating. English remained the universal language of instruction in Welsh schools until the 1950s. In 1957, the first Secondary school was founded with all instruction in Welsh. Today, there are large numbers of Welsh-medium Primary and Secondary schools, and Welsh is a compulsory subject even in English-medium schools in Wales.

If they attend Welsh-speaking schools, children are taught to read in Welsh, a transparent alphabetic orthography in which letter–sound relationships are relatively consistent and irregular words are virtually non-existent (see Spencer & Hanley 2003 for a detailed description of the nature of the Welsh writing system). There is a Welsh Academy, 'Academi Gymreig', which ensures that foreign words entering the language are given a spelling that reflects the rules of the Welsh writing system. Welsh spelling was standardized in 1928 and in 1977, when many irregular words were reformed.

Despite the differences in the transparency of the orthographies, the Welsh- and English-speaking children in our studies lived in the same area of North Wales, commenced reading instruction at the same age, and were taught by similar methods of instruction. Welsh syllables also contain consonant clusters that can occur either at the beginning or end of words. It is therefore possible to compare the acquisition of a shallow and deep orthography in children of a similar age whose languages contain words with complex syllabic structures, all of whom receive phonic instruction. Wales therefore offers a unique opportunity to investigate the influence of orthographic consistency on reading development.

Reading regular and irregular words

A study of children's single word reading during their second and third year of formal reading instruction was carried out between 1996 and 1998 (Spencer & Hanley 2003). All of the participants were children living in Wales. Children who are referred to as 'Welsh' came from Welsh-speaking families and were attending a Welsh-medium Primary school in Denbighshire. 'English' children came from English-speaking families and were attending an English-medium Primary school in Denbighshire. Welsh was the main language spoken in the home by all of the families of the Welsh children, and English was the main language spoken in the home by all of the families of the English children.

Initially, 74 Welsh-speaking children and 88 English-speaking children were tested when they were six years old during their second year of formal reading instruction. We retested 70 of the Welsh children and 75 of the English children a year later in 1997/8 on a more difficult reading test. In 2001/2, we again tested 46 of the Welsh children and 52 of the English children when their average age was ten years (Hanley *et al.* 2004). At all three times of testing, we compared reading of regular and irregular English words with their Welsh equivalents (all of which are regular in Welsh). We assumed that the pronunciation of regular words could be produced by word decoding skills that involved knowledge of letter–sound associations. Conversely, irregular words would require word-specific knowledge and could only be read if their written form had already been learnt by the child.

Results from the first two testing sessions are summarized in Table 9.1 and indicated that the English children read many fewer words correctly than the Welsh children. Although the differences were greatest for the words that were irregular in English, the differences between the Welsh and English children were statistically significant even for regular words. It therefore appears that both the sight vocabulary (written words that they have learned to recognise relatively

Table 9.1 The proportion of words read correctly by children learning to read Welsh and English

	Six years old (List 1)	
	Welsh children	English children
All words	0.81	0.59
Regular words	0.78	0.67
Irregular words	0.84	0.52
	Seven years old (List 2)	
	Welsh children	English children
All words	0.86	0.47
Regular words	0.86	0.53
Irregular words	0.86	0.41

automatically) and the decoding skills of the English children lagged behind those of the Welsh children at six and seven years old.

When the children were ten years old, we compared their reading accuracy on a set of 60 words that varied according to their regularity and their frequency (i.e. how often they occur in written English). For example, the words *horse* (*ceffyl*), *tooth* (*dant*) and *grill* (*gril*) are regular words of high, medium and low frequency, and *bowl* (*bowlen*), *glove* (*maneg*) and *sword* (*cleddyf*) are irregular words of high, medium and low frequency. The English children read the regular words and the high frequency irregular words as accurately as did the Welsh children (see Table 9.2). This suggests that the decoding skills of the English children have by now caught up with those of their Welsh counterparts. Significantly superior performance by the Welsh children was only observed on the medium and low frequency irregular words. The lower frequency irregular words will have been encountered less often in print and many of them do not yet appear to be part of the English children's sight vocabulary. If English children try to use decoding skills to read these words, they will pronounce them incorrectly. The absence of irregular words in Welsh means that Welsh children will be able to read aloud correctly the Welsh equivalents of these words even though they are equally unlikely to have encountered them in print very often.

It therefore appears to be the case that the opaque nature of the English orthography slows down the acquisition of decoding skills, but even when these skills have caught up at ten years old, children learning to read English have not received sufficient print exposure to many irregular words to allow them to be read accurately. Because of the absence of irregular words, a much larger reading vocabulary is available to readers of Welsh immediately they have developed competence in decoding.

Further evidence that the decoding skills of the English children at age ten had caught up was provided by their performance at reading non-words. Although, they had been much poorer at non-word reading at six and seven years of age, the average scores obtained by the ten-year-old Welsh and English children at reading

Table 9.2 The number of words read correctly by Welsh and English children at age ten as a function of regularity and frequency. For the Welsh children, 'irregular' refers to Welsh translations of words that are irregular in English. Standard deviations (sd) are in parentheses.

	Regular words			Irregular words		
	Hi Freq	Mid Freq	Low Freq	Hi Freq	Mid Freq	Low Freq
Accuracy (max = 10)						
English children	9.10	8.19	8.19	9.00	7.15	4.73
(sd)	(2.07)	(2.17)	(2.60)	(2.07)	(2.41)	(1.99)
Welsh children	8.78	9.04	8.07	9.48	9.11	8.46
(sd)	(1.26)	(1.24)	(2.25)	(1.13)	(1.12)	(1.87)

aloud a set of 24 non-words (20.7 and 20.1 out of 24, respectively) did not differ significantly. However, a finding that has consistently been observed in our data is that it is the least able quartile (25 per cent) of the English readers who appear to be the most disadvantaged by learning to read an opaque orthography. Conversely, the Welsh children at the bottom end of the distribution of reading ability consistently perform relatively well compared with the more able readers of Welsh. When we examined the performance of the lowest quartile, the ten-year-old English readers read significantly fewer non-words than their Welsh counterparts even though there were no differences between the other three quartile groups of Welsh and English readers (see Figure 9.1). There therefore appeared to be an underachieving tail amongst the English readers that did not exist amongst the Welsh readers. At ten years old, this underachieving tail also performed disproportionately poorly relative to the least able Welsh readers on tests of accuracy and comprehension when reading text (see Hanley 2010 for further discussion).

In conclusion, our investigation of reading in Wales enables us to rule out some possible reasons why young English readers performed worse than children from Continental Europe in cross cultural comparisons. The first of these is age. Even though the Welsh and English readers in our study were matched for chronological age, the English children performed much worse than the Welsh children at reading words and non-words at six and seven years old. Excellent acquisition of reading skills in our study by Welsh-speaking children whose reading instruction commenced when they were five, is inconsistent with the view that children in the UK are introduced to reading instruction when they are still too immature.

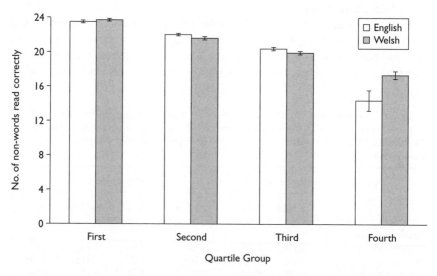

Figure 9.1 The number of non-words read correctly (maximum = 24) by quartile groups of Welsh and English children at age ten.

Both Welsh- and English-medium schools reported using approaches that were phonics-based. In the Welsh-medium schools, the focus was on teaching and blending the letter sounds of the Welsh alphabet, whereas the English teachers used synthetic phonics schemes such as *Jollyphonics*. We therefore found no evidence that the lower levels of word recognition observed in the English speaking children were associated with inferior teaching methods. Finally, the excellent word recognition skills of the Welsh children despite the existence of syllables that contain consonant clusters makes it unlikely that the complex nature of English syllables is the main reason why children's word recognition skills develops so slowly.

Our research clearly indicates that the English writing system itself is a major cause of low levels of attainment in children learning to read. The existence of irregular words appears to make it more difficult for English children to learn the decoding skills that would allow them to read regular English words. Moreover, individual irregular words take a long time to learn, with children struggling to read less frequent ones even at ten years of age. A particularly unfortunate additional outcome is that the least able readers appear to be disproportionately affected by the English writing system. We found evidence of an underachieving tail in the English readers but not in the Welsh readers. These children may never achieve the literacy skills in English that their counterparts achieve in Welsh.

Pedagogy

Improving children's reading attainment in the future by reform of the English orthography is clearly a utopian pipe-dream. Nevertheless, in the early 1960s, supporters of ITA (the Initial Teaching Alphabet) proposed a pedagogical solution to the opaque nature of English that was almost as radical (Pitman 1961). Young children first learnt a transparent version of the English alphabet (ITA) that comprised 44 distinct graphemes such that there was a discrete symbol to represent each English phoneme in a consistent fashion. Children were then taught to read words written in ITA rather than the standard alphabet. The children were eventually transferred to the standard orthography once decoding skills had been acquired by learning ITA. Research revealed that many children made rapid advances in reading the new script (Downing 1967). Unfortunately, some children encountered difficulties in the transition to standard orthography (Vernon 1967). There were also disadvantages for children moving into and out of schools that used ITA. A particularly important problem that Downing noted was that (in direct contrast to what we observed with Welsh), ITA seemed to be more beneficial for the most skilled readers. Unfortunately the least able readers appeared to derive relatively little advantage compared with children who had been taught the traditional alphabet. Despite early popularity, these factors led to the gradual abandonment of the use of ITA.

A more realistic strategy than reforming the orthography might be to acknowledge that English probably requires more extensive training in phonics than transparent orthographies. The English children in our study were taught by synthetic phonics yet their written word recognition skills took longer to develop than children who were learning a transparent orthography. The amount and type of phonics training that is sufficient to allow readers of transparent orthographies such as Welsh to learn grapheme–phoneme relationships may not be sufficient to produce rapid reading development in English readers. In our study of reading during the first year of formal instruction (Spencer & Hanley 2004), the English children had good knowledge of the phonemes represented by each letter of the alphabet. Nevertheless, the number of words they could read aloud improved very little over the course of the year. When they were asked to listen to spoken words, they had very poor knowledge of how many phonemes each word contained. This dissociation between letter knowledge and other literacy skills was not observed in the Welsh children whose decoding skills and phonological awareness improved rapidly once they had learnt the Welsh alphabet.

Although it is of a more informal nature, we have further evidence that is consistent with the claim that additional phonics training is particularly bene-ficial for English reading (Hanley 2010). When, six years after our original study, we returned to test a new cohort of six- to seven-year-old children in Wales in 2002, we found that the reading performance of English children had improved substantially. Although the National Literacy Strategy was not formally implemented in Wales in 1997, teachers told us that the amount of phonics instruction that the English children received had increased substantially during the intervening period. We have only anecdotal evidence that this is the case, and we have no information as to the type of additional phonics instruction that children received. Nevertheless, this does suggest that more extensive teaching of phonics is required for English reading development than for children learning a transparent orthography.

It is also possible that English requires a different type of phonic reading instruction. According to *grain-size* theory (Ziegler & Goswami 2005), teaching should not be exclusively focused on grapheme–phoneme correspondences. Children should also be made aware of correspondences between larger phonological and orthographic units. Most obviously, the correct pronunciation of many irregular words can only be taught by word-specific training. Nevertheless teaching a child to read an irregular word such as *friend* will allow him or her to read all words that contain 'friend' as their root morpheme (e.g. *friend, friendship, friendly, friendlier, unfriendly, befriend, friendliness,* etc.).

In some irregular words, however, there are higher order consistencies that provide information about how the irregular portion of the word should be pronounced. In particular, there are important orthographic consistencies at the level of onsets and rimes even in words that are irregular in terms of their grapheme–phoneme mappings (Treiman, Mullennix, Bijeljac-Babic & Richmond-Welty 1995). For example, the pronunciation of the *ea* vowel in *health* differs from the regular pronunciation of *ea* (as in *heat*). However, *ea* is pronounced as it is in *health* in all words in which —*ealth* is the rime segment (*wealth, stealth,* etc.). Consequently, if they are taught the correspondences between rime segments and their pronunciation, Ziegler and Goswami argue that children should be able to successfully decode words that contain consistently spelled rime segments even if they are irregular. A teaching schedule that concentrates exclusively on grapheme–phoneme relationships ignores this important source of information about the English writing system. There is evidence that phonic training interventions based on onset-rimes are no less effective than those based on grapheme–phoneme relationships. Walton *et al.* (2001) performed a training study in which children received 50 minutes of phonics training per week for 11 weeks. They compared the effects of phonics training that was based on graphemes and phonics training that was based on rime segments and found that both types of training were equally effective relative to a control group.

Morphemes (defined as the smallest units of meaning in a language) contain another important source of information about how English words are written because English orthography often preserves morpheme identity at the expense of phonology. For example, *the* is always spelled the same way even though its pronunciation differs according to whether it precedes a vowel or consonant. In a highly impressive series of studies, Nunes and Bryant (2006) provide a powerful demonstration that interventions based on the teaching of morphemes to children significantly improve their spelling ability. For example, they point out, teaching children that the plural inflection at the end of a word is consistently represented by the letter *s* should prevent them from spelling *rocks* as *rox* even if they have learnt to spell *fox* correctly. Furthermore, some morphemes are spelled differently even though they have the same sound (e.g. the endings of the words *magician* and *emotion*). Nunes and Bryant demonstrate that the number of errors children make when spelling this ending is significantly reduced if they are taught that — *ian* is correct if and only if only the word refers to an animate object such as a person.

In conclusion, it is evident that English is a particularly difficult writing system to learn. The transparent alphabetic orthographies that are commonly used in other European countries including Wales allow children to develop phonological awareness and decoding skills much more easily. Our study of reading development in Wales shows quite clearly that the advantages of a transparent orthography are not secondary to differences in teaching method, the ages of the children or the complex nature of English syllables. It appears that children learning English require more extensive phonics instruction than is required for children learning transparent orthographies. Some of this teaching should involve synthetic phonics (Rose 2006). However, the unpredictable nature of the English writing system can be reduced if children's attention is also drawn to the relationships between larger units than graphemes and phonemes (Nunes & Bryant 2006; Ziegler & Goswami 2005). Knowledge of the relationships between the orthography and phonology of onsets, rimes, and morphemes is likely to make it easier for children to achieve mastery over the notoriously complex English writing system.

Acknowledgements

The work reported in this paper was funded by the ESRC in the form of a project grant (No. R000238437) and an earlier research studentship to Llinos Spencer. I am grateful to Llinos Spencer, Jackie Masterson, and Dylan Evans for the contribution that they made to the research discussed in this chapter. I would also like to thank the teachers and staff of a number of primary schools in Denbighshire, North Wales for permission to test the children in their classes.

References

Bradley, L. & Bryant, P.E. (1983) 'Categorising sounds and learning to read: A causal connection', *Nature, 310*: 419–421.

Bruce, D.J. (1964) 'The analysis of word sounds', *British Journal of Educational Psychology, 34*: 158–170.

De Cara, B. & Goswami, U. (2002) 'Statistical analysis of similarity relations among spoken words: Evidence for the special status of rimes in English', *Behavioral Research Methods and Instrumentation, 34*: 416–423.

Downing, J. (1967) *Evaluating the initial teaching alphabet.* London, Cassell.

Hanley, J.R., Masterson, J., Spencer, L., & Evans, D. (2004) 'How long do the advantages of learning to read a transparent orthography last? An investigation of the reading skills and incidence of dyslexia in Welsh children at 10 years of age', *Quarterly Journal of Experimental Psychology, 57*: 1393–1410.

Hanley, J.R. (2010) 'Differences in reading ability between children attending Welsh- and English-speaking primary schools in Wales', in N. Brunswick, S. McDougall & P. de Mornay Davies (eds), *The role of orthographies in reading and spelling.* Hove: Psychology Press.

Liberman, I.Y., Shankweiler, D., Fischer, F.W., & Carter, B. (1974) 'Explicit syllable and phoneme segmentation in the young child', *Journal of Experimental Child Psychology, 18:* 201–212.

Morais, J., Cary, L., Alegria, J., & Bertelson, P. (1979) 'Does awareness of speech as a sequence of phones arise spontaneously?', *Cognition, 7*: 323–331.

National Institute of Child Health and Human Development (2000) *Report of the national reading panel. Teaching children to read: An evidence-based assessment of the scientific research literature on reading and its implications for reading instruction: Reports of the subgroups* (NIH publication no. 00–4754). Washington, DC: US Government Printing Office.

Nunes, T. & Bryant, P. (2006) *Improving literacy by teaching morphemes.* London, Routledge.

Office of Population Censuses and Surveys (1991) *1991 census report for Wales (Part 1).* London, HMSO.

Pitman, J. (1961) *Learning to read.* London, Initial Teaching Alphabet Foundation.

Reid, C., Zhang, Y., Nie, H., & Ding, B. (1986) 'The ability to manipulate speech sounds depends on knowing alphabetic spelling', *Cognition, 24*: 31–44.

Rose, J. (2006) *Independent review of the teaching of early reading.* Nottingham, DfES Publications.

Seymour, P.H.K., Aro, M., & Erskine, J.M. (2003) 'Foundation literacy acquisition in European orthographies', *British Journal of Psychology, 94*: 143–174.

Spencer, L. & Hanley, J.R. (2003) 'The effects of orthographic consistency on reading development and phonological awareness: Evidence from children learning to read in Wales', *British Journal of Psychology*, 94: 1–28.

Spencer, L. & Hanley, J.R. (2004) 'Learning a transparent orthography at 5 years old: Reading development of children during the first year of formal reading instruction in Wales', *Journal of Research in Reading*, 27: 1–14.

Treiman, R., Mullennix, J., Bijeljac-Babic, R., & Richmond-Welty, E.D. (1995) 'The special role of rimes in the description, use, and acquisition of English orthography', *Journal of Experimental Psychology: General*, 124, 107–136.

Vernon, M.D. (1967). 'Evaluations' in J. Downing (ed.) *The ita symposium*. Hove, UK, King Thorne & Stace.

Walton, P.D., Walton, L.M. and Felton, K. (2001) 'Teaching rime analogy or letter recoding reading strategies to pre-readers: Effects on pre-reading skill and word reading', *Journal of Educational Psychology*, 93: 160–80.

Wimmer, H. & Hummer, P. (1990) 'How German-speaking first graders read and spell: Doubts on the importance of the logographic stage', *Applied Psycholinguistics*, 11: 349–368.

Ziegler, J.C. & Goswami, U. (2005) 'Reading acquisition, developmental dyslexia and skilled reading across languages: A psycholinguistic grain size theory', *Psychological Bulletin*, 131: 3–29.

Chapter 10

Contextualised phonics teaching

Dominic Wyse

How children learn to read and – of particular significance to this chapter – how they can most effectively be taught to read is a concern for researchers, teachers, policy-makers, and societies in general. If a child does not learn to read they cannot play a full part in society once they reach adulthood, nor during childhood can they access the full school curriculum. In an ideal world these different groups of people with an interest in the teaching of reading would have sufficient shared understanding of how it is best taught. A shared understanding could allow people to act in ways that complemented rather than contradicted each other in the best interests of supporting children's reading. It appears that this is indeed an ideal world because while theory and research has much to tell us about reading pedagogy the route from research evidence to policy and practice is one that is far from smooth.

The aim of the chapter is to explore *contextualised phonics teaching* at three different levels. The first level is an illustrative example which uses a short extract of children talking about text. This analysis enables some key features of contextualised phonics teaching to be identified. The second level is an analysis of a selection of experimental trials which investigated effective phonics teaching. Here an analysis of the pedagogy employed in the selection is considered. The third level is an analysis of literacy policy and its implementation, a vital component in efforts to improve reading teaching. This final section of the chapter explores contextualised phonics teaching at policy level by focusing on the National Literacy Strategy in England as a significant case internationally.

One way to understand contextualised phonics teaching is through a socio-cultural perspective. Learning to read is not simply a matter of acquiring knowledge about written language and skills in decoding, but becoming involved in cultural practices of meaning making (Hall 2003; Heath 1983; Street 1984). From this perspective reading is a practice which is 'socially, culturally, and historically situated [and] used for particular purposes in particular contexts' (Myhill & Fisher 2005: 1). Socio-cultural theory has much to offer our understanding of reading teaching, and particularly learning to read, but in addition to some socio-cultural considerations I wish to advance a theorisation of contextualisation which focuses on phonics teaching methods in particular.

The following extract of children talking with an adult took place in an early years setting for children aged three to four in England. The transcript of dialogue was part of a project carried out in the early years centre. Taking an ethnographic approach the research analysed the ways that the children engaged with print and texts, and what the implications were for practitioners. One of the children was working in the 'writing area' in his classroom. He had been folding a piece of sugar paper into an irregular structure to which he added some marks with felt pen. He turned to show the adult what he had done. In seeking to ensure that the photograph of the child and his writing was appropriately oriented the adult was drawn into a pedagogic role that centred on the children's good-natured disagreement about letters and phonemes.

Adult:	Oh that's good, a parcel for Ben [*Mark's friend who did not attend the same early years centre*], I like that. I'll take a picture of it like that.
Mark:	I want to hold it like that.
Adult:	Do you, that makes the writing upside down, is that alright? OK. You want to hold it. Well tip it back a bit so that I can get the writing. Look at the camera, you can see it . . . That looks like a letter M.
Michael:	No it's a /m/ [*Michael voices the sound*].
Adult:	It's a /m/ is it?
Michael:	/m/ for mummy. It's for my mummy.
Neil:	No it's M for mummy. [*Neil says the name of the letter.*]
Adult:	That's right, M is the name of the letter isn't it, and /m/ is the sound.
Neil:	No, M! [*spoken very firmly*]
Adult:	M's the name yes. They're both right . . . Is that mummy?
Neil:	Yes.

Pedagogy is revealed in many ways through this short extract. The teacher had organised a writing area with a range of resources to support children's mark-making, and the children were encouraged to use the area in a similar way to the other play-based areas in the classroom. The children were able to exercise choice over the kind of mark-making that they carried out. Mark had chosen to construct a parcel for his friend Ben, so in other words he had decided who the audience for his text was. Purposeful activity determined by the children, with, in Mark's case, a real audience in mind for his writing, was affected on occasion by the interaction of more expert language users – the adults who worked in the centre, including the researcher, but also the children's peers whose development of literacy varied due to their different home backgrounds.

The adult used the term M (the letter name) rather than the sound /m/, in part because of their view that learning about the distinction between letter names and the sounds associated with letters is an important feature of early years literacy learning. The ensuing discussion about letter names and sounds arguably represents significant learning about complex ideas, through a discussion led in a spirited way by children because they were interested in the topic. As a way of resolving the dispute, and to help the children's understanding, the adult intervened to offer some information to the children. The role of the adult as more expert language user was a facilitative one, but also one that involved a kind of direct teaching informed by ongoing formative assessment of the children's discussion.

To sum up, a series of understandings about reading and writing were addressed in the course of the interaction: a) texts can communicate meaning to specific audiences; b) text has to be oriented in a particular way; c) the letter M can be called M or /m/; d) the letter M is the first letter of the word 'mummy'; e) there is a complex relationship between letters and the sounds that they represent in English. The children's knowledge of this relationship was in the early stages but it is likely that such conversations would support their emerging understanding. From a socio-cultural perspective the example highlights some key features of pedagogy: a) children having some control over their learning within frameworks established by teachers; b) learning located in scenarios that are meaningful to children; c) the interaction of the adult as expert language user extending children's learning by responding to the children's interests with a clear understanding of, and high expectation of, the knowledge to be developed.

Effective phonics teaching

The example examined above provides illuminating evidence from the perspective of children's interaction in an early years setting; however, another way to explore phonics teaching is through consideration of evidence from experimental trials. Wyse and Goswami (2008) carried out a review of research internationally in response to a government-commissioned report on the teaching of early reading in England (Rose 2006). Part of their analysis included establishing categories for the effective phonics instruction pedagogy that was part of the experimental trials included in two systematic reviews (National Institute of Child Health and Human Development (NICHD) 2000; Torgerson, Brooks & Hall 2006). One category of studies was "contextualised phonics instruction". Further analysis of the pedagogy of these studies provides insights of relevance to the concerns of this chapter.

Table 10.1 summarises the key features of contextualised phonics teaching revealed in a series of studies (further information about the methods used in the studies can be found in Wyse and Goswami 2008). The key feature of the effective approach in the study by Berninger *et al.* (2003) was the combination of word recognition activities with comprehension teaching including language cueing at text-level as part of the lessons, although the word recognition training was contextualised in words rather than whole texts. The combination of phonics teaching with comprehension teaching was also a feature of the studies by Umbach *et al.* (1989) and Vickery *et al.* (1987). Similarly, Blachman *et al.*'s (1999) study featured the reading of connected text as a part of the lesson. Brown and Felton (1990) found that reinforcement of skills through use of whole texts was beneficial.

Table 10.1 The pedagogy of contextualised phonics teaching

Study	Overall teaching context	Key features of contextualised phonics teaching
Berninger et al. (2003)	Combination of explicit word recognition and reading comprehension was most effective. Reading comprehension training include language cueing at text level: e.g. 'Tell the plot or main events in the story so far'.	Combination of word recognition and comprehension teaching in reading lesson.
Blachman et al. (1999)	This study covered kindergarten through to, and including, grade one. Overall sequence: 1. Review of sound-symbol associations learned previously; 2. Phoneme analysis and blending skills; 3. Automatic recognition of words. 4. Ten to fifteen minutes of reading connected text.	High-frequency words selected from stories that the children would be reading and that are introduced as part of sessions. Reading of connected text. Writing to dictation so teacher could assess students' progress. Vocabulary development and comprehension not neglected. Children's understanding of words and their understanding of stories was supported.
Brown and Felton (1990)	The selection of reading programmes was based on those which were 'complete instructional programmes which emphasised both word identification and comprehension'.	Mastery of the skills taught was reinforced through the use of controlled readers and the coordination of reading and spelling.
Evans and Carr (1985)	General analysis of 20 classrooms. In these classrooms, reading was instructed primarily through basal readers and workbooks rather than student-generated stories, phonics drill rather than sight-word banking, and supervised practice at cloze-type prediction from context, using relatively unfamiliar reading materials.	Recognised the importance of helping pupils understand how to coordinate dual task performance such as word analysis with predictive context use.
Foorman et al. (1997)	Synthetic phonics group did activities including reading practice: 'Language, Alphabet, Reading, spelling decks, New Concept, Reading practice, Handwriting, Spelling, Review, Verbal expression, Listening' (p. 260).	The more successful phonics intervention is characterised as 'synthetic' but this was integrated as part of the daily lesson format which included reading practice.

(continued)

Table 10.1 Continued

Study	Overall teaching context	Key features of contextualised phonics teaching
Foorman et al. (1998)	Carried out during 90-min language arts period. Direct instruction in letter-sound correspondences practiced in decodable text . . . emphasis on phonemic awareness, phonics . . . and literature activities.	The more successful direct code approach mixed phonemic awareness and phonics with literature activities. The phonics rules are introduced using alliterative stories and controlled vocabulary text in order to practice. Skills in oral language comprehension and motivation for stories are developed.
Greaney et al. (1997)	*Reading Recovery* type lessons but with more flexibility.	The reading of familiar and less familiar books is an integral part of the programme.
Martinussen and Kirby (1998)	Programmes included broader features such as work with shapes, matrices, and sequential analysis. The reading of picture books by instructors was part of the programmes.	Phonics teaching was embedded in the reading of texts.
Santa and Hoien (1999)	The *Early Steps* programme has a particular emphasis on story reading, writing and phonological skills. Similar to *Reading Recovery*. The programme evaluated is *Early Steps*, an intervention with 1–1 tutoring and with particular emphasis on story reading, writing, and phonological skills . . . 'the program emphasises real book reading' (p. 62).	The programme represents what the researcher consider to be a balanced approach and one that fitted well philosophically with programmes already in place in the district. Included reading connected text and daily writing.
Tunmer and Hoover (1993)	*Reading Recovery* approach.	Work on phonological and visual similarities of words was used in the context of lessons to learn strategies about how and when to apply such knowledge. Wherever possible the teachers chose clear and memorable examples from texts that had been read. Children were encouraged to identify unfamiliar words in their reading using strategies they had been taught and to help with spelling words in writing.

Table 10.1 Continued

Study	Overall teaching context	Key features of contextualised phonics teaching
Umbach *et al.* (1989)	Broad approach which included teaching of text orientation, sounding-out, comprehension, and problem solving skills.	Argues for combined phonics and comprehension teaching.
Vickery *et al.* (1987)	Broader programme: Multisensory teaching approach for reading, spelling and handwriting (MTARSH).	Comprehension is part of programme. Attention to broader areas of learning is included.

Evans and Carr (1985) recognised the importance of using word analysis skills in combination with other tasks such as predicting meaning when using relatively unfamiliar reading materials. The studies by Foorman (Foorman *et al.* 1997 and 1998) were set in the context of language arts lessons which included literature activities. Phonics teaching was embedded in the reading of texts in the Martinussen and Kirby (1998) study in addition to the less common use of global and bridging tasks.

The studies by Santa and Hoien (1999), Tunmer and Hoover (1993), and Greaney *et al.* (1997) all based the pedagogy of the effective intervention on Clay's (1979) *Reading Recovery* approach with modifications. Reading Recovery teaching is well specified by Clay and also has the benefit of a particular high number of research evaluations (Brooks 2002) which enable in-depth understanding of the pedagogy. Although Reading Recovery has attracted some debate about its effectiveness, research continues to show its benefits, as in the recent meta-analysis by D'Agostino and Murphy (2004). Reading Recovery lessons begin and end with the use of whole texts. In summary, the teaching of sub-word level features such as phonemes, and the decoding of words, appears to be effective when embedded in whole texts.

Contextualised phonics teaching is effective because new understandings can be applied in real contexts in order to consolidate what are often complex areas of learning for pupils. The use of whole texts also enables systematic comprehension teaching to be very closely linked with phonics teaching. In addition, although the focus may be the teaching of reading, writing is frequently a part of the lessons. This enables pupils to understand the links between the decoding and encoding of language, something that once again consolidates their understanding.

From a socio-cultural methodological perspective there are, however, some limitations to the studies summarised above. The selection of experimental trials as a sole indicator of effective pedagogy excludes all other kinds of research including practitioner research, case study work, ethnography, etc. While it is generally agreed that questions about what is the most effective teaching method are particularly well served by experimental trials (Torgerson 2003) other methods can provide relevant findings in relation to effectiveness. Even if a trial shows a high effect size for a particular approach used in a particular context this does not mean that it will necessarily be effective when implemented on a larger scale or even on the same scale in a different context. One important feature of implementation of any pedagogy is the interaction between teacher and pupils, a feature that typically is not analysed as part of experimental trials but one that is increasingly seen as particularly important in relation to teaching quality. Methodologically, interaction has been evaluated well by socio-cultural methods (Mercer 2005) and interaction analysis studies using observation tools (Galton *et al.* 1999).

In spite of the increasing hegemony of the methodology of experimental trials, and the fact that these studies can be legitimately combined in meta-analysis in order to further generalise (Glass 1977) my analysis of the studies has revealed further limitations that are particularly relevant to a consideration of pedagogy. For example, the socio-economic backgrounds and other characteristics of the pupils in the studies is an important methodological variation. It can be seen in Table 10.2 that most interventions were carried out with children with reading difficulties (in general there appears to be a lack of experimental trials on reading pedagogy with typical readers) but even within this category the selected children varied from the bottom 1 per cent to the bottom 20 per cent of readers in the initial sample. Another variation is the overall length of the training that varies from two years in one study, to eight weeks in another, or is variable according to the progress that children make during the intervention. The duration of lessons varies from 15 minutes to one hour. The total number of lessons is not always clear in the studies but seems to vary from 17 to 44. The context for the teaching is more often small group or individual rather than whole class teaching. These variations are key ones for teachers and policy makers as they try and weigh up which is the most effective pedagogy.

It is probable that the most complete answers to effective pedagogy are likely to be found through a combination of: new research; systematic review including meta-analysis; and what is often called 'expert review' or 'narrative review', which can accommodate a wider range of methodologies.

The policy perspective

I have addressed contextualised phonics teaching at two levels: a) through the illustrative example of young children talking to an adult; and b) through a consideration of experimental trial evidence. If contextualised phonics teaching is to be successfully implemented it should be considered at a third level, i.e. educational policy. In the remaining sections of the chapter I show that although there is some evidence of recognition of the importance of contextualised phonics instruction at policy level the picture is complicated by a range of factors that work against this. I focus on the National Literacy Strategy in England as a significant

Table 10.2 Key socio-cultural methodological features of phonics instruction studies

Author	Participants	Length of training	Duration of lessons	Frequency per week	Total number of lessons	Individual (I), small group (sg) or whole class (wc)
Berninger et al. (2003)	'Poorest readers' nominated by teachers. Each participating child was at least 1 SD below the mean on either word-reading or pseudo-word-reading, and many were below that on the reading skill on which they qualified.	Twice weekly x 20mins	20	2	24	sg 2
Blachman et al. (1999)	Of the 21 elementary schools in the district, we chose four of the five schools in the district with the lowest achievement scores in reading on standardised tests. The mean PPVT-R phoneme segmentation, letter name and letter sound knowledge or word identification of the children was 101, and the children, who were from a mix of high-, middle, and low-income families, knew an average of 9 letter sounds when the intervention began.	Spread over 2 years. 11 weeks phonological awareness in K.	30	3 to 4	41	sg 4 to 5
Brown and Felton (1990)	Risk measures required that the child obtain, on at least three of the research measures, scores of one or more standard deviations below the group mean or in the bottom 16th percentile for the sample.	2 years	15 to 20	unknown	unknown	sg 8

(continued)

Table 10.2 Continued

Author	Participants	Length of training	Duration of lessons	Frequency per week	Total number of lessons	Individual (I), small group (sg) or whole class (wc)
Evans and Carr (1985)	Large suburban school district.	1 year	unknown	unknown	unknown	wc
Foorman et al. (1997)	Participants were all the second and third grade students with reading disabilities (RD) in 13 of 19 elementary schools in an urban school district in the Southwest. The sample size was 128. Children were included in the study only if their Basic Reading Cluster score was less than or equal to the 25th percentile.	1 year (6 or more months)	60	5	unknown	sg 8
Foorman et al. (1998)	Participants were 285 of the 375 children in first and second grades eligible for services under Title I funding in an urban district with 19 elementary schools. Low achievement was defined by school district officials as scores on the district's emergent literacy survey in the bottom quartile in first and second grade classrooms. The present sample represented the lowest 18% because of lack of funds for tutoring.	1 year	30	5	unknown	sg 3 to 5

Greaney et al. (1997)	57 'disabled' children. The children had been selected for intensive remedial instruction. The children fell in the bottom 1% to 2% of beginning readers.	11 weeks	30	3 to 4	11 weeks = 33 to 44	1
Martinussen and Kirby (1998)	48 students were originally selected on the basis of low performance on successive processing and phonological processing measures and teacher recommendation. Poor performers were those students in the bottom one-third of the distribution of the principal component scores.	8 weeks	20	2 to 3	17 to 20	sg 2 to 3
Santa and Hoien (1999)	Lowest 20%. The children from each experimental and control class were ranked from highest to lowest, and the 20% in each class with the lowest combined scores were selected as experimental or control subjects.	1 year (September to May)	30	5	September to May. 165 sessions	1
Tunmer and Hoover (1993)	Children were drawn from a large pool of at-risk readers from 30 schools across 13 school districts. From the pool the lowest ranked children in each school were given the Diagnostic Survey (Clay 1985) and the Dolch Word Recognition Test (Dolch 1939) at the beginning of first grade.	Depends on child	30	5	Depends on child	1

(continued)

Table 10.2 Continued

Author	Participants	Length of training	Duration of lessons	Frequency per week	Total number of lessons	Individual (I), small group (sg) or whole class (wc)
Umbach et al. (1989)	31 first grade students in a rural community in the Southeast. In the county of the school the Stanford Achievement Test scores usually were at or slightly below the state average, students in the school typically scored much lower than the county average especially in the reading and language areas. Students nominated by teachers as having difficulty with reading and needing extra help.	50 minutes daily for a year	50	5	180	wc
Vickery et al. (1987)	282 remedial and 144 non-remedial. During the four years covered in this study, 426 students were trained by the MTARSH programme; of these, 282 were enrolled in remedial classes and 144 in non-remedial classes.	1 year	Grade 1 25 minutes daily instruction; Grades 2 to 6, 55 mins daily instruction	5	180	wc and remedial sg

case before moving to a brief comparison with similar policy initiatives internationally.

In 2009 a UK government White Paper reported that 'As we move to our new model of how improvement support is delivered to schools, we will not renew the current, central contract for the National Strategies when it comes to an end in 2011' (DfCSF 2009: 59). Although this may appear to be a somewhat mundane sentence, something which its placement on page 59 of a 103-page document also seemed to reflect, it was highly significant because it marked the end of a period of 12 years of continuous government intervention in primary and early years literacy and numeracy education that was unique internationally (Earl *et al.* 2003). In 1997 when the New Labour government came to power Prime Minister Tony Blair signalled that 'education, education, education' would be at the heart of the New Labour project, and the teaching of literacy (and numeracy) in primary schools the most important part of this vision. The teaching of reading was central to the National Literacy Strategy (NLS) (and subsequently the Primary National Strategy, PNS). In the following section I address the extent to which the approach to reading reflected contextualised phonics teaching, and then consider the evidence on whether the NLS approach was effective.

The teaching approach of the NLS, described in the Framework for Teaching (DfEE 1998), had been developed between 1996 and 1998 as part of the National Literacy Project (NLP) that preceded the NLS. The NLP was a professional development initiative led by one of Her Majesty's Inspectorate. It involved Local Education Authorities and schools in England who had identified weaknesses in their teaching of literacy. The NLP established for the first time a detailed scheme of work with term-by-term objectives to be used by schools nationally. The objectives were delivered through the use of a daily literacy hour with strict timings for the different parts of the hour.

The NLP was originally conceived as a five-year project; after that time, an evaluation was to be carried out. In the event, the approach of the NLP was adopted by the New Labour Government and introduced as part of the National Literacy Strategy in 1998. This decision was taken before the results of any independent evaluation had been reported and long before the planned five-year extent of the National Literacy Project. The only independent evaluation of the project found some gains in standardised reading test scores but as there was no control group these could not necessarily be attributed to the teaching methods of the NLP (Sainsbury *et al.* 1998).

When the NLS was implemented from 1998 onwards the approach to reading was described as a *searchlights* model that consisted of four strategies: 'phonic (sounds and spelling); knowledge of context; grammatical knowledge; word recognition and graphic knowledge' (DfEE 1998: 3). The guidance said that, 'The range of strategies can be depicted as a series of searchlights, each of which sheds light on the text. Successful readers use as many of these strategies as possible' (1998: 3) Although the idea of combining strategies in order to understand the meaning of texts could be seen as similar to, for example, linking language cueing at text level with word recognition activities (one feature of contextualised phonics teaching), the model is different in most other respects, and features various inconsistencies. For example how graphic *knowledge* can be defined as a strategy, and how this might differ from the spelling aspect of phonic knowledge. Also 'phonic' or 'phonics' normally refers to a teaching approach rather than to a strategy or to a facet of knowledge.

The NLS approach cannot be described as contextualised phonics teaching primarily because of the over-complexity of the Framework for Teaching and the rather eclectic combination of ideas it contained. The structure of the daily literacy hour was one part of this complexity. The timed segments of the hour required the following:

1   Approximately 15 minutes shared reading and writing – whole-class;
2   Approximately 15 minutes word-level work – whole-class;
3   Approximately 20 minutes guided group and independent work;
4   Final ten minutes – plenary session with the whole class.

This structure was applied to reading *or* writing but the balance between the time for, and the timing of, the teaching of reading and writing was not made clear. A further layer of complexity was added by the decision to categorise all teaching objectives as word-level, sentence-level, or text-level (organised by primary school year group term-by-term from age 5 to age 11) with no apparent theoretical rationale for doing this. It is probable that a major reason for this eclecticism was that although it was claimed after implementation that some areas of research influenced its design there was a lack of systematic evaluation of research evidence prior to implementation (Wyse 2000, 2001, 2003; Wyse & Jones 2008).

The answer to the question of whether the NLS approach to teaching reading was effective suffers from the fact that the reading teaching method has not been subject to rigorous large-scale research. However there is a significant amount of evidence in general about the success or otherwise of the NLS: Wyse, McCreery and Torrance (2008; and Wyse & Torrance 2009) summarised this by looking at studies of primary classrooms and analysing trends in national test outcomes. Although reading showed slightly better gains than writing according to some sources, the overall trend in national test scores can be explained as modest gains from a low base as teachers learned to prepare pupils for statutory tests, then a plateau in scores as no further gains could be achieved by test coaching. Overall, the intense focus on testing and test results in the period of the NLS resulted in a narrowing of the curriculum, driving teaching in the opposite direction to that which research indicates will improve learning and attainment.

In 2006, concerns expressed by many in education that the NLS approach to reading teaching had not worked led to a government-commissioned review into the teaching of early reading in England. It was hoped that this might result in a more rigorous analysis of research evidence as the basis for a carefully considered approach to how to improve reading teaching. This unfortunately was not the case. The outcome of the review was the decision to prescribe synthetic phonics as the sole method for teaching reading, something that has caused controversy (see Ellis 2007; Goouch & Lambirth 2008; Kershner & Howard 2006; Lewis & Ellis 2006; Wyse & Styles 2007). As Wyse and Goswami (2008) point out the report did not draw sufficiently upon the large amount of high quality research evidence that was available.

The tension at policy level between narrow forms of reading instruction versus other forms such as contextualised phonics instruction can also be seen in other countries. In the United States the National Reading Panel (NRP) (NICHD 2000) concluded that reading teaching should not focus too much on the teaching of letter–sound relations at the expense of the application of this knowledge in the context of reading texts. Also, phonics should not become the dominant component in a reading programme, so educators "must keep the end in mind and insure that children understand the purpose of learning letter-sounds" (2–96). The importance of the cautions about phonics becoming a dominant component are given added weight if we consider the findings of Camilli *et al.* (2003). Camilli *et al.* replicated the meta-analysis from the NRP phonics instruction report and found a much smaller effect for systematic phonics instruction versus less systematic phonics instruction. They found that the effect for individual tutoring was larger than the effect for systematic phonics and that the effect for systematic language activities was slightly larger but comparable with that for systematic phonics. These findings resulted in their conclusion that 'systematic phonics instruction when combined with language activities and individual tutoring may *triple* the effect of phonics alone' (Camilli *et al.* 2003).

Unfortunately the measured and generally appropriate conclusions of the NRP and Camilli *et al.* may not have been sufficiently reflected in policy on reading pedagogy. Policy on the teaching of reading became strongly influenced by federal government through the legislation of No Child Left Behind. Phonics instruction frequently received more attention than other important aspects of reading pedagogy, sometimes to an extreme extent (Cummins 2007). Allington (2010) argues that federal education policy adopted a narrow, ideologically defined notion of 'scientifically-based reliable, replicable' reading research (SBRR). This determined the kind of reading pedagogy that states had to implement in order to receive federal funding. However, to date there is no compelling evidence that reading standards have improved as a result of the No Child Left Behind legislation which includes the requirement for SBRR, in fact there is some evidence of more limited reading curricula and decreased curricular and instructional coherence (Allington 2010).

The difficulties of maintaining research informed reading pedagogy in the context of policy formation and implementation are also revealed in Australia. The Commonwealth government in Australia carried out a review of research on literacy, influenced by the work of the NRP, but effectively restricted its focus to the teaching of reading. Although the report recommended that 'teachers [should] provide an integrated approach to reading that supports the development of oral language, vocabulary, grammar, reading fluency, comprehension and the literacies of new technologies' and that 'no one approach of itself can address the complex nature of reading difficulties. An integrated approach requires that teachers have a thorough understanding of a range of effective strategies, as well as knowing when and why to apply them' (Australian Government, Department of Education Science and Training 2005: 14), Sawyer (2010) argues that the approach to reading known as synthetic phonics, which does not represent contextualised phonics teaching, was foregrounded and particularly favoured by the report. Of particular concern to Sawyer was the use of the study by Johnston and Watson (2005) as the basis for the suggestion in the report that the research showing the significance of *balanced reading instruction* was 'assertion', whereas the case for synthetic phonics was clearly proven.

Reform of education systems globally has increasingly focused on teachers as a major factor in enhancing learning and educational quality. However, Tatto's (2007) thesis is that in many cases the top-down operationalisation of this focus has resulted in control of education being taken away from teachers and teacher educators. In the pursuit of 'standards', governments in England have increasingly influenced the teaching of reading through the mechanisms of the statutory testing system, although other factors such as changes to the inspection system have also strengthened top-down control. There are recent signs, however, that the 'standards' agenda is becoming exhausted and that top-down control has run its course. Test results have plateaued, and across the public services any benefits which centrally imposed targets may have produced are perceived as diminishing rapidly. Coffield *et al.* (2007) note that a new model of public service reform is being proposed that includes the idea of 'users shaping the service from below (PMSU 2006: 8)' but complain that the evidence base for the new model of public service reform is weak and that '[a] simple model has been arrived at by the expedient of understating all the difficulties and complexities inherent in each of its four main elements' (66). In view of the claims made about its world-class education system, the actual and potential influence of policy in England on other nations, and theories of education as an economic driver in a global market place, Tikly's (2004: 194) cautions are important. The hegemonic role of economics in developing educational programmes, with the associated targets and quantifiable indicators, often ignores the processes at the heart of education, namely those of the curriculum and pedagogy. Tikly describes such global economics-driven policy as a *new imperialism*.

Conclusions

The theory of contextualised phonics teaching privileges the holistic over the partial, the theorised over the instrumental, the complex over the simple, the nuanced over the crudely straightforward. It recognises the socio-cultural context in which the teaching of reading, like all teaching, is located but emphasises the pedagogical aspects of the socio-cultural context. Contextualised phonics teaching is an approach to the teaching of reading which involves the use of whole texts to locate teaching about the smaller units of language including letters and phonemes. The use of whole texts contributes to contexts that are meaningful to children and enables them to better understand the reading process, including the application of key reading skills. The teacher or other adult as expert language user facilitates children's learning by responding to their interests and building on these in ways which are informed by clear general aims for children's development of reading. This chapter has explored the implications of contextualised phonics teaching at different levels: the level of interaction between children and teachers/adults; the effective pedagogy investigated in research; and the ways in which reading teaching is too often negatively affected by the decisions of policy makers.

Research has provided significant evidence about effective reading pedagogy. For example, over at least a 20-year period evidence has been accumulated to clearly show that systematic phonics teaching of a variety of kinds is more likely to result in positive outcomes for children than unsystematic or no phonics teaching. However, questions remain about the best ways to implement systematic phonics teaching and other aspects of reading teaching including how this should be contextualised. Further advances in our understanding may come through mixed methods research, and systematic reviews that are able to combine evidence from experimental trials with other kinds of research evidence. Further research could usefully explore the extent of training that is necessary to deliver contextualised phonics teaching effectively, and whether reading recovery teaching might have some potential benefits for larger groups of children who do not have reading difficulties, particularly in the early years. As Wyse and Goswami (2008) point out there is also a need for further research which directly compares contextualised phonics teaching with approaches that isolate the phonics teaching, such as many synthetic phonics programmes.

The ways in which research evidence is adopted and used to inform policy is variable. However, in spite of a good knowledge base in some areas it is evident from the efforts by governments internationally that questionable decisions can be made which push teaching in directions that are undesirable. Short-term policy cycles and the relationship between policy and the media are possibly implicated in this, as are politicians' perceptions of globalisation and the resultant policy actions designed to minimise risk (Wyse and Opfer 2010). My review of the evidence in this chapter leads me to conclude that governments should ensure that contextualised phonics teaching has a central place in efforts to improve reading teaching. If this were to happen it is possible that greater shared understanding of reading pedagogy might be developed to more effectively support children's reading.

References

Allington, R. (2010) 'Recent federal education policy in the United States', in D. Wyse, R. Andrews & J. Hoffman (eds), *The International Handbook of English, Language and Literacy Teaching*, London: Routledge.

Australian Government, Department of Education Science and Training (2005) *Teaching Reading: Report and Recommendations. National Enquiry into the Teaching of Literacy*, Barton: Australia.

Berninger, V. W., Vermeulen, K., Abott, R. D., McCutchen, D., Cotton, S., Cude, J., *et al.* (2003) 'Comparison of three approaches to supplementary reading instruction for low-achieving second-grade readers', *Language, Speech, and Hearing Services in Schools*, 34: 101–116.

Blachman, B., Tangel, D., Ball, E., Black, R., & McGraw, D. (1999) 'Developing phonological awareness and word recognition skills: A two-year intervention with low-income, inner-city children', *Reading and Writing: An Interdisciplinary Journal*, 11: 239–273.

Brooks, G. (2002) *What Works for Children with Literacy Difficulties? The Effectiveness of Intervention Schemes. DfES Research Report no. Rr380*, London: DfES.

Brown, L. & Felton, R. (1990) 'Effects of instruction on beginning reading skills in children at risk for reading disability', *Reading and Writing: An Interdisciplinary Journal*, 2: 223–241.

Camilli, G., Vargas, S., & Yurecko, M. (2003) 'Teaching children to read: The fragile link between science and federal education policy', *Education Policy Analysis Archives*, 11, 15: Retrieved 1 March, 2006, from http://epaa.asu.edu/epaa/v11n15/.

Clay, M. (1979) *The Early Detection of Reading Difficulties* (3rd ed.), Auckland, New Zealand: Heinemann Education.

Coffield, F., Steer, R., Allen, R., Vignoles, A., Moss, G., & Vincent, C. (2007) *Public Sector Reform: Principles for Improving the Education System*, London: Institute of Education.

Cummins, J. (2007) 'Pedagogies for the poor? Realigning reading instruction for low-income students with scientifically based reading instruction', *Educational Researcher*, 36, 9: 564–572.

D'Agostino, J. & Murphy, J. (2004) 'A meta-analysis of reading recovery in United States schools', *Educational Evaluation and Policy Analysis*, 26, 1: 23–38.

Department for Children Schools and Families (2009) *Your Child, Your Schools, Our Future: Building a 21st Century Schools System*, Norwich: The Stationery Office.

Department for Education and Employment (DfEE) (1998) *The National Literacy Strategy Framework for Teaching*, Sudbury: DfEE Publications.

Earl, L., Watson, N., Levin, B., Leithwood, K., Fullan, M., Torrance, N., *et al.* (2003) *Watching and Learning: Oise/Ut Evaluation of the Implementation of the National Literacy and Numeracy Strategies*, Nottingham: DfES Publications.

Ellis, S. (2007) 'Policy and research: Lessons from the Clackmannanshire synthetic phonics initiative', *Journal of Early Childhood Literacy*, 7, 3: 281–297.

Evans, M. & Carr, T. (1985) 'Cognitive abilities, conditions of learning, and the early development of reading skill', *Reading Research Quarterly*, 20: 327–350.

Foorman, B. R., Francis, D. J., Fletcher, J. M., Schatschneider, C., & Mehta, P. (1998) 'The role of instruction in learning to read: Preventing reading failure in at-risk children', *Journal of Educational Psychology*, 90: 37–55.

Foorman, B. R., Francis, D. J., Winikates, D., Mehta, P., Schatschneider, C., & Fletcher, J. M. (1997) 'Early interventions for children with reading disabilities', *Scientific Studies of Reading*, 1: 255–276.

Galton, M., Hargreaves, L., Comber, C., & Wall, D. (1999) *Inside The Primary Classroom: 20 Years On*, London: Routledge.

Glass, G. V. (1977) 'Integrating findings: The meta-analysis of research', In L. S. Shulman (ed.), *Review of Research in Education*, Itasca, Illinois: American Educational Research Association.

Goouch, K. & Lambirth, A. (2008) *Understanding Phonics and the Teaching of Reading: Critical Perspectives*, Maidenhead: McGraw-Hill/Open University Press.

Greaney, K., Tunmer, W., & Chapman, J. (1997) 'Effects of rime-based orthographic analogy training on the word recognition skills of children with reading disability', *Journal of Educational Psychology*, 89: 645–651.

Hall, K. (2003) *Listening to Stephen read: Multiple perspectives on literacy*, Buckingham: Open University Press.

Heath, S. B. (1983) *Ways With Words: Language, Life and Work in Communities and Classrooms*, Cambridge: Cambridge University Press.

Johnston, R. & Watson, J. (2005) 'The effects of synthetic phonics teaching of reading and spelling attainment: A seven year longitudinal study', Retrieved 10 December, 2006, from http://www.scotland.gov.uk/Resource/Doc/36496/0023582.pdf.

Lewis, M. & Ellis, S. (eds) (2006) *Phonics: Practice Research and Policy*, London: Paul Chapman Publishing.

Kershner, R. & Howard, J. (2006) *The Psychology of Education Review*, 30, 2: 1–60.

Martinussen, R. & Kirby, J. (1998) 'Instruction in successive and phonological processing to improve the reading acquisition of at-risk kindergarten children', *Developmental Disabilities Bulletin*, 26: 19–39.

Mercer, N. (2005) 'Sociocultural discourse analysis: Analysing classroom talk as a social mode of thinking', *Journal of Applied Linguistics*, 1, 2: 137–168.

Myhill, D. & Fisher, R. (2005) *Informing Practice in English: A Review of Recent Research in Literacy and the Teaching of English*, London: Office for Standards in Education (Ofsted).

National Institute of Child Health and Human Development (NICHD) (2000) *Report of the National Reading Panel. Teaching Children to Read: An Evidence-Based Assessment of the Scientific Research Literature on Reading and its Implications for Reading Instruction: Reports of the Subgroups (NIH publication no. 00–4754)*, Washington, DC: US Government Printing Office.

Rose, J. (2006) *Independent Review of the Teaching of Early Reading*, Nottingham: DfES Publications.

Sainsbury, M., Schagen, I., Whetton, C., Hagues, N., & Minnis, M. (1998) *Evaluation of the National Literacy Project Cohort 1, 1996–1998*, Slough: NFER.

Santa, C. & Hoien, T. (1999) 'An assessment of early steps: A program for early intervention in reading problems', *Reading Research Quarterly*, 34: 54–79.

Sawyer, W. (2010) 'English teaching in Australia and New Zealand', in D. Wyse, R. Andrews & J. Hoffman (eds), *The International Handbook of English, Language and Literacy Teaching*, London: Routledge.

Street, B. (1984) *Literacy in Theory and Practice*, Cambridge: Cambridge University Press.

Tatto, M. T. (2007) *Reforming Teaching Globally*, Oxford: Symposium Books.

Tikly, L. (2004) 'Education and the new imperialism', *Comparative Education*, 40(2): 173–198.

Torgerson, C. J. (2003) *Systematic Reviews*, London: Continuum.

Torgerson, C. J., Brooks, G., & Hall, J. (2006) *A Systematic Review of The Research Literature on the Use of Phonics in the Teaching of Reading and Spelling*, London: Department for Education and Skills (DfES).

Tunmer, W. & Hoover, W. (1993) 'Phonological recoding skill and beginning reading', *Reading and Writing: An Interdisciplinary Journal*, 5: 161–179.

Umbach, B., Darch, C., & Halpin, G. (1989) 'Teaching reading to low performing first graders in rural schools: A comparison of two instructional approaches', *Journal of Instructional Psychology*, 16: 22–30.

Vickery, K., Reynolds, V., & Cochran, S. (1987) Multisensory teaching approach for reading, spelling, and handwriting, Orton-Gillingham based curriculum, in a public school setting', *Annals of Dyslexia*, 37: 189–200.

Wyse, D. (2000) 'Phonics – the whole story?: A critical review of empirical evidence', *Educational Studies*, 26, 3: 355–364.

Wyse, D. (2001) Grammar. 'For writing?: A critical review of empirical evidence', *British Journal of Educational Studies*, 49, 4: 411–427.

Wyse, D. (2003) 'The national literacy strategy: A critical review of empirical evidence', *British Educational Research Journal*, 29, 6: 903–916.

Wyse, D. & Goswami, U. (2008) 'Synthetic phonics and the teaching of reading', *British Educational Research Journal*, 34, 6: 691–710.

Wyse, D. & Jones, R. (2008) *Teaching English, Language and Literacy* (2nd ed.), London: Routledge.

Wyse, D., McCreery, E., & Torrance, H. (2010) 'The Trajectory and Impact of National Reform: Curriculum and Assessment in English Primary Schools', in R. Alexander, C. Doddington, J. Gray, L. Hargreaves & R. Kershner (eds), *The Cambridge Primary Review Research Surveys*, London: Routledge.

Wyse, D. & Opfer, D. (2010) 'Globalisation and the international context for literacy policy reform in England', in D. Wyse, R. Andrews & J. Hoffman (eds), *The International Handbook of English, Language and Literacy Teaching*, London: Routledge.

Wyse, D. & Styles, M. (2007) 'Synthetic phonics and the teaching of reading: The debate surrounding England's "Rose Report" ', *Literacy*, 47, 1: 35–42.

Wyse, D. & Torrance, H. (2009) 'The development and consequences of national curriculum assessment for primary education in England', *Educational Research*, 5, 2: 213–228.

Part IV

Challenging research, policies and pedagogies

Chapter 11

What it takes in early schooling to have adolescents who are skilled and eager readers and writers

William H. Teale, Kathleen A. Paciga and Jessica L. Hoffman

Introduction

Influential research and policy documents on early literacy from the UK and the US (e.g., the Rose Report [Rose 2006]; the National Early Literacy Panel Report [NELP 2008]; and the National Reading Panel Report [NRP 2000]) have stressed that when it comes to early reading instruction, preparing teachers to implement 'the principles which define high quality phonic work' (Rose 2006: 4–5) is of critical importance. Though all of these reports take pains to acknowledge that there is more to literacy learning than phonics and phonological awareness skills, issues related to learning and teaching the code represent the core message that they deliver to policy-makers and practitioners involved in early childhood education. As a result, their practical impact in schools (and especially in US urban contexts with the highest concentrations of children at risk for reading difficulties) has been to center early literacy curriculum and instruction on the skills of phonological awareness, decoding, and reading fluency. This chapter supports fully the importance of teaching these 'word-related' skills but also addresses the shortcomings of such an approach when the resulting instruction neglects other equally, if not more, important components of literacy instruction for young twenty-first century learners.

We propose that in order for children to become capable, engaged, and eager readers and writers when they are older, early literacy programs that young children experience must be reoriented to stress what is foundational with respect to early literacy. It is our contention that more systematic attention must be given to content, comprehension, child engagement, and complex interactions with text if students are to be successful with literacy not only when they are in the early grades but as they progress through the remainder of primary and secondary schooling.

A vision of literacy achievement

This chapter is about early literacy curriculum and instruction – what happens in classrooms during the first years of schooling, between the ages of four and eight, related to helping children learn to read and write. To begin this discussion, however, we invite readers to think about the literacy of 17- or 18-year-olds, students who are at the point of finishing their secondary school education. The completion of secondary school by no means marks the end of literacy development, but it serves as a useful point at which to consider what the institution called school is intended to accomplish in the realm of literacy. Among the scholar readers of this chapter, as would be the case with the general public, policy-makers, or virtually any audience group, there are without doubt varying conceptions of what this 'outcome' should be. Our point here is not to argue for a particular vision, but to pose a general literacy end toward which schooling is headed. In this spirit we offer the following goals – that students graduating from secondary school in a technologically advanced country should be able to:

- access, understand, and critically analyze information and literary content in a variety of written and multimedia texts and synthesize information across texts;
- compose clearly and effectively in a variety of textual forms for a range of different audiences for purposes such as informing, persuading, conveying experience, and constructing an aesthetic experience;
- read most texts fluently enough to focus on making meaning, thus employing a wide variety of comprehension strategies – and where the reading is not fluent, employ 'fix-up' strategies that enable comprehension to occur;
- enhance their conceptual knowledge as a result of reading texts and apply that conceptual knowledge to life experience;

and that they should:

- collaborate with others across distance, time, and space in their literacy and problem solving activities;
- be positively disposed toward reading and writing so that they choose to engage in these activities for pleasure and in their careers throughout their lives.

   Think of these six bullet points as a representation of literacy knowledge, skills, and dispositions that we as educators aim for students to accomplish at the end of 12 or 13 years of schooling. With such a vision of the end point in mind, let us examine: (a) what literacy growth across the years from school entry to school graduation looks like; and (b) what is happening in many early childhood classrooms today as a result of language and literacy research and policy of the past decade and a half. Consideration of these two factors will help build an understanding of what it takes in preschool, kindergarten, and the first and second grades to make it most likely that a child will get to the end point represented by the vision of literacy achievement just presented.

The relation of literacy skill learning to achieving the vision

No one description of the developmental pattern for learning language, reading, and writing skills has been agreed upon by research. But there is an emerging consensus that in thinking about such development across the years – and what that means for early childhood in particular – it is helpful to distinguish between what Paris (2005, 2008) calls 'constrained' and 'unconstrained' skills. Constrained language and literacy skills develop to mastery in a relatively short period and typically at a fairly early age, whereas unconstrained skills develop over a longer period of time and, for all intents and purposes, are never fully mastered. Figure 11.1 depicts the differential growth trajectories for a number of these skills. The figure represents the ideas that within the realm of oral language, a constrained skill like Articulation is typically mastered by children during the first few years of life and thus exhibits a steep learning trajectory. Syntactic development, although taking somewhat longer to master, is similarly a constrained oral language skill. With respect to literacy, learning in the areas of Letter Knowledge, Phonological Awareness, and Decoding typically starts in preschool, also exhibits steep learning curves, and is usually mastered by second or third grade. On the other hand, such areas as Vocabulary, Reading Comprehension, and Composing develop much more gradually and over considerably longer periods of time.

We raise the distinction between constrained and unconstrained skills to illustrate two points. First, as is emphasized in most developmental conceptions of literacy/language (e.g., Chall 1996), at different periods of the individual's development different aspects of literacy learning are ascendant. During the initial years of schooling, for example, it is clear that issues related to 'cracking the code' – letter knowledge, phonological awareness, letter–sound and sound–letter

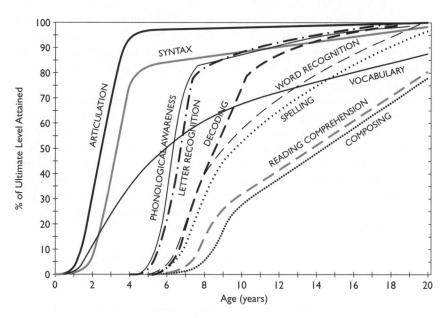

Figure 11.1 Growth trajectories for selected dimensions of language and literacy.

correspondences – occupy more of the focus of learning than they do past the ages of nine or ten. Conversely, during the teenage years, development in areas such as composing, comprehending, and vocabulary is typically more active than learning related to decoding or spelling skills. This being said, it is equally important to emphasize the second point illustrated in Figure 11.1: that *all* of the reading and writing skills depicted begin developing in early childhood.

Where we are now: the early literacy instruction model we have

The good news is that a robust body of research in beginning reading (and to a lesser extent in beginning writing) is now available and that the public as well as policy-makers realize the crucial importance of the early childhood period for success in becoming literate in an alphabetic written language like English. As a result, attention to and support for early literacy instruction in school has never been stronger. The 'reading wars' (Lemann 1997; Pearson 2004) are over for all except the ideologically minded. Researchers and teachers overwhelmingly take the stance that deliberate instruction in the alphabetic code, in reading comprehension, and in writing are all part of high-quality early literacy instruction, both in the regular elementary/primary school language arts curriculum (e.g., Pressley, Allington, Wharton-McDonald, Block, & Morrow 2001; Pressley, Wharton-McDonald, Allington, Block, Morrow, Tracey, Baker, Brooks, Cronin, Nelson, & Woo 2001) and in early literacy intervention programs (e.g., Taylor, Pearson, Clark, & Walpole 2000; Taylor & Ysseldyke 2007). Even in preschool education programs for three- to five-year-olds, there is a broad consensus that emergent literacy skills can and should be focused in intentional, developmentally appropriate ways (e.g., Barone & Morrow 2003; Justice & Vukelich 2008; Vukelich & Christie 2009).

The bad news is that a robust body of research in beginning reading (and to a lesser extent in beginning writing) is now available and that the public as well as policy-makers realize the crucial importance of the early childhood period for success in becoming literate in an alphabetic written language like English. Why do we say bad news? A close look at the impact on classroom practice of all the policy-maker attention to, and funding of, early literacy indicates that what is currently promoted on the national level in both the US and the UK as best instructional practice for the early years of schooling comes up short in two significant respects:

- It is based on a simplistic view of literacy development that fails to take into account what the differences between constrained and unconstrained skills imply for instruction.
- It ignores aspects of learning that are vitally needed in order to attain the end-of-school vision of literacy achievement outlined above, especially for children who fundamentally depend on schooling for their academic learning.

The simple view of literacy development and the resulting skills gap

The current prevailing view about what constitutes good early literacy instruction is based heavily upon research syntheses conducted within the past decade, especially the Reading Review (Rose Report, Rose 2006) and the reports of the National Reading Panel (2000) and the National Early Literacy Panel (2008). These syntheses were, overall, consistent with one another in (1) the factors identified as influencing early literacy and predicting later literacy skill (NELP and NRP); and (2) the conclusions drawn regarding the effectiveness of common instructional practices for early reading (NELP, NRP, Rose), with specific focus in the Rose Report on instruction related to synthetic phonics. The main conclusions emanating from these reports were as follows:

- During the preschool years, alphabet knowledge; phonological awareness; rapid, automatic naming of a random sequence of letters or digits, as well as objects or colors; writing one's own name; and phonological memory are moderate to strong predictors of later conventional literacy skills.
- During the K-3 years, instruction in phonological awareness, phonics, vocabulary, fluency, and a variety of text comprehension strategies are all central to success in early reading.
- It is smart to teach skills related to alphabetics systematically and well during early schooling – phonological awareness in preschool through grade 1 and phonics during the K-2 years – especially in first grade where effects are greatest.

These reports have been used by policy-makers (on the national as well as regional and [in the US] state levels) and by schools to create or adjust their early literacy programs to be 'scientifically based' (McCardle & Chhabra 2004). We firmly believe that the content dimensions of early literacy identified in these reports – alphabet knowledge, phonological awareness, phonics, vocabulary, reading fluency, and text comprehension – are indispensable components of a quality early literacy program. However, our visits to classrooms as well as our conversations with curriculum directors, reading specialists, literacy coaches, and teachers indicate that the 'translation' of these reports' findings into practice has resulted in many instances of less-than-ideal instruction, especially in US urban and rural schools that have large proportions of children from low-income homes.

The problem we have observed is this: early grades literacy instruction in these situations has been focused largely on the constrained skills involved in literacy development – letter knowledge, phonological awareness, phonics, and isolated word identification – and, in many instances, a restricted conception of reading fluency that emphasizes only rate and accuracy. In other words, a simple view of literacy development has predominated, one that regards learning in an area like literacy as proceeding from one skill to another in a cumulative, linear flow. Such a view operates on the assumption that the constrained skills of literacy are somehow more basic and only when these constrained skills have been mastered should instruction 'shift' to a higher level.

This simple view of literacy development appeals considerably to common sense, and as a result has blinded us to the more nuanced reality of what occurs in language and literacy learning during the initial years of schooling. Although literacy development does move from one phase to another as was discussed above, it bears repeating that *all* of the aspects of literacy included in Figure 11.1 have their roots in early childhood. Moreover, if the abilities and dispositions that are so central to realizing the vision that was outlined of a mature reader/writer at the end of schooling are to develop as fully as needed, unconstrained literacy skills – vocabulary, composing, and text comprehension – must be as systematically and well taught in early childhood as are the constrained skills.

Here is a statement from Rose (2006): '. . . children should have a secure grasp of phonics which should be sufficient for them to be fluent readers by the age of seven. This review therefore concentrates upon provision and practice up to the end of Key Stage 1' (7). At other points the report says things like, 'It is widely agreed that reading involves far more than decoding words on the page' (4). This example provides insight into what has so frequently happened as the research translates through policy into practice, in essence operating on what we have called a simple view of development. It may be 'widely agreed' that there is 'far more' to reading and reading development and therefore to what is needed instructionally at this phase of development. But the curriculum directives that ultimately reach most early childhood teachers in their classrooms as a result of statements like the above is that phonics is what you really need to concern yourself with at this stage because the 'far more' stuff doesn't really matter until later. As Teale, Paciga and Hoffman (2007) pointed out in discussing recent trends in literacy instruction in urban schools in the United States:

> . . . the message that large numbers of K–3 teachers in urban schools have taken . . . is that reading instruction in the early grades is exclusively about children learning phonological awareness, how to decode, and how to read words accurately and fluently.
>
> (345)

However, a facet of literacy like comprehension, for example, does not begin to be learned at the point when children have mastered phonics; and therefore, we cannot afford to delay deliberate instruction in comprehension until children are in third or fourth grade or until they are considered fluent on some standardized assessment of reading. Instead we need to operate from the more nuanced view of development that recognizes the learning interplay of both constrained and unconstrained skills in order for children to accomplish all of the dimensions of literacy that are so necessary during the early years of schooling. In other words, comprehension, composing, and complex oral language skills are just as much foundational to literacy achievement as are code-related skills.

A simple view of development implies a linear progression from letter/word-related learning to text-related learning (the infamous, misguided idea that first children learn to read and then they read to learn). Such a view undermines chances of achieving the ultimate vision of a capable secondary school reader/writer described above for many children, especially those who do not live in home environments that promote rich, complex interactions with language and text during their early years. If these children have to wait until their third or fourth year in school for such skill experiences, it will be too late for most of them. Development in early childhood language and literacy does not move from the smaller (letter, word) to the larger (text). Instead, it is fundamentally a process of recursive interplay in which the constrained and unconstrained skills identified earlier interact with each other to build both automaticity in areas like letter, letter–sound, and word recognition as well as the abilities to understand content, shades of meanings, and other complex word and text features and to construct clear, effective messages orally and in print. It is certainly the case that the constrained skills represented by the code elements of literacy need to be emphasized in early grades instruction, but it is also the case that intentional instruction in the unconstrained skills needs equal attention.

As a final footnote to this section, we also want to suggest that engagement is a crucial element of early literacy learning. Developing automaticity in foundational literacy skills requires practice. Practice requires sustained attention. For young children especially, sustained attention is much easier to achieve when activities are meaningful rather than merely repetitious, as is the case with so many commercially published skills worksheets and workbooks. Doing it again and again does not have to be boring – but it often is when a narrow view of skills guides the curriculum.

The short-term view of literacy learning and the resulting knowledge gap

The second way in which the current prevailing approach to early literacy instruction comes up short is a lack of attention to the relationship between content instruction (the development of broad and deep background knowledge) and early literacy learning. We attribute this problem to a short-term vision of literacy achievement that says having all children reading and writing on grade level by the third grade is a matter of teaching them the skills of reading and writing in their first years of schooling. Even if one were to take a charitable view of such a line of thinking and assume that what is meant by the 'skills of reading and writing' includes both constrained and unconstrained skills, a fundamental problem exists with the implementation of such a policy/conceptual model. When we reexamine the six points outlined previously that represent a vision of literacy achievement for the school leaver, it is clear that the definition of literacy implied in these points fundamentally involves deep and rich content knowledge. In other words, literacy achievement is not merely about gaining control over a set of literacy skills; it is about the integration of knowledge with literacy skills. To read well or write well, one draws continually on what one knows.

In a sense, the short-term vision of literacy achievement treats literacy as a content area. What do we need to teach? Reading. Writing. But reading or writing what? Reading or writing about what? We applaud the current emphasis on literacy instruction in kindergarten through grade 2, but we also are concerned about some results of this emphasis. In 2007, the Center on Education Policy (CEP 2007) in the US surveyed 349 school districts and conducted additional in-depth district- and school-level interviews in 13 school districts. Results showed that in the previous five years over 60 per cent of districts overall and 77 per cent of urban districts had increased time for English language arts instruction considerably; *and* that to enable this increase, almost half of districts substantially reduced instructional time in other subject areas. Moreover, the lower the overall achievement of children in the district/school, the greater was the reduction in instruction in other content areas.

As a result, increasing numbers of young children – especially those in urban and rural US schools where poverty levels are highest and achievement levels lowest – are getting shortchanged on domain-specific knowledge during the early grades. But, some argue, that is alright because it is offset by the fact that they are getting a better foundation in literacy in the early years. Are they really getting a better literacy foundation? Teale *et al.* (2007) have suggested that:

> It could appear that way, and it may even show up that way in mandated K–3 assessments: Scores on phonics tests, word recognition, and word reading speed and accuracy may well rise a bit (at these grade levels) in the short run. But what happens in fourth or seventh or tenth grade when what it takes to be a good reader depends on vocabulary knowledge, domain knowledge, and the ability to comprehend a variety of genres of text at a deep level? Our prediction is that the initial 'bump' will . . . fade away. . . .
>
> (346)

Research has consistently shown that instructional time is related to achievement (e.g. Greenwood 1991; Seidel & Shavelson 2007); this is a primary reason why so many programs have chosen to spend more time teaching reading and mathematics in the early grades. But to understand what time should be spent on requires consideration of reading and writing as thinking activities. What children need during the early grades to be good readers and writers in later grades is intimately connected with what they know, whether conceptualized as knowledge in traditional domains like science and history (e.g., Alexander 1997, 2005; Shanahan & Shanahan 2008) or in knowledge domains such as those explored in software engineering (e.g., Hjørland & Albrechtsen 1995; Shiffrin & Börner 2004).

In other words, educating young children in literacy for the long term is not simply educating them in literacy skills; it involves tying reading and writing instruction closely to content instruction throughout the early years of school. What happens when there is a lack of instructional attention to building children's knowledge in the early grades? For children who come from advantaged homes, the consequences may not be so severe because they have access to other sources that foster their background knowledge – they are taken on trips, have music or art lessons, go to camps, experience the theater and concerts, and so forth. The children hurt the most by the short-term view of literacy learning are precisely the children who depend the most on school for their knowledge of the world – those from populations 'at-risk for reading failure.'

Where we need to be

We do not pretend to have a formula for, or portrait of, what an early childhood classroom should look like with respect to literacy instruction, either at a preschool level or for the initial years of schooling, because different contexts (student population, teacher characteristics, resources, etc.) must necessarily result in different curricular configurations, literacy materials, room set-ups, and so forth in settings where the mission is to teach children rather than to adopt a curriculum or implement a program. However, the ideas we have put forth up to this point in this chapter are consistent with the set of principles and a general approach to early literacy practices and policy that we present below. Based on the research available and our work in preschool-grade 2 classrooms around the United States, we offer the following as guiding principles and practices that are most likely to result in high levels of children's literacy achievement as well as positive dispositions toward reading and writing, both during early childhood and throughout the remainder of children's schooling.

For preschool and kindergarten

Principles

- *Literacy is experienced as part of the everyday life and activities of the classroom.* The classroom exists as a context in which literacy is routinely used to help get a wide variety of things done. Thus, reading and writing become inherently interesting because of the information, the sense of wonder, and the communicative opportunities they unlock for children.
- *Children are viewed as active constructors of their own literacy knowledge and strategies.* The teacher engages in deliberate and systematic instruction and always leaves 'spaces' in lessons because she recognizes that young children's early literacy learning is not centrally about memorizing and copying but rather is fundamentally about children making the knowledge and skills being taught their own. The many rich, open-ended dramatic play and center activities the teacher orchestrates provide a variety of chances for children to explore and employ reading and writing in many different ways.

- *A variety of developmental paths into literacy learning are recognized and supported.* Because there is no single developmental progression that young children go through in becoming literate (Sulzby 1991), the classroom provides a range of instructional and assessment activities in order to provide for children of different abilities, cultures, and language backgrounds.
- *The curriculum offers integrated experiences.* Research indicates that listening, speaking, reading, and writing are learned interrelatedly rather than sequentially by young children (Teale & Sulzby 1986; Whitehurst & Lonigan 1998). Thus, the classroom provides learning/teaching experiences in all of the language arts simultaneously rather than first concentrating on oral language and then on reading and finally on writing. In addition, content from areas such as science and social studies is routinely integrated into language arts instruction.

Instructional literacy practices

- The classroom is a *print-rich environment*, and *literacy is embedded* throughout children's daily activities: formal lessons, structured play, and the other, more informal times of the day like snack, lunch, outside time, activity transition times, and even bathroom time as well as across classroom contexts – large group, center, small group, and independent activities.
- The teacher provides many *demonstrations of forms and functions of reading and writing* through explanations of, and think alouds about, a variety of literacy materials and processes. In addition, there are multiple opportunities in a variety of contexts for children to practice the forms and functions of reading and writing, independently and with teacher support.
- *Intentional instruction* is provided on both constrained and unconstrained language/literacy skills, especially listening comprehension, vocabulary, phonological awareness, letter knowledge and letter–sound relationships, print awareness, and writing.
- The *key literacy instructional activities* include both formal and informal, child-centered activities:

  - read alouds: reading books to children and discussing them to develop listening comprehension skills and knowledge about basic concepts of print (directionality, word boundaries, etc.);
  - children's self-selection of books for browsing and emergent reading;
  - word play and phonological awareness activities;
  - children writing emergently for a variety of audiences and purposes;
  - dramatic play structured in ways that includes opportunities for emergent reading and writing as well as oral language development.

- Development of *rich background knowledge* in subject areas such as science, social studies, math, art, and music.
- Attention to promoting deep *engagement* in and *positive dispositions* toward literacy through all of the above activities and out-of-school experiences as well.

For kindergarten–grade 2

Principles

- *Literacy is experienced as part of the everyday life and activities of the classroom.*
- *Children are viewed as active constructors of their own literacy knowledge and strategies.*
- *A variety of developmental paths into literacy learning are recognized and supported.*
- *The curriculum offers integrated language arts experiences.*
- *Children experience written and oral texts that reflect grade level concepts and language in addition to texts at their reading level.* This is especially important for children who experience difficulties with reading in early childhood. Lessons and lots of independent practice with texts at an appropriate reading level are critically important for children. But, in addition, the information, vocabulary, and language structures consistent with grade-level standards are equally important for enabling satisfactory academic achievement in these early grades and – especially – beyond.

Instructional literacy practices

- The classroom is a *print-rich environment,* and *literacy is embedded* throughout the variety of children's daily activities.
- The teacher provides many *demonstrations of forms and functions of reading and writing,* through explanations of, and think alouds about, a variety of literacy materials and processes.
- *Intentional instruction* is provided on both constrained and unconstrained language/literacy skills, especially reading comprehension skills and strategies, vocabulary, phonics, reading fluency, and writing.
- The *key literacy instructional activities* include both formal and informal, child-centered activities:

  - read alouds: reading books to children and discussing them to develop comprehension skill, vocabulary, and literary understanding;
  - children's independent reading of books and online materials to provide practice using constrained and unconstrained skills with connected text;
  - children writing for a variety of audiences and purposes;
  - systematic instruction in decoding;
  - guided reading to apply decoding skills, build automaticity in word recognition and fluency, and experience scaffolded support in text comprehension and vocabulary learning;
  - inquiry projects that foster information literacy skills and higher level reading, writing, and online skills.

- Development of *rich background knowledge* in subject areas such as science, social studies, math, art, and music.

- Attention to promoting deep *engagement* in and *positive dispositions* toward literacy through all of the above activities and out-of-school experiences as well.

Conclusion

Our experience in early childhood classrooms includes conducting Early Reading First projects in preschool classrooms where more than three-quarters of the children come from poverty level home situations. The goal of these projects is to develop centers of excellence in early literacy instruction (see http://www.uic.edu/educ/erf/). In addition, we have taught and worked in kindergarten, first-, and second-grade classrooms in a wide variety of urban and suburban schools in numerous parts of the United States. These experiences and observations have caused us to consider carefully what it takes to foster in children the desire to come back to school each year eager to read, write, and learn, and able to develop the habits of mind, positive dispositions toward reading and writing, the self-regulation, and literacy skills that make academic success and social adjustment a reality both in their early years and throughout their schooling (as well as into their careers). We have seen that there is no one answer to this, no one program or set of 'best practices' to point to. But, in circumstances in which young children experience a content-rich curriculum that is structured with activities that engage them in critical thinking in a variety of contexts, that embed authentic literacy activities throughout the school day rather than designating only a stand-alone block of time for reading and writing instruction, and that pay attention to making reading and writing rewarding (sometimes fun and sometimes very hard work but ultimately rewarding), children succeed – both in the short term and in the long term.

References

Alexander, P. A. (1997) 'Mapping the multidimensional nature of domain learning: The interplay of cognitive, motivational, and strategic forces', in M. L. Maehr & P. R. Pintrich (eds) *Advances in motivation and achievement*, Greenwich, CT: JAI Press.

Alexander, P. A. (2005) 'The path to competence: A lifespan developmental perspective on reading', *Journal of Literacy Research*, 37: 413–36.

Barone, D. M. & Morrow, L. M. (eds) (2003) *Literacy and young children: Research-based practices*, New York: Guilford Press.

Center on Education Policy (2007) 'Choices, changes, and challenges: Curriculum and Instruction in the NCLB era'. Available from http://www.cep-dc.org/index.cfm?fuseaction=Page.viewPage&pageId=484 [Accessed 29 December 2007].

Chall, J. S. (1996) *Learning to read: The great debate*, New York: McGraw-Hill.

Greenwood, C. R. (1991) 'Longitudinal analysis of time, engagement, and achievement in at-risk versus non-risk students', *Exceptional Children*, 57: 521–535.

Hjørland, B. & Albrechtsen, H. (1995) 'Toward a new horizon in information science: Domain analysis', *Journal of the American Society for Information Science*, 46, 6: 400–425.

Justice, L. & Vukelich, C. (eds) (2008) *Achieving excellence in preschool literacy instruction*, New York: Guilford.

Lemann, N. (1997) 'The reading wars', *The Atlantic Monthly.* Available from http://www.theatlantic.com/issues/97nov/read.htm [Accessed 14 April 2004].

McCardle, P. & Chhabra, V. (2004) *The voice of evidence in reading research,* Baltimore, MD: Paul Brookes.

National Early Literacy Panel (2008) *Developing early literacy: Report of the National Early Literacy Panel,* Washington, DC: National Institute for Literacy.

National Reading Panel (2000) *Teaching children to read: An evidence-based assessment of the scientific research literature on reading and its implication for reading instruction,* Washington, DC: National Institute of Child Health and Human Development.

Paris, S. G. (2005) 'Reinterpreting the development of reading skills', *Reading Research Quarterly,* 40, 2: 184–202.

Paris, S. G. (2008) 'Constrained skills – So what?'. Paper presented at the 58th annual meeting of the National Reading Conference, 3–6 December, Orlando, FL.

Pearson, P. D. (2004) 'The reading wars', *Educational Policy,* 18: 216–252.

Pressley, M., Allington, R., Wharton-McDonald, R., Block, C. C. & Morrow, L. M. (2001) *Learning to read: Lessons from exemplary first grades,* New York: Guilford Press.

Pressley, M., Wharton-McDonald, R., Allington, R., Block, C. C., Morrow, L. M. & Tracey, D. (2001) 'A study of effective first-grade literacy instruction', *Scientific Studies of Reading,* 5, 1: 35–58.

Rose, J. (2006) *Independent review of the teaching of early reading,* Nottingham: Department for Education and Skills. Available from http://www.standards.dcsf.gov.uk/ phonics/report.pdf [Accessed 23 January 2009].

Seidel, T. & Shavelson, R. J. (2007) 'Teaching effectiveness research in the past decade: The role of theory and research design in disentangling meta-analysis results', *Review of Educational Research,* 77, 3: 454–499.

Shanahan, T. & Shanahan, C. (2008) 'Teaching disciplinary literacy to adolescents: Rethinking content-area literacy', *Harvard Educational Review,* 78, 1: 40–59.

Shiffrin, R. & Börner, K. (2004) 'Mapping knowledge domains', *Proceedings of the National Academy of Sciences,* 101, Suppl 1: 5183–5185.

Sulzby, E. (1991) 'The learner develops: The development of the young child and the emergence of literacy', in J. M. Jensen, J. Flood, D. Lapp & J. R. Squire (eds) *Handbook of research on teaching the English language arts,* New York: Macmillan.

Taylor, B. M., Pearson, P. D., Clark, K. & Walpole, S. (2000) 'Effective schools and accomplished teachers: Lessons about primary grade reading instruction in low-income schools', *The Elementary School Journal,* 101, 2: 121–166.

Taylor, B. M. & Ysseldyke, J. E. (2007) *Effective instruction for struggling readers, K–6,* New York: Teachers College Press.

Teale, W. H., Paciga, K. A. & Hoffman, J. L. (2007) 'Beginning reading instruction in urban schools: The curriculum gap ensures a continuing achievement gap', *The Reading Teacher,* 61: 344–48.

Teale, W. H. & Sulzby, E. (1986) 'Emergent literacy as a perspective for examining how young children become writers and readers', in W. H. Teale & E. Sulzby (eds) *Emergent literacy: Writing and reading,* Norwood, NJ: Ablex Publishing Corporation.

Vukelich, C. & Christie, J. (2009) *Building a foundation for preschool literacy: Effective instruction for children's reading and writing development,* Newark, DE: International Reading Association.

Whitehurst, G. J. & Lonigan, C. J. (1998) 'Child development and emergent literacy', *Child Development,* 69: 848–872.

Chapter 12

Classroom interaction and reading pedagogy in the early years of school

Henrietta Dombey

Introduction

It is widely assumed that education in general and literacy education in particular, should be interactive. But what does the term 'interaction' mean when applied to classroom literacy teaching? Interactive teaching is rather like motherhood – approved by all. But there are many different ways of mothering and more than one way of interacting in the classroom. Is the approach currently in official favour in England the best for all educational purposes? This chapter attempts to answer this question, with particular reference to research on the interaction promoted within England's Literacy Hour.

I begin by briefly considering what interactive teaching is and where it has come from. I then discuss different types of classroom interaction in literacy learning. After considering how a view of classroom interaction shaped England's National Literacy Strategy, I look at the forms interaction has taken in England's classrooms in recent years. Having discussed how reading itself is now seen as an interactive enterprise, I argue that this means it does not sit easily with Recitation, the form of interaction dominant in most classrooms. There follows an examination of the key features of Recitation and contrasting discourse patterns, as identified in two important research studies. I then use these to examine closely a classroom interaction in which young children are not restricted to the responding role of Recitation, but instead initiate and pursue their own lines of enquiry through textured discussion. I conclude by arguing that different styles of interaction imply fundamentally different potentials for promoting reading as a thinking activity and fundamentally different conceptions of the purpose of education.

What is interactive teaching and where has it come from?

The view of teaching as one-way transmission of knowledge and skills is rooted in the very distant past and has dominated for most of the modern era. But interactive teaching also has a long history, traceable back to Socrates' dialogic method. Early in the last century, a concern with education for democracy in the US turned attention to interactive teaching. It then came to prominence in the 1920s

(Delamont 1983), when child development researchers were investigating the limits placed on pupils' freedom of speech. Since then it has gained power, at least in the world of research: from the early 1970s, Flanders' *Interaction Analysis* categories (Flanders 1970), constructed to foster children's participation in democratic society, were instrumental in shaping much research into teaching.

The publication in English of Vygotsky's *Thought and Language* (1962) and *Mind in Society* (1978) strengthened this interest, adding a further challenge to the hegemony of the view of teaching as straightforward one-way transmission of knowledge. It also undermined Piaget's view of learning as essentially the lone individual's encounter with the material world (Piaget 1951). Vygotsky's influence was instrumental in the re-conceptualisation of learning by nearly all educational theorists, as an essentially social process.

Vera John-Steiner, a noted Vygotskyan scholar, was one of the editors of *Mind in Society*. Even before its publication, with her colleagues in New Mexico, she set about the practice of interactive teaching (IT), focusing particularly on a literacy course for university freshmen. Drawing contrasts with anthology-based curricula on the one hand and reductionist, behaviourist approaches to literacy learning on the other, Elasser and John-Steiner wrote in 1977 of their pioneering programme for advanced literacy: 'an intricate interaction among teachers, learners, and social change, which in turn provides a dynamic of continuity and change that enhances the development of written communication' (Elasser and John-Steiner 1977: 365).

The concept of 'an intricate interaction among teachers, learners, and social change' is an idea that has endured. A path can be traced to the socio-cultural conceptions of learning of Courtney Cazden (1965) and Barbara Rogoff (1990).

At much the same time as the psychology of learning was becoming more social, the development of discourse analysis made it possible to identify patterns of verbal interaction. Almost by chance, much of the early work on verbal interaction patterns, especially that by Sinclair and Coulthard, focused on school classrooms. Their major contribution was to take the exchange rather than the individual utterance as the unit of analysis, so revealing more fully who was in control of the discourse (Sinclair and Coulthard 1975). Analyses of classroom interaction using these tools showed the majority of classrooms on both sides of the Atlantic to be dominated by what was termed the IRF or IRE exchange pattern. In this the teacher's 'Initiation' move is followed by the student's 'Response' move and the exchange is then completed by the teacher's 'Feedback' move, which often takes the form of 'Evaluation'. Such a pattern came to be known in the US as the Recitation format, the term I use in this chapter.

Meanwhile the democratic theme developed. Au and Mason (1981) highlighted the issue of student control over the discourse, advancing their balance of rights hypothesis, that 'higher levels of student behavior are probable if there is a balance between the interactional rights of the teacher and children' (Au and Mason 1981: 150).

The issue of student control of talk has also been central to the work of Douglas Barnes and colleagues in the UK. Their concern has been with student–student interaction, rather than student–teacher interaction. Their main focus is on what they term 'exploratory talk' – talk occurring in small group discussion without the teacher – which Barnes characterises as 'often hesitant and incomplete; it enables the speaker to try out new ideas, to hear how they sound, to see what others make of them, to arrange information and ideas into different patterns' (Barnes 1976: 126).

This then presents some rather different views of productive classroom interaction. At one extreme there is the highly patterned 'Recitation' lesson, under the close control of the teacher, while at the other there is the much more loosely structured 'exploratory talk', often producing unforeseen outcomes. In between we have Au and Mason's balance of interactional rights (Au and Mason 1981).

Different types of interaction in literacy lessons

With only a passing reference to the work of Sinclair and Coulthard, Chinn *et al.* present a strong challenge to the dominance of the Recitation format, in a complex and subtle study that contrasts two kinds of literature discussion in fourth-grade US classrooms (nine- to ten-year-olds) (Chinn *et al.* 2001). Drawing on the work of Au and Mason (1981), they compare the two types of discussion principally in terms of the amount of teacher and student talk, the character of teacher and student questions and the cognitive processes involved in the student talk.

By the researchers' definition, the two instructional frames involved, Recitation and Collaborative Reasoning, differ in terms of four dimensions – all concerned with the making of key decisions. These are: who decides the stance the discussion takes, who has interpretive authority, who controls turn-taking and who chooses the discussion topics. The teachers in the four classrooms involved (all rated as good), were initially videotaped using their habitual Recitation format. After a seven-week supported initiation into Collaborative Reasoning they were videotaped again.

Although there was no marked increase in turn length, the analysis of the transcripts shows the Collaborative Reasoning format to be dramatically more productive of student talk, in terms of the length of each discussion, the rate of words spoken per minute (111 as against 66) and the relative proportion of both words and turns spoken by the students. Meanwhile the teachers' questions were fewer than in the Recitation classes, and the proportion of questions of the assessment type was smaller, while there was a greater proportion of open-ended questions and questions challenging the students to substantiate observations. In these Collaborative Reasoning classes, the students made many more elaborations and predictions, provided evidence at ten times the rate of their Recitation classes and 'were much more likely to articulate alternate perspectives' (Chinn *et al.* 2001: 398). After commenting that the teachers' and students' inexperience in Collaborative Reasoning may have inhibited the students from producing more extended utterances, the authors conclude: 'The results of this study suggest the possibility that giving students greater control over interpretation, turn-taking and topic may generally enhance engagement and elicit a high rate of using beneficial cognitive processes' (Chinn *et al.* 2001: 408).

Yet some would argue that both types of classroom exchange studied by Chinn *et al.* could be seen as interactive. Not all conceptions of interactive teaching involve such matters as 'control over interpretation, turn-taking and topic', much less 'engagement and . . . beneficial cognitive process'. In simple terms of rapidity of exchange, a lesson proceeding through a sequence of questions and answers might be classed as highly interactive, particularly where the children are encouraged to respond at speed. In such terms the Recitation format is an interactive one.

But the educational value of such a conception of interactivity is questionable. An extensive survey of studies of classroom discourse finds that a slower pace of teacher questioning with extended wait times correlates with a greater number of student responses (Carlsen 1991). Another study finds such characteristics associated with sustained responses of greater complexity (Fagan, Hassler and Szabl 1981). We need to be clear about what we wish children to learn before deciding the kind of interaction we promote in the classroom.

Interactive teaching and the introduction of England's National Literacy Strategy

In 1998 Reynolds published a review of research, mainly from the US, on teacher effectiveness and school effectiveness in terms of literacy teaching, with the aim of identifying implications for contemporary educational policies (Reynolds 1998). Reynolds argues that the research demonstrates a link between whole-class interactive instruction and academic success. Interactive classrooms are defined as those in which every student is required to attempt a response, in contrast to those 'with a traditional lecturing and drill approach in which the students remain passive' (Reynolds 1998: 150). It is assumed throughout the survey that teacher questioning, apparently following the Recitation format, is the way to achieve interaction.

However, interaction is not the sole focus of this survey. It is one of a number of factors found to be associated with effective teaching. And there is only one passing reference in the studies surveyed to the 'pacing' of instruction, but no explicit statement that interaction should be fast-paced.

Reynolds' survey found favour with the architects of England's strategies for teaching numeracy and literacy, implemented by New Labour shortly after they assumed power in May 1997. Following his recommendation, this gives a prominence to whole-class 'interactive teaching', a practice very different from the norm in England's primary schools at the time.

In 1998 the 'Framework for Teaching', the document that set out in detail England's National Literacy Strategy (NLS), specified the most successful literacy teaching as being:

- discursive – characterised by high quality oral work;
- interactive – pupils' contributions are encouraged, expected and extended;
- well-paced – there is a sense of urgency, driven by the need to make progress and succeed;
- confident – teachers have a clear understanding of the objectives;
- ambitious – there is optimism about and high expectations of success.

(DfEE 1998: 8)

The importance accorded to interaction is evident in the first two descriptors. As the next two indicate, this is a view of interaction that, as in Reynolds' survey, places the teacher firmly in control of the discourse. It also places a premium on speed – rapid exchange Recitation. It seems some distance away both from the exploratory talk championed by Barnes and colleagues and also from Au and Mason's balance of interactional rights and the Collaborative Reasoning of Chinn *et al.* So it is interesting to examine the forms interaction has taken in England's classrooms before and after the introduction of the NLS.

Types of interaction found in literacy lessons in England's classrooms

Of the various studies of discourse in classrooms since the introduction of the NLS in 1998, the SPRINT study has the most comprehensive data (English *et al.* 2002). In addition to the products of their own fieldwork, English *et al.* draw on classroom interaction data from the two ORACLE projects, carried out in the mid-1970s and mid-1990s by Galton and colleagues (Galton *et al.* 1980; Galton *et al.* 1999). Over the 25 years involved, the three sets of data show marked changes in exchange patterns. If the data are representative of literacy lessons in England's primary classrooms, and if the trend has not since changed, children are now making significantly more contributions to their lessons than their predecessors did some 30 years ago. English *et al.* conclude: 'These data suggest that teachers have been very successful in making their literacy teaching more interactive. Pupil contributions were expected and encouraged twice as often as they were before the NLS' (English *et al.* 2002: 23).

But they go on to point out that this increase in the number of interactions may be at the expense of their duration. Their own data show a decline between 1996 and 2000 in the percentage of interactions with the same child or small group, lasting over 25 seconds, from 27 per cent of the total in 1996, to 5 per cent at KS2 and 2 per cent at KS1 in Literacy Hours in 2000. They also found significantly more (9 per cent) of these more sustained exchanges in small classes of 19 children or fewer, than in large ones (2 per cent).

A few years later, in a study of interactive teaching in the National Literacy Strategy and National Numeracy Strategy, Smith *et al.* found the average length of a pupil answer was five seconds (Smith *et al.* 2004). So, despite the positive presentation by English *et al.*, the encouraging picture of increasing participation appears to be marred by the increasing brevity of students' utterances.

Unsurprisingly, these studies have shown the Recitation pattern to predominate in school classrooms in England in the teaching of literacy, as in a wide range of other subjects (Galton *et al.* 1980; Galton *et al.* 1999; Smith *et al.* 2004). There may be some variation in the incidence and length of student responses, but none is shown in the basic pattern. What these studies do not make clear is whether this is evident to the same degree in the most effective school classrooms. If education in literacy is to become more powerful for more children, we need to know more about what happens in the most productive classrooms. But we need to be careful of the yardstick we use to measure productivity.

Citing Brophy and Good (1986), Reynolds reports: 'In general, effective teachers have been found to teach a concept, then ask questions to test children's understanding and, if the material did not seem well understood, to re-teach the concept, followed by more monitoring . . .' (Reynolds 1998: 150). For English *et al.*, 'interactivity depends on the ratio of [teacher] questions to [teacher] statements'. For both, a lesson proceeding through a sequence of questions and answers would be seen as highly interactive, disregarding the caveats and concerns of other researchers.

More recently, in his international study of the culture and pedagogy of primary education, Alexander claims that in the primary classrooms of Russia, France or India, children's classroom contributions are not marked by brevity to the extent that they appear to be in the UK and the US (Alexander 2000). The emphasis is not on universal participation, but instead, a few children are invited to make substantial responses and supported in the process.

The National Literacy Strategy itself may have contributed to the situation in English classrooms. Inherent contradictions, both practical and ideological, between the first two of the NLS's most successful literacy teaching characteristics and the third have been noted by a number of researchers with a more complex view of classroom interaction (e.g. Mroz *et al.* 2000; English *et al.* 2002). These three characteristics are:

- discursive – characterised by high quality oral work;
- interactive – pupils' contributions are encouraged, expected and extended; and
- well-paced – there is a sense of urgency, driven by the need to make progress and succeed.

(DfEE 1998: 8)

The recommended 'sense of urgency' may be inimical to thoughtful discussion. But this problem cannot be laid at the door of the NLS alone, which is only part of a much wider apparatus of direction and control of classroom teaching in England. As English *et al.* observe of three 'typical' case study teachers in their SPRINT study: '. . . in an educational climate dominated by monitoring, inspection and test results, teaching for understanding was regarded as an optional extra, permissible only once the learning objectives had been met' (English *et al.* 2002: 22).

The exhaustive lists of objectives of the NLS, combined with the apparatus of accountability (SATs scores, Ofsted inspections) pushes teachers into steaming on through lessons, pre-planned in detail, militating against 'passages of intellectual search' (Tizard and Hughes 1984). Quick-fire interaction appears to be the instrument of choice for shepherding children through a curriculum, but militates against the exploration of issues, ideas, implications and connections. The kind of interaction increasingly evident in England's primary classrooms since the introduction of the NLS seems to have little in common with the interaction inspired by the idea of democracy and collaborative meaning-making explored above.

Reading as an interactive enterprise

Since the early development of interactive teaching in the last century, outlined at the start of this chapter, the act of reading has been re-conceptualised. As recently as 40 years ago reading was seen by most who taught it or researched it as initially an essentially perceptual matter, followed by a process of comprehension, in which the good reader obediently and correctly registers the meaning of the text, rather like a negative exposed to the light. As in Cain's account (this volume), the process of reading is now seen as much more complex, shaped through interaction between the knowledge, inferences, experience and habits of mind of the reader and the assembly of words (and images) on the page or screen.

This implies that there cannot be one correct reading of any text. In 1959, arguing that spoken language is not governed by the laws of behaviourism, Chomsky reminded us that it is not possible to predict what a person will say in response to a given stimulus (Chomsky 1959). Similarly we now see that, because of what different readers bring to a particular text, although it may prompt many incorrect or unjustifiable readings, no text can generate only one correct reading. The explorations of Rosenblatt and Iser of the active role of the reader of literary texts, have both been enormously influential (Iser 1978; Rosenblatt 1978) in revealing the complex subtleties of the process of reading literature.

Bakhtin has argued that all understanding is essentially dialogic, which makes reading an essentially dialogic process – between the reader and the writer (Bakhtin 1981). Each reader must enter into a rather different dialogue with the author, since each approaches the text within her own set of concerns, values, understandings and experiences.

So we should look at interaction to see not just how much the students speak, but to what extent the sense they make of the text is shaped by their own concerns and experiences, or, conversely, to what extent they are being guided by the teacher to one 'correct' interpretation. Perhaps we need to trace where information and conceptions originate in such interactions, making use of some of the tools of discourse analysis, producing more complex information than numerical analyses of the words spoken.

Identifying the key features of Recitation and Discussion

The analytic framework of Sinclair and Coulthard is particularly informative. It shows us whose voice is dominant and the texture of the interaction, resulting, as Table 12.1 shows, in a taxonomy that extends far beyond the IRF format they identified, which has subsequently been shown to be predominant in most classrooms (1975). Their catalogue of exchange types is shown in Table 12.1.

This taxonomy proved useful to the work of Nystrand and colleagues, who set out to explore the patterns of interaction that were characteristic of highly effective English lessons at the secondary level (Nystrand *et al.* 1997). They approached this task recognising their debt to Vygotsky and Bakhtin for a view of learning as a dynamic, social and epistemic process of constructing and negotiating knowledge.

In their observations of some 450 lessons in 112 eighth- and ninth-grade classrooms, the largest study of classroom discourse carried out at that time, Nystrand and colleagues were concerned to identify 'the most important qualities of instruction that works'. We need to look carefully at what they mean by this, since Reynolds and others have also claimed a concern with what works. For Nystrand *et al.*, effective instruction in literature is:

> . . . instruction that helps students understand literature in depth, remember it and relate to it in terms of their own experience, and – most important for literature instruction – respond to it aesthetically, going beyond the who, what, when and why of non-fiction and literal comprehension.
>
> (Nystrand *et al.* 1997: 2)

To identify such instruction in the many classrooms they studied, they did not rely on pre-existing tests, but created their own tests of knowledge and understanding

Table 12.1 Possible exchange types (following Sinclair and Coulthard, 1975)

Teacher-initiated exchanges	*Student-initiated exchanges*
Teacher Direct [+Response] [+Feedback]/[+Follow-up]	**Student** *Direct* [+Response] [+Feedback]/[+Follow-up]
Teacher Inform [+Response] [+Feedback]/[+Follow-up]	**Student** *Inform* [+Response] [+Feedback]/[+Follow-up]
Teacher Elicit [+Response] [+Feedback]/[+Follow-up]	**Student** *Elicit* [+Response] [+Feedback]/[+Follow-up]

Key
Square Brackets [ ]   optional move
Forward slash /   alternative option

of literature, based on the texts studied by each class. These tests included such matters as internal motivation of characters, and relation of conflict and/or ending to theme. The results for each class were analysed in relation to the features of the classroom discourse. So the precise interactive patterns were not, as in the work of Chinn *et al.* (2001) a starting point for the study, but emerged from the data.

However, to analyse their data they found they needed more than the Sinclair and Coulthard taxonomy allowed. They needed to identify the status of the teacher and student speakers, in relation both to each other and to the content of the exchanges. They also needed, in an echo of Flanders' categories, to determine the function of any responding move from a teacher in terms of elaborating or extending the student's contribution on the one hand, or evaluating it on the other (Flanders 1970). These features are remarkably similar to those used by Chinn *et al.* to distinguish between the instructional frameworks of collaborative reasoning and recitation, namely: who decides the stance the discussion takes, who has interpretive authority, who will control turn-taking, and who chooses the discussion topics. However, Nystrand and colleagues also looked at patterning over larger stretches than the individual exchange.

They found that the most successful classes were characterised by three features: 'authentic questions', where the questioner did not know the answer already; 'uptake', where the teacher incorporated students' responses into subsequent questions, so that the course of talk was shaped by the students' responses; and 'discussion', where the students and the teacher together negotiated and jointly determined the discourse.

> In none of our analyses did we ever find that a higher cognitive level of instructional activities actually enhanced learning. Instead we could explain the relative effectiveness of different instructional activities only when we examined the ways teachers and students interacted as evidenced by authentic questions, uptake and especially discussion.
>
> (Nystrand *et al.* 1997: 57)

In these classes the Recitation format had no place: the teacher neither adopted the role of final arbiter over wrong or right answers, nor allocated to the students the role of obedient responders. Table 12.2 shows the paradigmatic contrasts of the two formats.

Nystrand *et al.*'s Discussion format is in marked contrast with the numerical view of successful interaction of English *et al.*, based on the Recitation format. It is nearer John-Steiner's view of 'an intricate interaction among teachers, learners, and social change'.

The distinction made between Discussion and Recitation also appears to approximate the distinction between Chinn *et al.*'s Collaborative Reasoning and their Recitation. Yet the two studies are the products of contrasting methodologies: while Nystrand *et al.* proceed inductively from studying the instructional patterning in highly effective classrooms, Chinn *et al.* intervene to induct teachers

Table 12.2 Key features of recitation and discussion

Paradigm	Recitation	Discussion
Communication model	Transmission of knowledge	Transformation of understandings
Epistemology	Objectivism: knowledge is a given	Dialogism: knowledge emerges from interaction of voices
Source of valued knowledge	Teacher and textbook authorities: excludes students	Includes students' interpretations and personal experience
Texture	Choppy	Coherent

(Nystrand *et al.* 1997: 19)

who are effective in the conventional Recitation format into the format of Collaborative Reasoning. Yet, despite the different approaches (and age groups) involved in the two studies, there seems to be no important difference between the two conceptions of Recitation. Additionally, Nystrand's Discussion could almost be equated with Chinn *et al.*'s Collaborative Reasoning: neither one appears to have features that conflict with the definition of the other.

Yet the sets of identifying features are not identical. As set out earlier, the four key features Chinn *et al.* advance are: who decides the stance the discussion takes (whether to treat the literary text as a work of art, or quarry it for pieces of information), who has interpretive authority, who controls turn-taking, and who chooses the discussion topics. While interpretive authority could be seen as catered for by the paradigm that Nystrand *et al.* term 'source of valued knowledge', Chinn *et al.* have something distinct to add: an explicit concern with control of the discourse. In addition to the issue of interpretive authority, they see the fundamental discriminator that sets Recitation apart from Collaborative Reasoning to be the allocation of authority to take decisions – about the topics discussed, the stance of the discussion and turn-taking within it. These features remain implicit in the work of Nystrand *et al.*

As stated earlier, Bakhtin sees understanding as essentially dialogic (Bakhtin 1981). Yet he recognises that much discourse is monologic in form, not seeking to take account of the point of view or experience of discourse partners. The distinctions drawn by Nystrand *et al.* between Recitation and Discussion, and by Chinn *et al.* between Recitation and Collaborative Reasoning, echo the opposition articulated by Bakhtin. So we might usefully term the two contrasting forms Monological and Dialogical teaching.

Dialogical teaching in the literacy education of young children

But is this too far removed from the literacy learning of young children? Chinn *et al.* (2001) carried out their study with fourth-grade ten-year-olds. Nystrand *et al.*

(1997) studied high school students. Both were concerned with literature lessons. This is surely very removed from learning to read in the early stages of formal schooling. Can dialogical teaching ever be appropriate for young children in the early stages of literacy learning?

It is certainly not inappropriate for early language learning. Around 30 years ago we were shown, by Cazden, Wells and others, that reciprocity characterises the interactions of caretakers with more rapid young language learners (Cazden 1965; Wells 1978). Children who learn most rapidly tend to initiate most of the exchanges, while adults support and extend the meaning of the children's initiations.

A few years later, Tizard and Hughes (1984) showed that pre-school children from varied class backgrounds were engaged in more sustained and challenging dialogue with their mothers at home than they were with their teachers in the nursery classes they attended. The characteristics of the home dialogues are broadly similar to the key features of dialogical teaching set out above. All these successful interactions are concerned with the negotiation rather than the transmission of meaning.

As to lessons in school, the answer depends, in part, on how early literacy learning is conceived. If it is thought of in narrow terms as instruction in phonics, then there is less room for a dialogical approach, since there is a fixed body of knowledge to be transmitted. The teacher is the undisputed arbiter of wrong and right answers. However, the complex orthography of English suggests it is wise to allow children in the early stages of learning to read to supplement their use of phonics with other approaches to word identification – in particular, analogy with known spelling patterns and guessing from context (see Goswami's chapter in this volume). Here a collaborative problem-solving approach to word identification in running text may well be productive.

And if early literacy learning is held to include making sense of whole texts, then it seems there is a clear place for dialogical teaching. In the US, Sipe has shown children in first- and second-grade classes developing 'a rich, textured literary understanding' through oral interaction during 'read aloud' sessions of picture story books. He writes of the teacher with whom he worked: 'Both of us placed a high value on children's free responses during the reading of stories and were less interested in pursuing a set agenda than in listening to what the children had to say' (Sipe 2000: 261).

In my own work, I have shown highly successful teachers of Year 1 classes engaged in collaborative meaning-making with the children (Dombey 2003a). What follows is an extract from a transcript of a lesson taught by one of these teachers, Julie, reading Martin Waddell's *Farmer Duck* with a Year 1 class. I have selected an extract typical of the whole in terms of its patterns of interaction. Julie has prefaced the reading by asking the children 'What can you tell me from the pictures about the story?' They are inspecting page 9, and one of the children, Charlie, has just put his hand up.

1	*Teacher:*	Charlie.
2	*Charlie:*	The, it's, the, it's so much it's rain.
3		That might be flooded.
4	*Teacher:*	D'you think it's rain down here?
5	*Charlie:*	No, it's flooded.
6	*Teacher:*	What does anybody else think?
7		Charlie thinks it's rain, it might be flooded.
8		What d'you think, Robert?
9	*Robert:*	I think it's snow.
10	*Teacher:*	Yeah I thought maybe it was snow.
11		Maybe it's turned colder.
12	*Teacher:*	Harvey, you had your hand up, didn't you?
13		What did you want to say?
14	*Harvey:*	Nathan's being silly.
15	*Teacher:*	Oh well, I'm glad he's stopped now.
16		Thank you, Nathan.
17		Yes Sam.
18	*Sam:*	But how could water leave the people's print foots?
19	*Teacher:*	Oh well done!
20		What a detective!
21		If there are footprints, they can't be in rain, can they?
22		So we must be right about the snow.

Despite Harvey's interruption at 14, these interactions exhibit a number of the key features of Discussion identified by Nystrand *et al.*

- In addition to two tag questions, the teacher asks two authentic questions at 6 and 13, soliciting the children's ideas, and one question at 4 inviting elaboration. There are no pseudo-questions.
- The teacher makes use of 'uptake' at 7, 8, 10 and 11, incorporating the children's earlier responses into subsequent invitations to extend the discussion, so the children are shaping the course of the talk.
- Although the overall agenda has been determined by the teacher, she and the children are together negotiating and jointly determining the discourse, which can therefore be determined Discussion in the terms of Nystrand *et al.*

The interactions also show key features of the Collaborative Reasoning of Chinn *et al.*

- The teacher asks a number of open-ended questions at 4, 6, 8 and 13, but no 'assessment type' questions.
- The students are articulating alternative perspectives.

I would add that the teacher eschews the role of interrogator of the children, but instead invites them to take on the role of active interrogators of the text.

If we look at the paradigms exemplified, the communication model is transformation rather than transmission of knowledge. The source of valued knowledge clearly includes the students' interpretations. The texture of the discussion is coherent rather than choppy and the teacher and children share control of the direction of the discourse.

This transcript extract is far from unique. While the Recitation pattern remains dominant in England's classrooms, a number of excellent teachers of young children are shaping their literacy lessons in more dialogical ways (Dombey 2003b), demonstrating that young children can certainly be engaged in dialogical literacy learning. We need to explore its potential if we are to enable our children to develop rich understandings of the texts of a rapidly changing world.

Here we should return to a consideration of the kinds of education promoted by Monological Teaching on the one hand and Dialogical Teaching on the other. Bourdieu and Passeron (1990) distinguish between Cultural Reproduction and Cultural Transformation. The aim of Cultural Reproduction is to pass on an unchanged culture to one's successors, whereas the aim of Cultural Transformation is to enable those successors to understand, think, perceive and do things differently, in response to changes in the physical and social worlds in which we all move. One is concerned with initiating students into a set of unchanging practices and the other with enabling them to work to develop changing practices. Monological Teaching can be seen as an instrument of Cultural Reproduction, whereas Dialogical Teaching is essentially an agent of Cultural Transformation.

To assess classroom interaction solely in terms of the rate and duration of children's answers to teachers' questions is to restrict the notion of interactive teaching to Cultural Transmission. At any time we should be wary of so restricting the process of education. At a time of vast physical, technological and social change, we should be very cautious indeed.

References

Alexander, R. (2000) *Culture and Pedagogy: International Comparisons in Primary Education*, Oxford: Blackwell.

Au, K.H. and Mason, J.M. (1981) 'Social organizational factors in learning to read: The balance of rights hypothesis', *Reading Research Quarterly*, 17: 115–152.

Bakhtin, M. (1981) *The Dialogic Imagination*, Austin: The University of Texas Press.

Barnes, D. (1976) *Communication and Curriculum*, London: Penguin.

Bourdieu, P. and Passeron, J-C. (trans. R. Nice) (1990) *Reproduction in Education, Society and Culture*, Revised edition, London: Sage.

Brophy, J. and Good, T.L. (1986) 'Teacher behavior and student achievement' in M.C. Wittrock (ed.) *Handbook of Research on Teaching*, New York: Macmillan.

Carlsen, W.S. (1991) 'Questioning in classrooms: A sociolinguistic perspective', *Review of Educational Research*, 61: 157–178.

Cazden, C. (1965) *Environmental Assistance to the Child's Acquisition of Grammar*. Unpublished doctoral dissertation, Harvard University.

Chinn, C.A., Anderson, R.C. and Waggoner, M.A. (2001) 'Patterns of discourse in two kinds of literature discussion', *Reading Research Quarterly*, 36: 378–411.

Chomsky, N. (1959) Review of Skinner's Verbal Behavior, *Language*, 35, 1: 26–58.

Delamont, S. (1983) *Interaction in the Classroom*, London: Routledge.

Department for Education and Employment (DfEE) (1998) *National Literacy Strategy Framework for Teaching*, London: DfEE.

Dombey, H. (2003a) 'Interactions between teachers, pupils and texts in three primary classrooms in England', *Journal of Early Childhood Literacy*, 3, 1: 37–58.

Dombey, H. (2003b) 'Moving forward together', in E. Bearne, H. Dombey and T. Grainger (eds) *Classroom Interactions in Literacy*, 36–48, Maidenhead: McGraw-Hill Education and Open University Press.

Elsasser, N. and John-Steiner, V. (1977) 'An interactionist approach to advancing literacy', *Harvard Educational Review*, 47, 3: 355–369.

English, E., Hargreaves, L. and Hislam, J. (2002) 'Pedagogical dilemmas in the National Literacy Strategy: Primary teachers' perceptions, reflections and classroom behaviour', *Cambridge Journal of Education*, 32: 9–26.

Fagan, E.R., Hassler, D.M. and Szabbl, M. (1981) 'Evaluation of questioning strategies in language arts instruction', *Research in the Teaching of English*, 15: 267–273.

Flanders, N. (1970) *Analyzing Teacher Behavior*, New York: Addison Wesley.

Galton, M., Simon, B. and Croll, P. (1980) *Inside the Primary Classroom*, London: Routledge & Kegan Paul.

Galton, M., Hargreaves, L., Comber, C., Wall, D. and Pell, A. (1999) *Inside the Primary Classroom – 20 years on*, London: Routledge.

Iser, W. (1978) *The Act of Reading: A theory of aesthetic response*, London: Routledge & Kegan Paul.

Mroz, M., Smith, F. and Hardman, F. (2000) 'The discourse of the Literacy Hour', *Cambridge Journal of Education*, 30, 3: 379–390.

Nystrand, M. with Gamoran, A., Kachur, R. and Prendergast, C. (1997) *Opening Dialogue: Understanding the dynamics of language and learning in the English classroom*, New York: Teachers' College Press.

Piaget, J. (1951) *The Child's Conception of the World*, London: Routledge & Kegan Paul.

Reynolds, D. (1998) 'Schooling for literacy: A review of research on teacher effectiveness and school effectiveness and its implications for contemporary educational policies', *Educational Review*, 50, 2: 147–162.

Rogoff, B. (1990) *Apprenticeship in Thinking: Cognitive development in social context*, Oxford: Oxford University Press.

Rosenblatt, L. (1978) *The Reader, the Text, the Poem: The transactional theory of the literary work*, Arbondale and Edwardsville: Southern Illinois University Press.

Sinclair, J. and Coulthard, M. (1975) *Towards an Analysis of Discourse*, London: Oxford University Press.

Sipe, L. (2000) 'The construction of literary understanding by first and second graders in oral response to picture storybook read-alouds', *Reading Research Quarterly*, 35, 2: 252–275.

Smith, F., Hardman, F., Wall, K. and Mroz, M. (2004) 'Interactive whole class teaching in the national literacy and numeracy strategies', *British Educational Research Journal*, 30, 3: 395–411.

Tizard, B. and Hughes, M. (1984) *Young Children Learning: Talking and thinking at home and at school*, London: Fontana.

Vygotsky, L.S. (1962) *Thought and Language*, Cambridge, MA: MIT Press.

Vygotsky, L.S. (1978) *Mind in Society: The development of higher psychological processes*, M. Cole, V. John-Steiner, S. Scribner and E. Souberman (eds), Cambridge, MA: Harvard University Press.

Wells, C.G. (1978) 'What makes for successful language development?' in R. Campbell and P. Smith (eds) *Recent Advances in the Psychology of Language*, 449–469, New York: Plenum.

Chapter 13

Dyslexia lessons

The politics of dyslexia and reading problems

Janet Soler

Introduction

This chapter examines how the historical construction of dyslexia as a concept and field of inquiry has influenced recent debates and the professional discourse/ practice surrounding dyslexia. It also presents an alternative perspective to the narrative of a successful progression towards a more accurate description of dyslexia, which has underpinned historical and biographical accounts of dyslexia written by researchers as professionals working within neuro- and cognitive psychology (see for example Miles and Miles 1999).

The academic field of dyslexia emerged from research at the end of the nineteenth century, which was grounded in medical approaches arising from early neurologists' investigations of the strange symptoms that were often exhibited by individuals who had survived traumatic head injuries. In many cases these injuries resulted in brain disorders leading to a loss of speech and the ability to translate words into speech; however, sometimes these brain-damaged patients might speak and understand English quite well but be unable to read. Historically, therefore, the professional and 'expert' discourses related to dyslexia can be traced from its roots in medicine and clinical studies in the 1860s to the emergence of broader psychologically, and LD/SpLD-based understandings of dyslexia and their use by educators in the 1980s. As we shall see in the following sections of this chapter, current professional discourses related to the development of dyslexia as a construct have continued to draw upon 'scientific' medical and psychological discourses, which has in turn impacted upon the ability to identify and implement specialist provision.

In recent decades, the causes of dyslexia have increasingly become seen as linguistically based rather than visual. There has also been an increasing emphasis upon the identification of the cognitive abilities related to the reading process. Dyslexia assessments and teaching programmes are therefore commonly linked to lexical problems and key related areas such as 'orientation, naming or repeating long words, arithmetic difficulties, list of items (forward or reverse), letter reversals, etc.' (Javier Guardiola 2001: 19). While theories related to visual effects have continued in the work of Thomson (1984) and Stein and Fowler (1982), more influential theories have focused upon deficits in phonological and isolated word recognition skills.

The interest in this field led to similarities being noted between these patients and uninjured school children who were considered to be of 'normal intelligence' in nearly every respect except that they experienced difficulties in language and literacy skills. This initiated attempts to find the specific brain dysfunctions responsible for dyslexia. The pursuit of this agenda led to the study of dyslexia emerging in the 1980s as a mainly psychologically based field related to reading skills and the distribution of reading ability and disability in the school population inextricably linked to the labels LD/SpLD (Learning Disabilities/Specific Learning Disabilities). Initially these labels implied that the student was viewed as having normal or above intelligence with 'deficits that are specific rather than generalised'. Given this emphasis the labels did not take into account the students' cultural or familial background (Ferri 2004: 511). 'Clinical' models based upon 'scientised forms of normative judgement' have, therefore, been persistent and pervasive in providing the explanatory and 'executive' framework for thinking about LD/SpLD aspects of literacy pedagogy (see for example Cook-Gumperz 1986).

Defining dyslexia: reconstructing professional discourse/practice

While definitions of dyslexia were originally based upon medical models, and came to embody the notion that dyslexia applies to individuals who have difficulties in reading and writing even though they are of 'normal' or 'above normal' intelligence, theorists working from within critical literacy and New Literacy Studies have drawn attention to the need to consider literacy pedagogy and literate practice in relation to socio-cultural contexts. This conceptualisation of literacy and literacy difficulties stands in stark contrast to the heritage of medically based understandings of literacy problems and the more recent development of 'clinical' and autonomous, and neutral models of dyslexia (Green and Kostogriz 2002). From a socio-cultural and New Literacies perspective it is possible to argue that the disciplinary heritage which informed the historical development of dyslexia as a concept and field of knowledge has inextricably been linked to notions of deficiency and neuropsychological deviancy. This background has made it very difficult for definitions of dyslexia to take into account the socio-cultural complexities of literacy learning, because from this viewpoint literacy learning is much broader than the 'autonomous model' (Street 1993), which emphasises the skills taking place in individual minds to decode printed text. From a socio-cultural perspective literacy learning can be viewed as embedded in culturally crafted, meaning making practices and discourses taking place within social groups. The problems and issues arising from the 'autonomous' model of literacy, which has become implicit in the 'scientific' medical and psychological professional discourse/practice surrounding dyslexia, will emerge as a key feature of the politics of literacy assessment and classification in the following sections of this chapter.

The construction and reconstruction of dyslexia over the previous three decades provides evidence of the tensions arising from increasingly complex clinical models put forward by neuroscientists and cognitive psychologists, and practitioners' and specialist assessors' need for clear descriptive and diagnostic categories. As dyslexia research moved towards systematically identifying the differences between normal and 'dyslexic' readers, the definitions were changed and adapted to accommodate environmental factors such as 'socio-cultural opportunities' as well as 'adequate intelligence'. This was evident as early as the late 1960s as shown by the definition reached by consensus at the 1968 World Federation of Neurology:

> [Dyslexia is] a disorder manifested by difficulty in learning to read despite conventional instruction, adequate intelligence and socio-cultural opportunity. It is dependent upon fundamental cognitive disabilities, which are frequently of constitutional origin.
>
> (Cited in Snowling 2000: 15)

This definition, however, fell out of use as it defined by exclusion and clinicians were unable to find objective data to 'diagnose' a person as dyslexic. For example what is 'conventional instruction' and how much 'intelligence' and 'socio-cultural opportunity' is deemed to be 'adequate'?

Snowling (2000) argues that subsequent definitions of dyslexia have rested on differentiating between 'generally backward readers' and people who have 'specific reading difficulties'. However, in 1996 Stanovich produced findings that questioned the usefulness of this distinction and it became evident that it was not possible to link discrepancies in IQ and reading attainment even if the concept of an Intelligence Quotient was accepted as a given (in Snowling 2000: 23).

With this in mind the International Dyslexia Association (IDA) offered a definition in 1994 which noted that dyslexia could be seen as only one kind of learning difficulty that often co-occurs with other disorders which needed to be treated separately for clinical and theoretical purposes:

> Dyslexia is one of several distinct learning disabilities. It is a specific language-based disorder of constitutional origin characterized by difficulties in single-word decoding, usually reflecting insufficient phonological processing. These difficulties in single-word decoding are often unexpected in relation to age and other cognitive and academic abilities; they are not the result of generalized developmental disability or sensory impairment. Dyslexia is manifest by variable difficulty with different forms of language, often including, in addition to problems in reading, a conspicuous problem with acquiring proficiency in writing and spelling.
>
> (cited in Snowling 2000: 24–25)

This definition also stressed problems with word decoding rather than reading comprehension skills, and differentiated between children who have specific reading difficulties and those who have more global language impairments. Despite these refinements, this definition of dyslexia continued to create problems for clinicians and those who wanted to positively assess and identify 'dyslexic' individuals, as it was too vague and could not be falsified (Snowling 2000: 23).

By the early to mid-1990s in the UK, Tim and Elaine Miles's work in areas related to experimental psychology and clinical experience had led to dyslexia no longer being seen as synonymous with reading difficulty. The prevailing view advocated by neuroscience-based researchers in the research journal *Dyslexia* was that it should be seen as a neurologically based syndrome with the implications that 'diagnostic assessment should include tests of reading, spelling and intelligence, but also neuropsychological evaluation' (Frith 1999: 193).

This influenced the development of Uta Frith's Three Level 'neutral' framework which was developed to demonstrate the compatibility of different theories and causal models of dyslexia and incorporate environmental aspects as well as biological, cognitive and behavioural aspects (Frith 1999: 193–4). Thus by the late 1990s it was increasingly difficult to have a simple definition and diagnostic categories for dyslexia. Dyslexia was increasingly being seen as a complex disorder which operated on a number of levels. It was seen to be linked to biological, cognitive, behavioural and environmental factors which can influence the causal pathway which influences the decoding of print. Cognitive-neuroscience based understandings of dyslexia were becoming more complex and endeavouring to account for interactions with the wider environment and cultural influences.

Once again, this created problems for clinicians and those who wanted to positively assess and identify 'dyslexic' individuals. UK-based educational psychologists saw themselves working as 'scientific practitioners' focused on 'making valid formulations in relation to descriptive and diagnostic categories'. They wanted to be able to accurately define and identify dyslexia as their work in Local Educational Authorities (LEAs) involved the identification of special educational needs (SEN) as specialist assessors (Regan and Woods 2000).

Practitioners' inability to clearly define dyslexia was a key factor leading to the convening of a Working Party by the Divisions of Educational and Child Psychology (DECP) of the British Psychological Society (BPS) to review current research and practice (BPS 1999). Commentators, however, have viewed the report produced by the Working Party as a 'professional' report primarily intended for those who were responsible for carrying out educational assessments, determining policy and allocating resources:

> It appears that this report is intended mainly for those carrying out professional assessments – educational psychologists, senior teachers in schools, Special Education Needs Co-ordinators (SENCOs), advisory teachers from local county teams and local Education Authority offices and others who will

determine the allocation of resources . . . The report then is essentially a professional one for professionals.

(Cooke 2001: 48)

In the Report, the Working Party proposed an inclusive working definition which is commonly used and forms the basis of much of LEA policy:

Dyslexia is evident when accurate and fluent word reading and/or spelling develops very incompletely or with great difficulty.

This focuses on literacy learning at the 'word level' and implies that the problem is severe and persistent despite appropriate learning opportunities. It provides the basis for a staged process of assessment through teaching.

(BPHS 1999: 64)

Soon after the release of the report, the definition cited above was critiqued by practitioners and clinicians publishing in *Dyslexia*, a journal which aims to bring 'together researchers and practitioners in the field of dyslexia' (*Dyslexia* 2009). In an article which was published as a critical review of the DECP Report, Anne Cooke from the Dyslexia Unit, School of Psychology, University of Wales, argued that the definition was not inclusive enough to allow a wide enough range of children and adults considered by teachers, educators and practitioners to have dyslexia to gain access to resources (Cooke 2001: 49). She also stated that it did not address the need for a causal explanation to help practitioners bring about changes in behaviour (Cooke 2001: 50).

Rea Reason, the Chair of the DECP Working Party on dyslexia, who was based in the School of Education at the University of Manchester, provided a critical response to Anne Cook's letter in which she acknowledged that her letter had 'worried me a great deal' because '[i]f Anne whose knowledge and experience I so respect, had misunderstood the rationale of the report then we, the authors, had not managed to make our meanings clear enough'. Reason also acknowledged that the working definition had stolen the 'limelight'. She argued that the definition was a 'neutral' starting point and stressed that it was a 'descriptive *working* definition and not an operational *definition*' because:

We could not resolve issues of how long to wait before deciding that accurate/fluent word reading and/or spelling was developing 'very incompetently' and with 'great difficulty'. This depended on the age and developmental stage of the learner and the amount of instructional effort involved.

(Reason 2001: 174)

Despite this pragmatic defence of the Report and the definition, researchers and practitioners have continued to critique the definition of dyslexia. Critics continued to argue that it is too general, all-embracing and inclusive. This results in it encompassing all forms of reading decoding and spelling difficulties, which has made it problematic for educational purposes.

In 2002, Michael Thomson, the Principal of East Court School, a specialist school for dyslexic children in Ramsgate, Kent, in a letter to the Editor of *Dyslexia* noted that the Report did not acknowledge the discrepancy model of assessment of dyslexia. He pointed out that this created difficulties for identifying and providing provision for children who have 'specific learning difficulties' rather than 'simply poor reading decoding':

> . . . Recently, those attending East Court School for reviews of children state that intelligence should not be used as a factor in deciding what level of special educational need provision a given dyslexic child might need. They quote the BPS Report in support of this argument. Obviously, if one defines dyslexia as simply poor reading decoding, then only those children whose reading levels fall in the Mass below the second centile based on their chronological age are eligible for specialist schooling provision or equivalent . . . I am afraid the reality at the chalk face is that this means that less children are being identified as having specific learning difficulties and appropriate provision is not being made. In many ways, it is like going back to the 1970s where children are identified as having general reading difficulty.
>
> (Thomson 2002: 53–54)

In the immediate years following the release of the Report further doubts about utilising the definition in the BPS (1999) report to categorise children and adults as dyslexic were raised in practitioner-orientated 'guide books' (see for example Fitzgibbon and O'Connor, 2002: 9) and research journals. Regan and Woods (2000), for example, argued that it includes too wide a range of decoding and spelling difficulties and noted that '[u]nder the proposed definition, all children with reading difficulties could be described as "dyslexic" where this is the most appropriate/"best fit" categorical description' (Regan and Woods 2000: 334).

Dyslexia discourse/practice: challenges, contestations and new discursive spaces

In recent years the 'shifting nature' of the LD/SpLD discourse/practice in the UK and its construction and reconstruction in relation to the culture within which it is embedded has intensified and is increasingly being played out in the mass media and newspapers as well as in professional contexts and publications. A number of voices, both supporting and resisting the dominant medical and deficit approaches to dyslexia and LD/SpLD, have been appearing within the mass media. This shift is particularly evident in the period surrounding the broadcasting of the programme 'The Dyslexia Myth' on Channel 4 in September 2005.

'The Dyslexia Myth' was screened at a time of increasing public concern for a working definition and access to the provision for children and adults who could be seen to have 'specific learning difficulties' rather than 'simply poor reading decoding'. The passing of the Special Educational Needs and Disability Act in May 2001 had resulted in Higher Education establishments being expected to provide appropriate support and make adjustments to include disabled students including those who could be categorised as dyslexic. In order to distribute funding and resources to 'meet the needs of students in a proactive way', and to demonstrate provision for students who have disabilities such as dyslexia, there was increased reliance in England on diagnosis and appeals to the Office of the Independent Adjudicator (OIA) which had been set up by higher education institutions in March 2004 (see for example Garner 2004; Hoare 2007). This reliance on diagnosis and more specific identification of LD/SpLD dyslexic individuals in turn raised issues related to the prioritisation of dyslexia over other literacy difficulties, and the 'over diagnosis' of dyslexia in undergraduate students (see for example, Bunting 2004).

During the same period, there had also been a study by school inspectors which highlighted 'the lottery families face in getting the support they need' (Barnard 2004: 3). These policies and reports increased the perceived need for dyslexia assessment and resulted in a number of calls supporting an increase in dyslexia assessments (Barnard 2004: 3).

With these developments in the background and related concerns over dyslexia assessment being increasingly reported in the press it was clear that this was a very controversial area, which would generate significant interest amongst a wider public audience. Professor Julian Elliott who featured in the screening of 'The Dyslexia Myth' stated in a later interview that the programme had come about because the Executive Producer had read a review he had published in a book and felt that this 'reflected his own understanding of a very muddled field'. The Producer had then spoken to other UK and North America academics in the field in order to produce the programme (Shaughnessy 2005).

Elliott also indicated that he was well aware of the 'explosive' nature of his viewpoint, as prior to the screening he had written a small piece for teachers in the *Times Educational Supplement* which had been picked up by national newspapers and a variety of television and radio programmes (Shaughnessy 2005). Elliott, however, maintained that he was not arguing that dyslexia did not exist. Rather than question its validity, he wanted to highlight the way that difficulties in the definition and understandings of dyslexia were leading to difficulties in its utilisation.

A published interview with a secondary school Special Educational Needs coordinator (SENCO) published a few months after the screening of 'The Dyslexia Myth' further clarified Elliott's position. In this interview he stated that the main issue was to achieve agreement about what is meant by the term dyslexia, rather than question whether it exists or not:

> For those who have not followed the debate, it is important to reiterate that it is not a case of whether or not dyslexia exists or not (this is not a meaningful

question) but, rather, it is essential that everyone is agreed about what we mean by this term. At present, dyslexia is used as a catch-all construct that has no significant value for guiding educators to the most appropriate forms of intervention beyond those approaches that are suitable for all struggling with literacy. However, the label often has an important function for families that transcends its relevance to everyday educational practice and you need to be alert to this.

(Elliott 2005: 9)

The screening of the documentary immediately created a strong reaction amongst fellow researchers, practitioners, dyslexia campaigners, and representatives from dyslexia initiatives and parents. A major concern for the last group was that the programme promoted Elliott's views which they saw as misleading, undermining literacy interventions and threatening the availability of resources for dyslexics (Hewlett 2005). The programme was seen to have 'angered many dyslexic people and dyslexia organisations' who saw the argument as damaging and unhelpful while the British Dyslexia Association (BDA) stated it had been inundated with calls from people worried about trying to overcome their dyslexia. Some researchers defended the 'scientific basis' for dyslexia (Kirkham 2005). Jack Rack who was head of research at the Dyslexia Institute at York had stated that 'we know which of the chromosomes are involved and some of the genes that are involved as well as some of the brain differences you observe when looking at a dyslexic child'. Other researchers supported Elliott's contention that there needed to be agreement and clarification of the term dyslexia. Michael Rice, a dyslexia and literacy expert from the Institute at Cambridge University, was quoted as stating 'People feel a sense of justification when they are diagnosed, and it becomes almost defining of who they are. It gets them off the hook of great embarrassment and feelings of personal inadequacy' (Kirkham 2005).

The contestations, struggles and the embedded power relationships related to the debate over the definition of dyslexia following the screening of 'The Dyslexia Myth' were also evident in a range of educational events and publications. They were also heightened by the coverage of key participants and commentary about the debate which was characterised as a battle in the media. Warwick Mansell reporting in the *Times Educational Supplement* on the provocatively titled 'Death of Dyslexia?' Conference, held in October 2005, after the screening of 'The Dyslexia Myth', reported that there were two rival camps in the debate. The conference was 'expected to be one of the most contentious educational events for years' as it had 'ramifications for the lives of millions'. He noted that at the conference Maggie Snowling of York University, who had also featured in the documentary, 'has been at odds with Professor Elliott' (Mansell 2005).

An outline of Margaret Snowling's paper given at the conference was posted on the BDA website on 27 September 2005. In it she stated that she wanted to make her position on the debate clear. She noted that 'it is not in doubt that the term is over used' but added that there is 'strong scientific evidence concerning the nature, causes and consequences of dyslexia' and that '[d]yslexia is a brain-based disorder with consequences that persist from the pre-school years through to adulthood'. She also stated that diagnosis of dyslexia was 'continuously distributed in the population' and directly related to social, cultural and institutional contexts:

> Modern conceptions of developmental disorder view such difficulties as dimensional rather than categorical. It is no longer relevant to ask 'who is dyslexic and who is not'. Rather, the skills underlying the acquisition of reading are continuously distributed in the population, such that some people find learning to read and write a trivial matter whereas others, notably children with dyslexia, have extreme difficulty. Whether or not a child is diagnosed 'dyslexic' depends on their age and stage of development, the context and language in which they are learning and the criteria adopted by the educational system in which they are schooled.
>
> (Snowling 2005)

She noted that dyslexia was clearly related to phonological processing and that phonological abilities were not dependent on IQ although there were genetic links. She explained that the problem was 'easier to detect in those of higher ability who do not show other learning problems'. She also supported the identification of dyslexia by educated professionals and argued that its potentially negative effects can be ameliorated (Snowling 2005).

During this period the *Psychologist*, the official monthly publication of the British Psychological Society, also published comments by Rod Nicolson, professor of Psychology at the University of Sheffield on the Channel 4 programme and the subsequent media coverage, and a reply by Julian Elliott. In his article in the November edition, Rod Nicolson acknowledged the 'ongoing outpouring of emotion and criticism in the media and websites'. He stated that he was clearly presenting 'a more considered view' on behalf of qualified psychologists.

In the first section of his article, Nicolson presented arguments against Elliott's contention that 'the term dyslexia is not helpful because dyslexic children have such wide-ranging difficulties'. He acknowledged that Elliott did have some valid points in relation to this issue. He agreed with Elliott that dyslexic children show phonological difficulties and noted that they were a major cause of their difficulties in learning to read. He also noted the resourcing issues associated with dyslexia and the need for early interventions:

> Dyslexia is one of the most common special needs, with a prevalence of at least 5 percent. Dyslexia support is indeed a major drain on the resources of the education system, and a major financial and emotional drain on the resources of the families involved. Early problems learning to read do frequently lead to a vicious circle of disaffection and reading avoidance.

Interventions at the age of six are much more effective than interventions at age eight, than at age ten and so on; and a systematic, well-planned intervention with trained staff and whole school implementation is going to be more effective than ad hoc interventions.

(Nicolson 2005: 658)

Nicolson agreed that there were difficulties in diagnosing dyslexia and that there was 'no complete consensus' about how this was to be done. He also acknowledged the way in which dyslexia was linked to business opportunities and embedded in a wider culture of entrepreneurship:

Finally, it is true that dyslexia is big business, with major financial opportunities for anyone inventing a more effective intervention. There are various 'lobbies' whose existence and lobbying distorts the 'normal science' investigations. These are usually beneficial but can also be counter-productive, by stimulating research in artificially small domains without encouraging consideration of the broader picture. The lobbies almost always distort research by introducing a political and an adversarial dimension.

(Nicolson 2005: 658)

As dyslexia clearly had a genetic basis, Nicolson argued, it could not be a 'myth'. He did not feel that there were inequities arising from identifying and diagnosing dyslexic children in the UK since 1994 as the Special Educational Needs (SEN) Code of Practice passed in 1994 ensured that there was equal support for all SEN children in the UK. Dyslexic children were, therefore, not advantaged over other poor readers. He also disagreed with the assumption that dyslexia was a meaningless term because children with low IQ can be helped with reading just as much as children with high IQ. He also disagreed with the assumption that there could be multiple causes of dyslexia, because it was not clear what the underlying cause of the phonological deficits was (Nicolson 2005: 629).

Elliott, in his reply in the December edition of the *Psychologist*, responded to Nicolson's article by emphasising at the beginning that he was not arguing that dyslexia was a myth (Elliott 2005: 728). In another interview he indicated that his argument had been misinterpreted by the media and incorrectly headlined as 'Academic claims that dyslexia doesn't exist' because:

. . . the arguments were too subtle for media purposes so that 'in talking with journalists, it proved hard to explain the difficulties of dealing with social constructs such as this and persuade them that the Manichaean world they wished to present was an oversimplification.

(Shaughnessy 2005)

Elliott pointed out once again that he was not questioning the existence of dyslexia, nor was he questioning the view that dyslexia was a brain-based disorder. The issues to which he was drawing attention had strong resonances with the issues surrounding the problems associated with defining, diagnosis and intervention which had earlier been raised by practitioners in *Dyslexia*. He also referred to the breadth of the BPS Report (1999) and the definition contained in the Report to support his use of the term 'myth'. From his point of view 'the common understanding of dyslexia is a myth which hides the scale and scandal of true reading disability'. Like the earlier critiques he asked how the position taken in the BPS definition could 'be reconciled with the many very different definitions (and symptoms) employed by others, and what relevance . . . these have for clinical/educational intervention' (Elliott 2005: 728).

The important point, which he felt that Nicolson had accepted, was that 'diagnosing dyslexia is not the objective process that many are led to believe, neither does it point to appropriate forms of treatment'. He also stated that the programme did stress the heritability features of dyslexia, but that they were 'questioning whether children with dyslexia (as traditionally defined) respond differently to intervention from those with generalised learning problems'. In 'The Dyslexia Myth' programme, they had rejected this claim because of the 'absence of clear evidence that there exists a particular teaching approach that is more suitable for a dyslexic subgroup than for other poor readers' (Elliott 2005: 728).

He also questioned that assumption that the existence of the Code of Practice necessarily leads to a reduction in the inequities resulting from a dyslexia diagnosis:

> While his [Nicolson's] point about the Code of Practice is true up to a point, I am puzzled that Nicolson doesn't recognise the more subtle ways that a dyslexic diagnosis can influence both teachers and gatekeepers to resources. Teachers are increasingly wary of litigation and may seek to project themselves against legal challenge. It would be naïve to underestimate the power of the label to access additional resources, a point recently noted by school SEN coordinators (SENCO-Forum, 2005).
>
> (Elliott 2005: 729)

The final paragraphs in Elliott's article once again highlighted the power relationships and the engagement with different identities and practices engaged in during the debate. He argued that Nicolson was making a 'simplistic distinction' between educational and 'academic' psychologists, and that this was 'neither helpful or meaningful' as educational psychologists might ascertain the 'causes of a problem (even if this were possible)' but it is 'not very helpful for guiding intervention' (Elliott 2005: 729).

Elliott concluded by reiterating his main argument that given the current state of knowledge about brain function and genetic studies, the diagnosis and definition of dyslexia did not necessarily have any 'practical value' for addressing reading problems and also raised resourcing problems:

Hopefully, such work will ultimately provide valuable guidance in developing increasingly effective interventions. At the current time, however, splitting poor readers into two groups – dyslexic sheep and ordinary poor-reading goats – has little practical value for dealing with literacy problems. Rather than pouring resources into dyslexic assessments, we would at the current time, be wiser to target all poor readers at an early age for intervention.

(Elliott 2005: 729)

Conclusion

The professional practice/discourses, which emerged in the debates outlined above, reveal the complexity and fluidity of positions and relationships between researchers, clinicians and practitioners. This raises questions in relation to how some discourses related to dyslexia and learning disabilities (LD/SpLD) come to maintain their authority so that some 'voices' get heard and others are silenced. In relation to power/empowerment/disempowerment, it also raises the questions: where do tensions arise, whose perspective is adopted, and with what consequences?

The issues and tensions and power relationships in the professional discourse/ practice debates over the definition of dyslexia have been rooted in dynamic interactions between medically, psychologically and neuroscience research-based discourses surrounding dyslexia. The historical evolution of the debates over definitions and the pubic examination of the 'Myth of Dyslexia' programme demonstrate the dynamic way in which discourses over LD/SpLD respond to the shifting nature of the wider culture in which it is embedded. They are linked to the wider culture through, for example: legislation, lobby groups, business interests, and parental and public views and concerns. The construction and reconstruction of the definition of dyslexia has been driven by the need to take account of these in educational, institutional and professional practices.

This chapter illustrates how the professional discourse and practice which surround concepts such as dyslexia undergo change through resistance, challenges and contestation and are inextricably linked to the ongoing formation of identities and practices. For instance the provision of an inclusive and all-embracing solution to defining dyslexia appears to have been designed to resolve conflicts and struggles over the need to include socio-cultural issues for practitioners. However this pragmatic solution in turn created further tensions, invited challenges and attracted resistance. The recent engagement of the mass media in the debates and dilemmas related to the professional discourse/practice surrounding dyslexia, has also served to highlight the tensions and further complicated the relationships between researchers and practitioners, through the insertion of the voices of public lobby groups, the general public and media representatives.

The definition of dyslexia, and the assessment and classification of literacy difficulties are discursive spaces for ongoing resistance, challenges and contestation, because they are key aspects in the construction of social and personal identities associated with dyslexia and LD/SpLD. As indicated in the 'voices' of the researchers, practitioners and lobbyists cited above, they are central to the professional/discourse surrounding dyslexia, because of their inextricable links to professional identity, power relationships and the access to resources.

References

Barnard, N. (2004, October 15) 'Losers in Wait-and-Fail Lottery', *The Times Educational Supplement*: 3.

British Psychological Society (BPS) (1999) *Dyslexia, Literacy and Psychological Assessment*. Leicester: British Psychological Society.

Bunting, C. (2004, July 23) 'Worrying case of can't write, won't write?' *Times Higher Education*, available at: http://www.timeshighereducation.co.uk/story.asp?storyCode= 190254&sectioncode=26 (accessed 26 October 2009).

Cook-Gumperz, J. (1986) 'Literacy and schooling: An unchanging equation?', in J. Cook-Gumperz (ed.) *The Social Construction of Literacy*, 16–44. Cambridge: Cambridge University Press.

Cooke, A. (2001) 'Critical response to "Dyslexia, Literacy and Psychological Assessment (Report by a Working Party of the Division of Educational and Child Psychology of the British Psychological Society)": A view from the chalk face', *Dyslexia*, 7, 1: 47–52.

Elliott, J. (2005, November 4) 'What diagnosis?', *The Times Educational Supplement*: 9.

Elliott, J. (2005) 'The dyslexia debate continues', *The Psychologist*, 18, 12: 728–729.

Ferri, B. A. (2004) 'Interrupting the discourse: A response to Reid and Valle', *Journal of Learning Disabilities*, 37, 6: 509–515.

Fitzgibbon, G. & O'Connor, B. (2002) *Adult Dyslexia: A guide for the workplace*, Oxford: Blackwell.

Frith, U. (1999) 'Paradoxes in the definition of dyslexia', *Dyslexia*, 5, 4: 192–214.

Garner, M. (2004, September 10) 'Universities exaggerate dyslexia epidemic for own gain, expert claims', *Times Higher Education*, available at: http://www.times highereducation.co.uk/story.asp?storyCode=191053&sectioncode=26 (accessed 26 October 2009).

Green, B. & Kostogriz, A. (2002) 'Learning difficulties and the New Literacy Studies: A socially critical perspective', in J. Soler, J. Wearmouth & G. Reid (eds) *Contextualising Difficulties in Literacy Development: Exploring politics, culture, ethnicity and ethics*, 102–114, London: Sage.

Guardiola, J. G. (2001) 'The evolution of research on dyslexia', *Annuario de Psicologia*, 32, 1: 3–30. English version available at: http://ibgwww.colorado.edu/ ~gayan/ch1.pdf (accessed 26 October 2009).

Hewlett, K. (2005, September 16) 'Why I believe that dyslexia is not a myth', *The Times Higher Education Supplement*, Opinion: 16.

Hoare, S. (2007, February 20) 'Education: Turning Points: What to do when things go wrong: the resolution of student complaints used to be a hit-and-miss process. It's now a lot easier, thanks to a new judicial review', *The Guardian*: 4.

Kirkham, S. (2005, September 3) 'Anger as experts claim dyslexia is a myth', *The Guardian*: 7.

Mansell, W. (2005, October 28) 'Fact and fiction about dyslexia', *The Times Educational Supplement*, News: 17.

Miles, T. R. & Miles, E. (1999) *Dyslexia a Hundred Years On* (2nd Edition). Buckingham: Open University Press.

Nicolson, R. (2005). 'Dyslexia: Beyond the myth', *Psychologist*, 18, 11: 658–659.

Reason, R. (2001) Letter to the Editor, *Dyslexia*, 7, 3: 174.

Regan, T. & Woods, K. (2000) 'Teachers' understandings of dyslexia: Implications for educational psychology practice', *Educational Psychology in Practice*, 16, 3: 333–347.

Shaughnessy, M. (2005, September 12) 'An interview with Julian Elliott: About "dyslexia" ', *EdNews*, available at: http://ednews.org/articles/professor-doubts-scientific-validity-of-dyslexia-.html (accessed 26 October 2009).

Snowling, M. J. (2000) *Dyslexia*. Oxford: Blackwell.

Snowling, M. (2005, September 27) 'The British Dyslexia Association: Dyslexia is not a myth', available at: http://www.bdadyslexia.org.uk/news17.html (accessed 15 April 2009).

Stein, J. & Fowler, S. (1982) 'Diagnosis of dyslexia by means of a new indicator of eye dominance', *British Journal of Opthalmology*, 66, 5: 69–73.

Street, B. D. (1993) *Cross-Cultural Approaches to Literacy*, Cambridge: Cambridge University Press.

Thomson, M. (2002) Letter to the Editor, *Dyslexia*, 8, 1: 53–54.

Thomson, M. E. (1984) *Developmental Dyslexia*, Baltimore, MD: Edward Arnold. Also available at the University of Sheffield website: http://www.shef.ac.uk/disability/extrain/2_legislation.html (accessed 27 November 2008).

Chapter 14

The use of evidence in language and literacy teaching

Sue Ellis

Literacy education deserves evidence-based decisions. Low literacy costs the British economy between £1.73bn and £2.05bn per year (KPMG 2006) and the social and emotional costs are equally high. Yet we know that children who struggle with literacy can make fast progress when the instructional content and pedagogy closely match their needs. This chapter describes some of the paradigms and problems associated with the use of evidence in language and literacy education, with examples from specific interventions and programmes. It raises issues about how literacy teachers are professionalized to attend to evidence, both the evidence in front of them and the research evidence 'out there'. It argues that to support teachers in using evidence effectively, we need to frame the research evidence about effective content, pedagogy and learning in ways that recognize the power and limitations of different evidence paradigms. To ensure that all children make fast progress, we need to appreciate how teachers develop broad and diagnostic understandings of literacy and literacy learning and of how policy and curriculum frameworks impact on the classroom decisions they make.

The problem of evidence-based education

For one group of researchers, solving the problem of evidence-based literacy education is straightforward: 'Use what works. . . . Focus on research-proven programmes and practices' (Slavin 2008). The suggestion is that the 'evidence' issue in education boils down to two problems: first, the paucity of properly evaluated programmes and second, the problem of ensuring that teachers, school managers and policy-makers know how to select for implementation only those programmes that have demonstrated a high impact (Torgerson & Torgerson 2001; Chalmers 2003; Slavin 2008; Tymms *et al.* 2008; Chambers 2008). This view of evidence-based literacy education gained impetus in the USA from that government's *Strategic Plan for Education 2002–2007* in which education research was criticized for lacking rigour and lacking the cumulative studies that generate knowledge about procedures that can be transferred across different classroom contexts, schools and education systems:

> . . . unlike medicine, agriculture and industrial production, the field of education operates largely on the basis of ideology and professional consensus. As such, it is subject to fads and is incapable of the cumulative progress that follows from the application of the scientific method. . . .
>
> (US Department of Education 2002: 59)

The solution proposed in the *US Strategic Plan* was to set out a model for education research and evaluations that would ensure the quality of evidence. Although the initial proposal was for a complex and not necessarily hierarchical model, government grants were made available only to states, districts and schools that used 'proven methods' of reading instruction and the federal *No Child Left Behind Act* mandated that districts use 'scientifically proven' instructional methods. In practice, the various research designs rapidly became ranked with Randomized Controlled Trials (RCT) at the top, followed by controlled cohort studies, case study series, individual case studies and, at the bottom, professional observation (Eisenhart and Towne 2003).

The Randomized Controlled Trial (RCT) was ranked highest because it is replicable. A well-designed RCT identifies one variable for investigation (for example, the educational programme being implemented) and controls for others that may influence the outcome. It requires random allocation of pupils, strict compliance measures, blind assessment so that assessors do not know which children are in which group and it determines the levels for a significant response independently at the start of the trial. In education, meeting the conditions for a full RCT is problematic – children cannot be randomly allocated to schools and classes, or randomly allocated to follow different programmes within a class – and many education researchers use cluster randomization at the level of class or school rather than the individual pupil (e.g. Tymms *et al.* 2008).

Problem 1: compliance

The rhetoric of the scientific RCT approach is seductive, particularly its focus on sorting out the literacy programmes that are effective from those that are not. It offers a vision of certainty in which teachers and policy-makers can get clear-cut advice about what to do, based on hard-nosed evidence that it will work. In practice, however, successful RCTs tend to lose their impact when rolled out to wider groups of schools (Datnow *et al.* 2002). One reason for this is that when researchers conduct evaluation studies, the intervention or programme has a high profile and research procedures ensure that compliance measures are met. On roll-out, the programme has a lower profile, it must compete with other programmes for curriculum space and teacher attention and it is more likely to be adapted or implemented in ways that compromise its design.

Two Scottish studies of children with severe and persistent language difficulties illustrate these problems (Boyle *et al.* 2007; McCartney, Ellis & Boyle 2009). Like many other countries, Scotland's policy of social inclusion is premised on a socio-cultural model of learning support. Mainstream schools are seen to offer rich learning environments for social and language development and children with severe and persistent language difficulties are encouraged to attend them. Speech and language therapists (SLTs) advise education staff about how to address the needs of individual pupils but the schools have the legal responsibility for ensuring that pupils' educational needs are met.

The first study, a full RCT on 161 language-impaired children in mainstream schools, showed that both individual and group language intervention could make a significant difference to these children's expressive language. The intervention activities were delivered directly by SLTs or by assistants (SLTAs) who were given a small amount of training and specific language targets by the SLT and activities and advice from a manual developed for the project. Additional support in the form of meetings, phone calls and written communications was also available. Standardized tests (CELF–3 UK, Semel et al. 2000) before and immediately after the intervention showed that all intervention groups made significantly more progress than a control group given 'usual therapy' (Boyle et al. 2007). It did not matter whether the intervention activities were delivered in a group or individually or by the SLT or the SLTA.

These results seemed to indicate that a positive intervention was possible and the training and the manual developed for this project could help teachers and classroom assistants work with SLTs to support language impaired children in school. It would help the schools meet their legal responsibilities and deliver an intervention of proven impact. Delivery by school staff offered further potential benefits because teachers and classroom assistants have wide opportunities to harness more general classroom activities to meet the children's needs.

A cohort study of 38 children in 19 schools was devised (McCartney, Ellis and Boyle 2009). The children for this study met the same inclusion criteria as for the RCT and it used the same consultancy and training model. The SLT provided specific language targets for each child and helped school staff (class teachers, learning support teachers and classroom assistants) to identify suitable activities and advice from the manual. The teachers and head teachers agreed to implement the activities on the same schedule as the RCT and to log each contact session. The children were pre-tested and then tested immediately after the intervention using the same standardized test as the RCT.

However, analysis of the test scores for this cohort intervention showed no significant impact on the children's expressive or receptive language. Analysis of the teachers' logs detailing the sessions children had been given indicated that, whereas the RCT provided 45 contact sessions over 15 weeks (an average of three contacts per week), the cohort study averaged only one or two contacts per week. Teachers generally planned for the agreed three activities a week, but not all were delivered. The logs identified a range of issues that prevented the activities from occurring, including difficulties in planning, in managing time and in accessing and managing the support staff allocated to work with the children.

This cohort study yielded important information about the operational issues that teachers face in schools, information that did not emerge from the RCT. It showed that the involvement of class teachers did not compensate for the lack of dedicated sessions. Also that the common-sense principle whereby school staff assumed that part-delivery of the intervention had some worth (on the basis that 'half a cake is better than no cake') was not well-founded; one or two sessions a week had no significant impact on the children's language, and unless schools could ensure three sessions per week the programme was probably not good use of time.

In terms of evidence-based practice, the RCT showed that, with the right support, children with severe and persistent language difficulties can make progress. However, the cohort study showed that evidence about how a programme actually operates in the real world is vital. The data highlights the need for a model of intervention that is more complex than simply specifying the content and operational parameters of a programme. An effective intervention model must address several levels of policy implementation within the school, employing planning and record keeping systems that incorporate a range of prompts and checks to ensure that school managers and classroom practitioners prioritize and deliver the intervention activities.

However, designing for compliance in this way risks producing a 'top-heavy' system in which the internal focus is on monitoring to ensure delivery and the external focus is on a package of activities. It is an empirical question whether working in this way would enhance teachers' understanding or their ability to recognize and use evidence diagnostically to better match core teaching content to children's needs. Moreover, the approach assumes that intervention programmes operate as 'sealed units' in which the context of implementation has no impact and it could position school staff as peripheral, complicating factors to be controlled or circumvented whenever possible.

Problem 2: the context of implementation

Intervention programmes do not operate as sealed units and the context of implementation affects their impact even when delivery and compliance are closely monitored. The evidence from the evaluation of Reading Recovery in Northern Ireland shows this (Munn and Ellis 2005).

Reading Recovery was devised in New Zealand by Marie Clay in the 1970s as an intervention to impact on the lowest attaining pupils. Its research base is rooted not in RCT evidence, but in a substantial series of case studies into the mechanisms of learning to read. It is not a programme per se, but a tight framework for teaching in which specially trained teachers withdraw children for individual tuition. They use generic activities and highly structured observation and analysis techniques to provide instruction that is carefully tailored to the individual needs of each child and they coach struggling readers to use knowledge flexibly and develop reading behaviours that are self-sustaining and self-expanding (Clay 1991). Clay always claimed that Reading Recovery works regardless of its context of implementation and most studies have focused on it as a stand-alone intervention (see for example, Brooks 2002; Gardner *et al*. 1998; Shanahan and Barr 1995).

The operational parameters of Reading Recovery are designed to ensure high compliance and fidelity and to withstand the pressure to adapt exerted by the school contexts. Thus, Reading Recovery teachers are supported and monitored by Reading Recovery tutors who are in turn supported by trainers from the Reading Recovery National Network. These trainers are not employees of the school district and are accountable only to the International Reading Recovery Network. They operate a highly effective 're-direction system' to ensure that Reading Recovery is delivered as specified and resists adaptation and colonization by the various 'host' systems in which it operates.

Our evaluation study in Northern Ireland showed that even these strict compliance measures could not completely mitigate the effect of school context on the efficacy of Reading Recovery interventions (Munn & Ellis 2005). A wide range of schools had taken on Reading Recovery and, although some had actively sought involvement, many were involved because they had a long 'tail' of underachievement or were linked to a secondary school with such a 'tail'. These schools wanted to address underachievement but not necessarily to change their core literacy curriculum. Reading Recovery was therefore operating in a wide range of literacy contexts, some of which were highly attuned to the intervention's approach, some were indifferent to it and some were rather hostile. The evaluation study collected quantitative data from 114 Reading Recovery teachers on the nature and scope of their involvement with classroom teachers and on literacy practices in their school as well as data on 1,552 children who had been through the system. This data included discontinuation status, entry and exit book levels, the number of lessons each child had received and the number of weeks spent in Reading Recovery.

Although Reading Recovery was effective in all contexts, it worked more quickly (on average requiring ten fewer lessons) when classroom literacy teaching practices dovetailed closely with Reading Recovery methods. This made Reading Recovery more cost-effective and efficient in some contexts than others (Munn & Ellis 2001; 2005).

Problem 3: 'horses for courses'

There are further problems associated with prioritizing RCT knowledge about 'what works'. RCTs are excellent for building and interrogating theoretical knowledge and they provide robust evidence of a programme's impact once the variables associated with specific contexts or populations are ironed out. However, evidence of impact on a general population, whilst interesting, may be less useful to practitioners than knowing its impact on a particular type of pupil cohort. Schools are not perfectly located with randomized catchment areas but tend to represent skewed populations and highly localized implementation contexts. Evidence about the impact on particular pupil cohorts is crucial to understanding whether a programme will be effective in a specific school context.

Gathering this information requires a different type of trial, a controlled cohort study (Sackett *et al.* 2000). Here, the characteristics of the participants or context are clearly defined so that progress can be compared, either to cohorts and contexts with different characteristics, or to similar cohorts following different interventions or programmes. Robust cohort studies identify, document and measure any characteristics of the cohort or the context of implementation that could affect the outcome. Despite their ability to take account of different cohorts and contexts, cohort studies are considered less reliable than RCTs in the US ranking because unacknowledged factors associated with the non-randomized sample might generate misleading information.

However, a large body of evidence indicates with remarkable consistency that socio-economic status, gender and race are all closely related to how quickly and easily children learn to read and write. We know from ethnographic (e.g. Gregory 2008; Lareau 2003; Moss 2007) and survey (e.g. D'Angiulli *et al.* 2004; McCoach *et al.* 2006; Topping *et al.* 2003) research that children begin school with different amounts of literacy experience, and different knowledge and skills and that they respond differently to the literacy education that schools offer. For example, children living in less-advantaged socio-economic circumstances are likely to begin school with a poorer phonological awareness and alphabetic knowledge, to have had less experience of books and digital technologies, to have poorer access to books, different understandings about the purposes and uses of literacy, a more limited knowledge of the world, poorer oral language and vocabulary skills, and a less secure grasp of narrative, and are more likely to have mothers and care-givers who are less well educated and poorly positioned to support them in learning to read and write (Zill and Resnick 2006). Also, Stanovich's work on 'Matthew effects' shows that a poor start to the most 'visible' aspect of reading – decoding words – can have lasting and compounding effects throughout a child's school career (Stanovich 1986). This would suggest the value of research paradigms that acknowledge different understandings and experiences.

The implications of children's different skill levels for the literacy curriculum are the starting-point for the work of Carol Connor and her colleagues (Connor *et al.* 2004; Connor *et al.* 2005). In a series of cohort studies, they investigated the optimum balance between phonics and reading-for-meaning activities, and also between child-directed and teacher-directed learning opportunities. The optimum 'literacy learning mix' depended on children's pre-existing letter–word reading and vocabulary skills. Those starting school with above-average vocabulary scores made greatest gains when they spent more time engaged in meaning-focused and self-directed activities such as independent reading; children starting school with below-average vocabulary scores made greater gains when given teacher-directed phonics activities at the start and increased self-directed, reading-for-meaning, activities as the year progressed. However, the picture is complex: children requiring less phonics instruction in Grade 1, benefited from more teacher-directed phonics work in Grade 2 (Connor *et al.* 2007a). To take the guesswork out of teaching phonics, the team developed algorithms that calculate the optimum amount of time that children with different literacy and language skill profiles should spend on each kind of instruction and learning activity to maximize progress.

This is an important shift in the view of evidence-based teaching. Rather than producing evidence about the 'best programme' regardless of the pupil cohort, Connor offers teachers access to complex data to help them plan the most effective ways to implement their existing reading and phonics curriculum. It is a different vision of the teacher's role in driving literacy education. It does not focus on compliance to a programme designed, trialled and chosen by others, but uses technological advances in information handling to harness research evidence as part of the teacher's planning process. This positions teachers' everyday use of evidence in a positive and symbiotic relationship to the evidence produced by researchers and creates the possibility of pulling the 'evidence in the classroom' and the 'research evidence out there' into greater alignment. This work illustrates the power of a series of cohort studies to map the terrain and develop a complex model in which teachers and teaching are seen as part of the solution rather than a complicating factor in the problem.

How teachers are positioned in relation to evidence-based teaching matters. RCT programme evaluations inevitably tend to see any contextual analysis, including teachers' professional judgement, as a threat to compliance procedures. They offer little incentive to take a diagnostic view of learning and no clear mechanisms for adapting programmes in the light of such evidence. Although some researchers express irritation with school cultures which, they feel, privilege professional judgement and encourage teachers to cling to ineffective practices, teachers are equally irritated by initiatives that, they feel, neither expect nor allow them to respond to the children in front of them but promote rigid curriculum frameworks and narrow models of teaching or literacy.

The evidence promoting programme adaptation

Yet there are strong imperatives for teachers to attend to the ecology of the whole curriculum rather than implementing discrete programmes. The language and literacy curriculum has to meet wide (and frequently changing) sets of goals. For example, children must learn to read, but they may also need to learn to work together or to use their reading skills in specifically creative, critical or entrepreneurial ways. A series of atomistic programmes is rarely an effective way to deliver diverse policy outcomes, and programmes are often adapted to take account of these wider goals.

The evidence on pupil engagement also highlights the importance of adapting programmes to link curricular areas and to contextualize and present activities in ways that pupils find relevant and interesting. Reading engagement matters because high engagement mitigates the worst effects of socio-economic status on reading attainment (Topping *et al.* 2003). Teachers, who can do nothing to change the socio-economic factors that impinge on children's lives, can limit its impact on literacy attainment by actively promoting reading engagement. Moreover, avid readers develop richer vocabularies, better verbal reasoning skills, and wider general knowledge, which drives up attainment across the curriculum (Cunningham & Stanovich 1998).

In a meta-analysis of the research evidence on reading engagement, Guthrie and Humenick (2004) show that, to produce engaged readers, the literacy curriculum must promote *curricular coherence* (so that pupils see the links between subjects and tasks), *strategy teaching* (so that pupils know how to apply the skills and knowledge gained in one task on others), *intrinsic purposes* (so that tasks are meaningful and have outcomes that the pupils believe are worthwhile), *choice* (so that pupils can influence the learning tasks, their timing, their sequence, their outcomes and materials) and *collaboration* (so that pupils' learning is social, which aids their persistence and perseverance with challenging tasks). These elements are not about individual programmes, but are about how teachers create coherent links between programmes, how they link literacy teaching to other areas of the curriculum, and how they contextualize literacy tasks to make them interesting and intrinsically motivating for pupils. This evidence implies that the impact of a programme is not solely affected by its content and design but by how it is adapted to complement other programmes and to dovetail with the core concerns and interests of the pupils. It sits in almost direct opposition to the compliance-measures required by RCTs. The challenge is to employ programmes in ways that respect the ecology of the curriculum, the policy goals of the school, the evidence from research and the learning needs of the pupils.

Understanding how teachers use evidence

Perhaps the key issue is to develop a better understanding of how teachers use the evidence of research and of pupil performance in this complex process, and of the ways that staff development, school systems and curriculum frameworks can prompt better use of this evidence.

Although modern schools have more data about pupil performance than ever before, it does not always make a positive difference to what teachers actually do. Some research indicates that this is due to factors such as lack of time or difficulties in accessing the information in a usable form (Wayman & Stringfield 2006). A number of studies indicate that teachers make fairly accurate judgements about language and literacy attainment (e.g. Williams 2006) but less accurate diagnostic judgements (Cabell *et al.* 2009). The accuracy may depend on the specific aspect of language and literacy that is being considered. Nation and Angell (2006) indicate that teachers overlook reading comprehension difficulties, especially when the pupil has strong decoding skills, but that they do notice decoding difficulties. Screening procedures that could help teachers identify pupils with problems often lack the sensitivity to accurately identify pupils with problems when used alone and, although using two screening tests can increase their sensitivity, their specificity (i.e. their accuracy in *not* identifying those who do not have problems) and their predictive power are too poor to form a reliable basis for intervention (Fletcher *et al.* 2001).

The few studies that have been done on effective evidence-use by teachers highlight the need for schools and local authorities to have a deliberate agenda for getting teachers to think about the formal data that schools keep on pupils and to agree common understandings of how it can be used in relation to their professional judgement and diagnostic analyses (Symonds 2003; Wayman 2005; Zhao & Frank 2003). They suggest that teachers are enthusiastic about evidence when it provides useful information for their classroom practice and that establishing a rationale for the use of particular types of evidence, modelling such use, and structuring time for teachers to learn about how to use it can be a helpful way forward. Any debate will be complicated by the cross-disciplinary nature of literacy learning research. Psychology, linguistics, sociology, literature and philosophy all directly and indirectly inform classroom pedagogy. Each values different types of evidence and promotes different discourses around that evidence.

We also know that teachers differ in their ability to plan and organize their work; in an RCT of their phonics algorithm software, Connor *et al.* found that some teachers struggled to manage the group planning and organization elements recommended by the software. Teachers also differed in how frequently they accessed the data to plan their lesson content and delivery. Those who were most diligent and organized in using the software had classes with greater reading gains (Connor *et al.* 2007b).

Pedagogical expertise apart, ethnographic studies indicate that teachers have different views about what learning to be literate involves, what constitutes high-quality evidence and what is appropriate use of that evidence. Some teachers focus on evidence of the child's understanding and skills but others focus on what it tells them about the learning processes, pupil engagement, the suitability of course content or the impact of their teaching. These differences are found to exist in the classroom and at every level of policy implementation in the education system (Coburn & Talbert 2006).

Coburn (2001; 2003) and Stein and Coburn (2008) show that some staff development approaches prompt more effective use of evidence about pupil learning than others. The most powerful specify 'big ideas' about teaching content and provide brief tutorials where necessary, but importantly clarify the purpose of the learning activities. Less effective strategies focus on instructional routes through programme material and tend to generate discussions about pupil throughput or the programme's management and organization. Effective strategies produced conversations that focused on teaching and learning and prompted teachers to discuss teaching in the context of specific pupils, their responses to lessons, their understanding and attitudes and the evidence of their learning. This led to new understandings of the teaching content, new insights into the evidence of pupils' learning and a better grasp of the teaching issues (Stein & Coburn 2008).

National policies and evidence-based education

Given this evidence and the evidence of diverse pupil populations, the wisdom of making blanket recommendations about the 'best' teaching programmes and pedagogies is questionable. Yet in countries with centralized literacy curricula, this is exactly how literacy policy often operates. A further complication comes because evidence is often understood and used differently by politicians, policy-makers and practitioners. For example, the discussion of phonics teaching in England, Australia and the US recently focused on a rather polarized debate about the relative efficacy of synthetic or analytic phonics teaching. Two meta-analyses of the research yielded no clear advantage for either approach, simply that systematic phonics programmes were all more effective than non-systematic ones (NICHD 2000; Torgerson *et al.* 2006) and the data is complex and needs careful interpretation (Wyse & Goswami 2008). Despite this, a policy review in England cited successful initiatives in, amongst other places, Clackmannanshire, Scotland to recommend that all schools adopt discrete, systematic synthetic phonics programmes (DfES 2006). The Clackmannan evidence is, at best, contradictory; whilst psychology tests showed an average three-and-a-half-year gain in decoding words, national reading test attainment was disappointingly average in the two largest and most advantaged schools (which accounted for over half the pupils involved in the study) and there was marked variation amongst the other schools involved, with some doing exceptionally well but others rather poorly (Ellis 2007).

Moss and Huxford observe, 'Phonics in the policy context is not the same as phonics in the research context or phonics as a focus for a political campaign' (2007: 74). In England, phonics was a lever for opposition politicians, pressure groups such as the *Reading Reform Foundation*, some phonics researchers and sections of the media to challenge the government's *National Literacy Strategy*. The government was vulnerable because attainment in early literacy had levelled out. The teaching-and-learning solution to this might require detailed and complex conversations about the characteristics and trajectories of particular pupil cohorts, the intricate nature of the early reading curriculum and how phonological development interacts with comprehension, phonics and wider issues of reading engagement. However, the political and policy imperatives required the exact opposite: a quick and clear position statement and an unambiguous plan of action to prevent further political fallout. Thus, new curriculum advice was issued for schools and the Prime Minister's Strategy Unit suggested 'The best response may be for the government to take a top-down approach and require the adoption of best practice' (PMSU 2006: 58). The government established a committee to establish which commercial phonics schemes met the new curriculum requirements (Brooks 2006) and requested details of the phonics content of university initial teacher education courses.

Such policy actions form the backdrop for teachers' work in schools, and set the tone and agenda for educational debate in the media. They help define how teachers and everyone involved in the education system thinks about literacy teaching. They do not focus teachers on the evidence in front of them or on the research evidence out there but exert considerable pressure on them to deliver programmes and comply with the latest government policy. It is a rather depressing thought that centralized curriculum decisions will *always* be under wider policy and political pressure to deliver clear, definitive answers and, consequently, will always distract the teaching profession from the more nuanced and complex debates about teaching and learning, and about how to use evidence more effectively to teach literacy in particular contexts with particular children and teachers.

Conclusion

Issues undoubtedly exist surrounding teachers' use of evidence. Researchers and those who fund and use education research have a responsibility to ensure that designs that generate contextual information are not undersold. Policy-makers, managers and teachers themselves have a responsibility to promote discussions that deepen diagnostic understandings and prompt effective action. To make real progress in these tasks however, we need wider discussion of how teachers are professionalized to attend to the research evidence out there and to the evidence of the children in front of them. This demands a better understanding of what impacts on teachers' use of evidence and of how wider policy and curriculum structures support or undermine this process.

References

Brooks, G. (2002) 'What works for children with literacy difficulties? The effectiveness of intervention schemes', *Research Report No. 380, Department for Education and Skills*. Norwich: HMSO.

Brooks, G. (2006) Personal communication during discussion at ESRC seminar: Pedagogy and Curriculum in Early Reading – Multidisciplinary perspectives, The Open University, Milton Keynes, November.

Boyle, J., McCartney, E., Forbes, J. & O'Hare, A. (2007) 'A randomized controlled trial and economic evaluation of direct versus indirect and individual versus groups modes of speech and language therapy for children with primary language impairment', *Health Technology Assessment*, 11, 25: 1–158.

Cabell, S.Q., Justice, L.M., Zucker, T.A. & Kilday, C.R. (2009) 'Validity of teacher report for assessing the emergent literacy skills of at-risk preschoolers', *Language Speech and Hearing Services in Schools*, 40, 2: 161–173.

Gardner, J., Sutherland, A. & Meenan-Strain, C. (1998) *Reading Recovery in Northern Ireland: The first two years*. Belfast: The Blackstaff Press.

Chalmers, I. (2003) 'Trying to do more good than harm in policy and practice: The role of rigorous, transparent, up-to-date, replicable evaluations', *Annals of the American Academy of Political and Social Science*, 589: 22–40.

Chambers, B. (2008) 'A response to Tymms, Merrell & Coe', *The Psychology of Education Review*, 32, 2: 9.

Clay, M. (1991) *Becoming Literate: the construction of inner control*. Auckland, NZ: Heinemann.

Coburn, C. (2001) 'Collective sense-making about reading: How teachers mediate reading policy in their professional communities', *Educational Evaluation and Policy Analysis*, 23, 2: 45–70.

Coburn, C. (2003) 'Rethinking scale: Moving beyond numbers to deep and lasting change', *Educational Researcher*, 32, 6: 3–12.

Coburn, C.E. & Talbert, J.E. (2006) 'Conceptions of evidence-based practice in school districts: Mapping the terrain', *American Journal of Education*, 112, 4: 469–495.

Connor, C.M., Morrison, F.J. & Katch, E.L. (2004) 'Beyond the reading wars: The effect of classroom instruction by child interactions on early reading', *Scientific Studies of Reading*, 8, 4: 305–336.

Connor, C.M., Son, S., Hindman, A. & Morrison, F.J. (2005) 'Teacher qualifications, classroom practices, family characteristics and preschool experience: Complex effects on first graders' vocabulary and early reading outcomes', *Journal of School Psychology*, 43: 343–375.

Connor, C.M., Morrison, F.J., Fishman, B.J., Schatschneider, C. & Underwood, P. (2007b) 'The Early Years: Algorithm-guided individualized reading instruction', *Science*, 315, 5811: 464–465.

Connor, C.M., Morrison, F.J. & Underwood, P. (2007a) 'A second chance in second grade? The independent and cumulative impact of first and second grade reading instruction and students' letter–word reading skill growth', *Scientific Studies of Reading*, 11, 3: 199–223.

Cunningham, A.E. & Stanovich, K.E. (1998) 'What reading does for the mind', *American Educator*, 22, 1&2: 8–15.

D'Angiulli, A., Siegel, L.S. & Hertzman, C. (2004) 'Schooling, socioeconomic context, and literacy development', *Educational Psychology*, 24: 867–883.

Datnow, A., Hubbard, L. & Mehan, H. (2002) *Extending Educational Reform: From one school to many*. New York: Routledge Falmer.

DfES (2006) *Independent Review of the Teaching of Early Reading: Final report* (The Rose Review). London: DfES.

Eisenhart, M. & Towne, L. (2003) 'Contestation and change in national policy on "scientifically based" education research', *Educational Researcher*, 32, 7: 31–38.

Ellis, S. (2007) 'Policy and research: Lessons from the Clackmannanshire Synthetic Phonics Initiative', *Journal of Early Childhood Literacy*, 7, 3: 281–297.

Fletcher, J., Tannock, R. & Bishop, D.V.M. (2001) 'Utility of brief teacher rating scales to identify children with educational problems: Experience with an Australian sample', *Australian Journal of Psychology*, 53, 2: 63–71.

Gregory, E. (2008) *Learning to Read in a New Language: Making sense of words and worlds*. London: Sage.

Guthrie, J.T. & Humenick, N.M. (2004) 'Motivating students to read: Evidence for classroom practices that increase reading motivation', in P. McCardle and V. Chhabra (eds) *The Voice of Evidence in Reading Research*. New York: Erlbaum.

KPMG Foundation (2006) *The Long Term Costs of Literacy Difficulties* [Online]. Available at http://www.kpmg.co.uk/pubs/ECR2006.pdf (accessed 26 October 2009).

Lareau, A. (2003) *Unequal Childhoods*. Berkeley: University of California Press.

McCartney, E., Ellis, S. & Boyle, J. (2009) 'The mainstream primary classroom as a language-learning environment for children with severe and persistent language impairment: Implications of recent language intervention research', *Journal of Research in Special Educational Needs*, 9, 2: 80–90.

McCoach, D.B., O'Connell, A.A., Reis, S.M. & Levitt, H.A. (2006) 'Growing readers: A hierarchical linear model of children's reading growth during the first 2 years of school', *Journal of Educational Psychology*, 98, 1: 14–28.

Moss, G. (2007) *Literacy and Gender*. Abingdon: Routledge.

Moss, G. & Huxford, L. (2007) 'Exploring literacy policy-making from the inside out', in L. Saunders (ed.) *Exploring the Relationship between Educational Research and Education Policy-Making*. London: Routledge Falmer.

Munn, P. & Ellis, S. (2005) 'Interactions between school systems and reading recovery programmes: Evidence from Northern Ireland', *The Curriculum Journal*, 16, 3: 341–362.

Nation, K. & Angell, P. (2006) 'Learning to read and learning to comprehend', *London Review of Education*, 4, 1: 77–87.

NICHD (National Institute of Child Health and Human Development) (2000) *Report of the National Reading Panel. Teaching children to read: An evidence-based assessment of the scientific research literature on reading and its implications for reading instruction: Reports of the subgroups*. NIH Publication Number 00–4754. Washington DC: US Government Printing Office.

Prime Minister's Strategy Unit (PMSU) (2006) *The UK Government's Approach to Public Sector Reform: A discussion paper*, London: Cabinet Office.

Sackett, D.L., Straus, S.E., Scott Richardson, W., Rosenberg, W. & Haynes, R.B. (2000) *Evidence-based Medicine*. Edinburgh: Churchill Livingstone.

Shanahan, T. & Barr, R. (1995) 'Reading Recovery: An independent evaluation of the effects of an early instructional intervention for at-risk learners', *Reading Research Quarterly*, 20, 4: 958–995.

Slavin, R.E. (2008) 'What works? Issues in synthesizing educational programme evaluations', *Educational Researcher*, 37, 1: 5–14.

Stanovich, K.E. (1986) 'Matthew effects in reading: Some consequences of individual differences in the acquisition of literacy', *Reading Research Quarterly*, 21, 4: 360–407.

Stein, M. & Coburn, C. (2008) 'Architectures for learning: A comparative analysis of two urban school districts', *American Journal of Education*, 114, 4: 583–626.

Topping, K.,Valtin, R., Roller, C., Brozo, W. & Dionisio, M.L. (2003) *Policy and Practice Implications of the Program for International Student Assessment (PISA) 2000: Report of the International Reading Association PISA Task Force*. Newark, NJ: IRA.

Torgerson, C.J., Brooks, G. & Hall, J. (2006) 'A systematic review of the research literature on the use of phonics in the teaching of reading and spelling', *DfES Research Report 711*. London: DfES.

Torgerson, C.J. & Torgerson, D.J. (2001) 'The need for randomized controlled trials in educational research', *British Journal of Educational Studies*, 49, 3: 316–329.

Tymms, P., Merrell, C. & Coe, R. (2008) 'Educational policies and randomized controlled trials', *The Psychology of Education Review*, 32, 2: 3–8.

US Department of Education (2002) *Strategic Goal Four: Transform Education into an Evidence-based Field*, Washington, DC: US Department of Education. Available at: http://www.ed.gov/about/reports/strat/plan2002–07/plan.pdf (accessed 28 October 2009).

Wayman, J. (2005) 'Involving teachers in data-driven decision making: Using computer data systems to support teacher inquiry and reflection', *Journal of Education for Students Placed at Risk*, 10, 3: 295–308.

Wayman, J.C. and Stringfield, S. (2006) 'Data use for school improvement: School practices and research perspectives', *American Journal of Education*, 112, 4: 463–468.

Williams, C. (2006) 'Teacher judgments of the language skills of children in the early years of schooling', *Child Language Teaching and Therapy*, 22, 2: 135–154.

Wyse, D. & Goswami, U. (2008) 'Synthetic phonics and the teaching of reading', *British Educational Research Journal*, 34, 6: 691–710.

Zhao, Y. & Frank, K.A. (2003) 'Factors affecting technology users in schools: An ecological perspective', *American Educational Research Journal*, 40: 807–840.

Zill, N. & Resnick, G. (2006) 'Emergent literacy of low-income children in Headstart', in D.K. Dickinson & S.B. Neuman (eds) *Handbook of Early Literacy Research Vol. 2*. New York: Guildford Press. Chapter 25: 347–374.

Chapter 15

Why do policy-makers find the 'simple view of reading' so attractive, and why do I find it so morally repugnant?

Colin Harrison

In answering the two questions that form the title of this chapter I aim to talk about what governments need in terms of clear, simple one-page policy, what Phil Gough actually said about the Simple View of Reading (Reading = decoding × linguistic comprehension, or R = D × LC), how the Simple View has been taken up by right-wing groups in the USA such as the Core Knowledge Foundation, for example (Davis 2006), and how it has become associated with the 'first, fast and only' model of phonics, and a technicist view of the pedagogy of reading. Then, most importantly, I want to give attention to all the things that might get missed with such a narrow emphasis, including fluency, vocabulary, cognitive flexibility, and morphology. My conclusion will be that the Simple View is elegant and compelling, and partly correct, but dangerously over-simple, with shortcomings as well as some merits.

Introduction: the Simple View and the 'elevator pitch'

In an opening address at the annual research conference of the British Educational Communications and Technology Agency, Jon Drory (2006), a former senior civil servant, argued that educational researchers are desperately poor at simplifying their findings in such a way as to maximise their impact on those who create and shape policy. He suggested that researchers needed to become more skilled at presenting their work in a variety of formats, but particularly, if they wanted it to influence policy, in smaller chunks – the 30-second 'elevator pitch' that succinctly captures the attention and leaves an enduring memory trace in the mind of the hard pressed minister, or ministerial advisor. Conversely, Drory pointed out, ministers and their advisors are not won over by research findings that leave questions unanswered, or that leave competing theories in a dialogic balance. Their primary job is to deliver money to their department, and to get that money, they need to win arguments with the Treasury, and to win those arguments, they need not research, but research-informed opinions that are clear, cogent, compelling and confident (whether they need to be alliterative was not dealt with, but I'm guessing that's a plus).

Were evidence needed that Drory's analysis is spot on in relation to the literacy field, in England at least, we need look no further than the clear, cogent, compelling, confident and Clackmannanshire-informed views that shaped the Rose Report (Rose 2006), as the following words reveal:

> Despite uncertainties in research findings, the practice seen by the review shows that the systematic approach, which is generally understood as 'synthetic' phonics, offers the vast majority of young children the best and most direct route to becoming skilled readers and writers.

If we decode this message, Rose is telling us three things: that the research results he encountered were equivocal, that he regards the terms 'systematic phonics' and 'synthetic phonics' as equivalent, and that his analysis of how the nation should teach reading has not been based on research data, but on the good practice he saw during his school visits. Of course this is only part of the story; Rose was impressed by the good practice he witnessed, but he was no doubt also compelled by the cogent and confident arguments of the Clackmannanshire researchers and the Reading Reform Foundation.

But how the Rose Report arrived at its final position on synthetic phonics is not the primary focus of this chapter. The issue I want to consider is the Rose Report's stance on the 'Simple View of Reading' which we are told 'has increasingly been adopted by psychologists researching reading development since it was first proposed in 1986' (Rose 2006: 78). This is an interesting assertion: it is most certainly the case that the Simple View of Reading has been increasingly adopted by policy-makers, and it has most certainly been adopted by the psychologists who advised Jim Rose, notably Morag Styles and Rhona Stainthorp. But the Simple View of Reading has also been roundly attacked by other psychologists, and we shall look at some of the arguments that challenge the simple view later in this chapter.

Four questions about the Simple View

There are four questions in my mind at this point, the first of which is: 'Is the Simple View of Reading broadly speaking correct?'; the second, 'Is it attractive to government simply because it's simple?'; the third, 'Is the Simple View simplistic?'; and the fourth, 'If the Simple View is broadly speaking correct, why do I still have a feeling of repugnance towards it?'

Let's take these questions in turn. First, is the Simple View of Reading broadly correct? Figure 15.1 shows the diagram presented in the Rose Report of the Simple View of Reading, and Figure 15.2 the Searchlights Model that preceded it in the government's advice to teachers of reading. The assumptions of the Simple View are transparent: there are two key components to reading, word recognition and language comprehension, and thus for reading to be successful, a child needs to be good at both. This would seem to be uncontestable: each is a necessary but

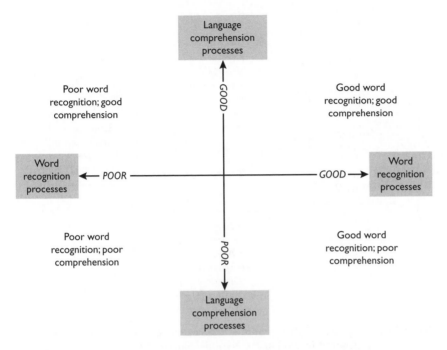

Figure 15.1 The Simple View of reading, as presented in the Rose Report (2006).

not sufficient condition for print to be understood. Are they separate processes? Well again, the intuitive answer would seem to be 'Yes'. The very fact that many people can do one but not the other would seem to confirm that the two processes are fundamentally different. And two sets of research evidence would also seem to confirm this difference. One was Ron Carver's finding that word recognition and comprehension still factor out as different skills even in adult fluent readers (Carver 2000). The other is the research of Watson and Johnson in Clackmannanshire, which found that their programme was successful in teaching word recognition, in that children's abilities improved by an average of three years, but only had a minor effect on the development of comprehension, which improved by an average of three months (Johnson and Watson 2005). If children get better at reading, but do not improve on comprehension, this would seem to confirm that the two are different processes. So on this analysis, the Simple View of Reading would seem to have much to commend it.

My second question, 'Is the Simple View attractive to government simply because it's simple?', is unlikely to be settled by empirical evidence. And in posing it I am not intending to insult policy-makers, either by suggesting that civil servants are incapable of dealing with complexity, or by suggesting that they believe teachers are incapable of dealing with complexity. But clearly its simplicity was an

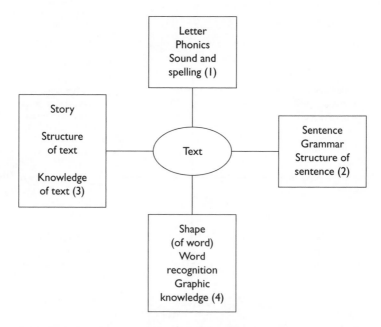

Figure 15.2 The 'Searchlights' model of the reading process, as originally presented in the English National Curriculum.

attraction. We need to remember that the Simple View was replacing the Searchlights Model of reading, which was not only more complex, but perceived by academics as well as civil servants as flawed in a number of ways. The Searchlights Model wasn't a model that had testable properties, and it is not at all clear how its elements fitted together. There is no indication in the Searchlights Model of how the separate processes pass control to each other, and (in a text box that is perhaps the least well-informed by research, box 4) there seems to be an assumption that words are recognised by 'shape', without any letter processing, which would be challenged these days. Worst of all, from a pedagogical point of view, in box 4, 'word recognition' appears but is not connected to and in fact is diametrically opposite to the 'phonics, sound and spelling' box, thereby possibly suggesting that phonics and word recognition are unconnected. Somehow, 'Graphic knowledge' has found its way into the 'Word recognition' box, but appears to be separated from 'Letter, phonics, sound and spelling' of box 1. As I shall argue in the next paragraph, phonics and word recognition are different but related processes. By contrast, the Simple View emphasises a fact just about all experts agree on, namely that, for children learning to read in English, learning to decode is important and necessary, since reading will not occur without it. So the simplicity is attractive, and it is also understandable that those in government (and those working for government who want to advise teachers) should seek it.

To the third question, 'Is the simple view simplistic?' in that it ignores or glosses over some absolutely crucial aspects of the process of reading, my answer is 'Yes', and I shall talk about the evidence for this claim in some detail below. The main point that I shall attempt to sustain is that it is at best inaccurate and at worst misleading to suggest that if a child has mastered decoding then he or she will be able to read. There are really two parts to this argument. The first is to make it clear that decoding and word recognition are not the same thing, or to put it another way – there is much more to word recognition than meets the eye. Part of the argument concerns fluency and prosody. The Simple View would suggest that once words are decoded from print the brain is able to recognise and interpret them as directly as if they were spoken. There is a good deal of evidence around that suggests that this is not the case. The second area of challenge relates to the assumption built into the Simple View that decoding and comprehension are independent processes. I shall discuss evidence that challenges this, and that in my view makes it clear that the Simple View, though elegant and engaging, oversimplifies the reading process. As Patrick Proctor (2006) put it, the Simple View is 'far too simple to make a meaningful difference in understanding the vast complexities that individual learners bring to the reading process'.

My fourth question, 'if the Simple View is broadly speaking correct, why do I still have a feeling of repugnance towards it?', is a tricky one to answer, because feelings of repugnance are not about scholarly argument, but about feelings and beliefs. There is much in the Rose Report that I would fully endorse. The following, for example:

> Two components of reading identified in the simple view of reading first put forward by Gough and Tunmer (1986) are 'decoding' and 'comprehension': according to these authors, 'Reading is the product of decoding and comprehension'. We would not want to suggest accepting this statement as a complete description or explanation of reading; rather, we want to advocate the good sense of considering reading in terms of these two components.
>
> (Rose 2006: 76).

Here, the Report explicitly states that reading is more than decoding and comprehension, but my anxieties are precisely around the fact that the Simple View does not bring these complexities to the fore. There is indeed 'good sense' in giving close attention to decoding and comprehension, but the Simple View diagram reproduced as Figure 15.1 has only two axes. In fact, the Rose Review version of the Simple View that it presents in a diagram does not label the axes with Gough's variables, but puts 'Word Recognition' and 'Language Comprehension Processes', which is an implicit acknowledgement that the Simple View is indeed inadequate, and needs broadening beyond 'Decoding'. The Report quotes with approval the words of Max Coltheart, who also stresses the importance of looking not only at the 'simpler component parts' but of trying to build a full picture of 'real reading':

> If we start off by investigating 'real reading', seeking for example to discover how readers develop an understanding of what life might have been like in Imperial Russia as they read *The Brothers Karamazov*. No one has any idea about how to carry out such an investigation; so more tractable reading situations have to be studied first. This is done by breaking up 'real reading' into simpler component parts that are more immediately amenable to investigation, with the hope that as more and more of these component parts come to be understood we will get closer and closer to a full understanding of 'real reading'.
>
> (Rose 2006: 75–76; original source: Coltheart 2006)

But there is something wrong here. Is it really the case that 'no one has any idea about how to carry out . . . an investigation' of 'real reading'? Didn't Louise Rosenblatt show us how we could investigate 'real reading' 70 years ago (1938), with her work on reader response? Hasn't Doug Hartman (1995) done work on intertextuality that showed in some detail how readers brought their knowledge of a range of texts and genres to bear when they were doing 'real reading'?

And here we come directly up against the nub of the Simple View issue: although I truly believe that we should learn all we can from psychological research, as a teacher I become very uneasy when I read that the intention is to focus on the aspects of the reading process that are more 'immediately amenable to investigation' in more 'tractable reading situations', with the hope of getting back to more of the 'component parts' of 'real reading' later on. This is because, while it's fine, if not essential, for psychologists to focus on a subset of the 'component parts' in order to advance our collective knowledge of the reading process, as a teacher I get very worried when I encounter a view that suggests that it is therefore desirable for teachers to focus on the same limited set of 'component parts' in order to teach reading. The psychologists who advised Jim Rose, and who guided the hand of those who wrote the scholarly sections on the reading process would perhaps be mortified at the suggestion that the Simple View is 'morally repugnant', and would find that idea difficult to understand. From their point of view, making it clearer to teachers that they have two important, but rather different jobs to do in teaching reading – teaching decoding and teaching comprehension – is doing a service to the profession, and clarifying some key aspects of pedagogy that were confused and confounded in the Searchlights Model. My antipathy is even more difficult to explain since they know that I am a researcher as well as a teacher.

But it is the teacherly part of me that recoils from the Simple View, and it does so because of a strong negative reaction to an unexpressed but powerful inference that is buried just beneath the surface of the Simple View, which is that children come to school with 'linguistic comprehension', and that the teacher's job is simply to teach the 'decoding', and then all will be well. We could call this the 'Simple

View of Reading Instruction', and I think that it is this Simple View of Reading Instruction that I find morally repugnant. The authors of the Rose Review, of course, would totally distance themselves from such a position. The latter sections of the Report make it very clear that the authors have a very explicit goal of supporting teachers in the pedagogy of comprehension as well as the pedagogy of word recognition, through making them aware of a range of strategies as well as encouraging them to teach decoding effectively. But the spectre of those in power reducing the teaching of reading to the teaching of phonics, and of reducing teachers from evangelists for the joy of reading to technicians who need to be better schooled in the mechanics of teaching grapheme–phoneme correspondences is not only in the background, it is sometimes in the foreground. Some proponents of 'phonics first, fast and only' would have such a technicist view, as would the elementary school principal in California who threatened a teacher with dismissal for introducing real books into a beginning reading classroom before the children had completed their restricted vocabulary phonics course. A more balanced critique of the concept of 'first, fast and only' is provided by the Torgerson, Brooks and Hall (2006) review of research into the teaching of phonics. These authors argue that there is plenty of evidence supporting the need for phonics teaching 'first', but none from empirical studies supporting the need for it to be either 'fast' or 'only'.

These, then are some of the areas of debate around the Simple View. Let us turn now to a more detailed consideration of what the Simple View asserts, and to what those who have suggested that it is inaccurate or wrong have had to say.

The Simple View of Reading: a polarising force in the reading field

Patrick Proctor (2006) has described the Simple View of Reading as a 'polarising force in the reading field', one that has 'engendered anger' from researchers for two decades. It is interesting, therefore, that in presenting it as the theoretical and pedagogical hub of the 'renewed' literacy strategy in England, the Rose Review suggested that the 'simple view of reading has increasingly been adopted by psychologists researching reading development' (Rose 2006: 77). It is one thing to make use of the Simple View in researching reading development, but quite another to use it as the primary framework for instruction. Michael Pressley (2000) wrote the key chapter on how comprehension develops for the *Handbook of Reading Research*, and he had little time for the Simple View, which he regarded as a theory that was attractive to policy-makers because of its simplicity and its emphasis on teaching phonics, but a non-starter as a serious contender for representing the complexities of the reading process:

> Although skilled and eventually fluent word recognition certainly facilitates comprehension, it is not enough. This conclusion contrasts with the thinking of some in the educational policy-making community who view word-recognition instruction as a panacea for reading problems, a simple view that

reduces reading to recognizing words and listening to oneself read those words (e.g. Gough, Hoover, & Peterson 1996). If that were all there is to it, then, of course, the many other interventions discussed in the first section of this article would not be as potent as they are. Those who argue that comprehension problems can be solved by taking care of word-recognition problems are ignoring a lot of relevant data.

(Pressley 2001)

Much of that 'relevant data' deals with the argument that, far from being independent, phonological and semantic processes act concurrently in skilled reading (Pressley *et al.*. 2009; Cartwright 2007), and we shall consider some of this data later in this chapter. Before doing so, however, it is worth giving some attention to Patrick Proctor's work since it explores arguments about multiple influences on reading, but does so by examining the Simple View from a mathematical viewpoint.

Proctor (2006) offered a critique of the Simple View that was based on an intriguing approach – namely, to test the statistical adequacy of the formula $RC = D \times LC$ in a variety of experimental contexts. Proctor collected data on 137 Spanish–English bilingual fourth graders (i.e. readers aged nine to ten), the majority of whom had learned to read in Spanish, their native language, and to whom he had given tests of reading comprehension (RC) decoding (D here was pseudo-word reading), and listening comprehension (LC). Using multiple regression techniques, Proctor first asked whether it was indeed the case that $RC = D \times LC$, and whether there was a statistically multiplicative relationship between decoding and listening comprehension. What he found was that (D $\times$ LC) on its own did indeed significantly predict reading comprehension, and that students who were weak in decoding did poorly on reading comprehension, even if their listening comprehension scores were above average. However, Proctor points out that it was not the cross-product (D $\times$ LC) that was the key predictor, but rather the straightforward additive contribution of the two main effects of D (decoding) and listening comprehension (LC). When these two variables were put into an additive model (i.e. D + LC + (D $\times$ LC)), the additional effect of the (D $\times$ LC) component was non-significant. It explained less than 1 per cent of additional variance in reading comprehension. Put another way, the statistical analysis suggested that the statistical relationship between decoding, listening comprehension and reading comprehension was linear and additive, rather than interactive and multiplicative.

Proctor then went on to carry out some additional analyses (Proctor *et al.* 2005; Proctor *et al.* 2006), this time adding two new variables to the equation: real word reading rate and vocabulary knowledge. Using structural equation modelling, Proctor's group found that when they controlled for the effects of decoding ability and listening comprehension, students' vocabulary knowledge in Spanish made a significant additional and separate contribution to predicting reading comprehension ($R^2 = 0.30$, p<.01). This small but significant main effect was interpreted by Proctor as revealing that the Simple View is too simple, and omits some crucial variables. A further analysis seemed to confirm this. The measure of 'real word reading rate' was in effect an indication of the reader's fluency, and this variable, too, was seen to play an important additional role in predicting reading comprehension. When all the other variables were controlled, students who both read fluently and had a good Spanish vocabulary scored highly on reading comprehension. There was also an interaction effect: those students who were fluent decoders in English but who had a poor Spanish vocabulary scored much more poorly on the test of reading comprehension. In other words, both vocabulary knowledge and reading fluency seemed to be making independent contributions to predicting reading comprehension, in addition to what could be predicted from their decoding (as measured by non-word reading) and listening comprehension ability. As Proctor (2006) put it, 'reading as a process does not occur in a cognitive vacuum'.

Another researcher who would share Proctor's view is Kelly Cartwright (2007), who argues that what she terms 'graphophonological–semantic flexibility' (GSF) makes a unique and separate contribution to fluent reading, over and above the contributions of D and LC. Cartwright's starting point is cognition, and the wide agreement among scholars who study reading processes that a fluent reader is simultaneously and flexibly dealing with phonological, lexical, orthographic and semantic representations during the reading process. Indeed, she makes the point that it is less fluent readers who are able to deal with only a subset of the features of text that are before them, and who lack the 'flexibility' that is a hallmark of the fluent reader. To measure GSF, Cartwright gave readers a test that required simultaneous processing of phonological and semantic information. Participants had to classify into a 2×2 table of initial sound and meaning a set of 12 cards that were in two semantic groups (for example vehicles and animals) and that started with one of two initial phonemes (for example bike, turkey, tractor, boat, tiger, bird, etc.). What Cartwright found, in separate studies with both children and adults, was that GSF came out as a variable predicting reading comprehension performance even when intelligence, phonological processing and semantic processing had been taken into account. As in Proctor's study, adding Gough's '$D \times LC$' to the regression equation did not account for significant variance, but GSF, which Cartwright viewed as 'individuals' flexibility in handling concurrently multiple features of print' seemed to be identifying a 'third cognitive skill' in addition to D and LC that predicted and contributed to reading comprehension ability.

The final study to which I want to refer is one by Nagy, Berninger and Abbott (2006). These authors argue that the Simple View omits another very important factor, namely the unique contribution made by morphological awareness to word recognition. A morpheme is the smallest unit of language that affects meaning, so the —*s* in a plural and the —*ed* that turns a verb into the past tense in English are morphemes, but so are other prefixes and suffixes such as *trans*—(as in transplant) or —*est* (as in newest). What Nagy and his co-workers found was that children's morphological awareness made a significant and independent contribution to their word reading speed and accuracy at fourth, fifth, eighth and ninth grade levels. In other words, as Nagy put it, 'translating print into speech, at least in English, is not a purely phonological process'. But Nagy goes further than this: he advances the view that morphological awareness impacts comprehension as well as word recognition, in that it seems to be related to vocabulary growth, and one can readily see how this might work, and how it might be related to the continued influence of morphology in the middle years of schooling. What Nagy was thinking was that, as a reader becomes more experienced and more fluent, the ability to spot semantic relationships (between such words as *complete* and *completion*, for example) would impact comprehension as well as word recognition. And such relationships do not always overlap with phonetic information: a reader might correctly deduce a morphological semantic relationship between the words *nation* and *national*, even though the two words are pronounced differently, and making such a deduction would speed up the integration of the word into an emerging model of the situation being described in the text. So morphological awareness and oral vocabulary are related, but not the same thing; Nagy found the two variables to be correlated, but the statistical models showed that morphological awareness made a separate contribution to reading comprehension, above and beyond that of vocabulary.

The data from the study of Nagy and his colleagues adds to this list of variables that need to be added to the simple view, in order to gain a more accurate and complete understanding of the reading process. On this analysis, reading comprehension is the result of a complex interaction of processes that begin with letter analysis, but then include phonological processing, morphological processing that supports word recognition, which in turn may be related at least in part to Kelly's graphophonological–semantic flexibility, vocabulary knowledge, morphological processing that supports comprehension, fluency and linguistic comprehension.

The researchers who critique the Simple View generally concede that decoding and linguistic comprehension are indeed very important. As Proctor put it, these variables may form a 'psycholinguistic nucleus' of the reading process, but research also suggests that other factors need to be part of a 'complexification' of the simple view. Proctor argues rather provocatively that

> Even the most naïve pre-service teacher will begin to expound on the numerous contextual factors that affect a student's reading when she is presented with the notion that reading comprehension is simply the act of decoding matched alongside the listening comprehension of a learner.
>
> (Proctor 2006)

This may be an exaggeration, but in my view the point is a valid one: reading does not take place in a cognitive vacuum. It takes place in a social context, and in school it takes place in a pedagogical context, and both these contextual factors will impact whether and how readers engage with texts.

Conclusions

My own strong negative reaction to the Simple View is not related to any quarrel with Gough's emphasis on the 'psycholinguistic nucleus' of decoding and linguistic comprehension. I also sympathise with the intentions of the Rose Review in England that has used the Simple View to stress for teachers that they have two complex jobs – to teach children to decode and recognise words, but also to teach and develop comprehension. But I do believe that there is a danger that some commentators and some policy-makers will infer from the Simple View of Reading that there should be a Simple View of Teaching, in which the teachers are viewed as technicians whose fundamental role is to teach decoding, and then all the problems of low literacy will be solved. Such an inference would be both naïve and ill-judged, and it is that view that I find morally repugnant, because it misunderstands and misrepresents the complexity and multifaceted constellation of skills that a good teacher of reading brings to her job. Liz Waterland, whose somewhat notorious book *Read With Me* (Waterland 1988) was credited with helping to start the 'real books' movement in England (and thus thought by some to have helped to lower reading standards by reducing an emphasis on the teaching of phonics), was a teacher who turned to real books precisely because she had found that teaching phonics did not result in children's learning to read. Many of the children to whom she taught phonics did learn to decode, but they did not learn to read. They saw reading as a complex and mystifying chore, and having learned to decode they had no wish to use their skill to gain access to the wonderful world of books.

What I am advocating, therefore, is a Complex View of Reading, and a Complex View of the Teaching of Reading. A complex view of reading is needed to take account of the rich seam of research findings that augment and challenge the Simple View, and of which I have done no more than to present a sample in this chapter. A complex view of the teaching of reading is necessary to place appropriate emphasis on the skilled and effective teaching of phonics, but also to acknowledge the crucial importance of the teacher's role not only in teaching decoding, but also in developing comprehension and in leading children into enjoyable experiences with books in a range of pedagogical and social contexts. Such a view would do greater justice to the complexity and professional skills of the reading teacher, and would also contribute more effectively to raising standards in reading.

References

Cartwright, K.B. (2007) 'The contribution of graphophonological–semantic flexibility to reading comprehension in college students: Implications for a less simple view of reading', *Journal of Literacy Research*, 39, 2: 173–193.

Carver, R. (2000) *The Causes of High and Low Reading Achievement*, New York: Routledge.

Coltheart, M. (2006) 'Dual-route and connectionist models of reading: An overview', *London Review of Education*, 4, 1: 5–17.

Davis, M. (2006) 'The simple view of reading', *Common Knowledge: The newsletter of the Core Knowledge Foundation*, 19, 2. Available at: http://coreknowledge.org/CK/about/CommonKnowledge/v19II_2006/v19_II_2006_simpleviewofreading.htm (accessed 24 January 2009).

Drory, J. (2006) 'The Big Mismatch: Why good research goes unheeded'. Presentation at the Becta Annual Research Conference, International Convention Centre, Birmingham, November.

Gough, P.B., Hoover, W.A., & Peterson, C.L. (1996) 'Some observations on a simple view of reading', in C. Cornoldi & J. Oakhill (eds) *Reading Comprehension Difficulties* (1–13), Mahwah, NJ: Erlbaum.

Hartman, D.K. (1995) 'Eight readers reading: The intertextual links of proficient readers using multiple passages', *Reading Research Quarterly*, 30, 3: 520–561.

Johnston, R. & Watson, J. (2005) *The Effects of Synthetic Phonics Teaching on Reading and Spelling Attainment: A seven year longitudinal study*, The Scottish Executive Central Research Unit, February. Available at: http://www.scotland.gov.uk/Publications/2005/02/20688/52464 (accessed 26 October 2009).

Nagy, W., Berninger, V., & Abbott, R. (2006) 'Contributions of morphology beyond phonology to literacy outcomes of upper elementary and middle school students', *Journal of Educational Psychology*, 98: 134–147.

Pressley, M. (2000) 'What should comprehension instruction be the instruction of?' in M.L. Kamil, P.B. Mosenthal, P.D. Pearson, & R. Barr (eds), *Handbook of Reading Research: Volume III* (545–561), Mahwah, NJ: Erlbaum.

Pressley, M. (2001, September). 'Comprehension instruction: What makes sense now, what might make sense soon', *Reading Online*, 5, 2. Available at: http://www.readingonline.org/articles/art_index.asp?HREF=/articles/handbook/pressley/index.html (accessed 26 October 2009).

Pressley, M., Duke, N.K., Gaskins, I.W., Fingeret, L., Halladay, J., Hilden, K., Park, Y., Zhang, S., Mohan, L., Reffitt, K., Bogaert, L.R., Reynolds, J., Golos, D., Solic, K., & Collins, S. (2009) 'Working with struggling readers: Why we must get beyond the Simple View of Reading and visions of how it might be done', in T.B. Gutkin & C.R. Reynolds (eds), *The Handbook of School Psychology, Fourth Edition* (522–546). Hoboken, NJ: Wiley.

Proctor, P. (2006) 'The simple view as a psycholinguistic nucleus'. Paper presented at the National Reading Conference, 56th Annual Meeting, Los Angeles, CA, December.

Proctor, C.P., Carlo, M.S., August, D., & Snow, C.E. (2005) 'Native Spanish-speaking children reading in English: Toward a model of comprehension', *Journal of Educational Psychology*, 97, 2: 246–256.

Proctor, C.P., August, D., Carlo, M.S., & Snow, C.E. (2006) 'The intriguing role of Spanish vocabulary knowledge in predicting English reading comprehension', *Journal of Educational Psychology*, 98, 1: 159–169.

Rose, J. (2006) *Independent Review of the Teaching of Early Reading*, London: DfES.

Rosenblatt, L.(1938) *Literature as Exploration*, New York: Noble & Noble [1983].

Torgeson, C.J., Brooks, G., & Hall, J. (2006) *A Systematic Review of the Research Literature on the Use of Phonics in the Teaching of Reading and Spelling*, London: Department for Education and Skills.

Waterland, L. (1988) *Read With Me*, London: The Thimble Press.

Chapter 16

Policy and pedagogy

Proficiency and choice in the literacy classroom

Gemma Moss

Introduction

This chapter will consider the impact of policy-driven education reform on the social organisation of reading in school. Drawing on ethnographic data collected in English classrooms before and after the introduction of the National Literacy Strategy, it will identify some of the key dilemmas teachers face in managing pupils' transition into self-directed reading.

Literacy and pedagogy in context

Arguments over the content of the literacy curriculum are not new. What has changed the tenor of the discussion in England in recent times is the direct involvement of government in laying down what and how literacy should be taught. Opening definitions drawn up in the National Curriculum have been superseded by a series of revisions and additional policy interventions. The National Literacy Strategy, at one point seen as the clearest remedy for raising standards, now finds itself the object of further revisions, via the Rose Review of the teaching of reading in the early years (Rose 2005), and a subsequent enquiry into the primary curriculum more broadly (Rose 2009). In some respects the latter could be thought of as a tactical intervention, designed to soften any potential fallout from an independent review into the primary curriculum set in motion by Robin Alexander at Cambridge University, and engaging substantial contributions from a wide range of experts (Alexander 2009; Alexander & Flutter 2009). If government ever thought that publicly managing the education system using a combination of performance data and increased specification of what teachers should do would automatically lever up attainment and end inequalities in the system, they must be sadly disappointed.

In their interim report which forms part of a wide-ranging and critical review of current policy and practice in primary education (Alexander & Flutter 2009) the authors outline a series of dichotomies which underpin many of the arguments over the nature of the curriculum, and how its focus should be understood. These they variously describe as standards versus curriculum; the basics versus breadth; knowledge versus skills; and English versus literacy. They spend some time tracing these arguments back over time, highlighting how the balance between these contrasting elements has been drawn in different periods and how long such settlements last before the argument starts up again. Their purpose in addressing this history is to establish a better basis upon which to answer certain core questions (see Figure 16.1).

Their report operates as a serious and substantial intervention into the politics of literacy policy at a point when one revision after another seems to have left the curriculum overburdened with requirements, without any settled sense of purpose offering teachers and pupils a clear way through.

In this context I want to return to one of the fundamental distinctions at the heart of the reading curriculum, namely the contrast between viewing reading as a matter of proficiency, where what matters most is the level of skill children acquire, and viewing reading as a matter of choice, where what matters most is children's willingness to read and the pleasure they get from exercising that skill. Some of the intensity in debate over reading method maps onto this distinction, with some approaches emphasising the necessary skills required to read, and others emphasising the necessary motivation. Place the emphasis on the skills required to learn to read and the curriculum is driven by systematic instruction, focused on word-recognition skills or the processes involved in the comprehension of written language. Place the emphasis on children's use of the skills they acquire and a different set of priorities comes into play, centred on the enthusiasm, enjoyment, confidence and pleasure that children derive from the content of their reading, demonstrated by the fact that they want to read and find the time and place to do so.

Yet in practice the reading curriculum always enshrines both these aims. Even when debate is most highly polarised between those espousing a holistic approach to learning to read against those who take a more atomistic view, specifying the various component skills involved and the precise order in which they should be taught, the end point is the same: fluent readers who know what reading has to offer them and read in a self-motivated way. At root, the heat in the debate is about the sequence in which these two aspects need to be addressed; and about the necessary relationship between them. At one extreme, there is the proposition that skill must always come first, and that sufficient skill is the key to unlock the

---

- What do children currently learn during the primary phase?
- Do the current national curriculum and attendant foundation, literacy, numeracy and primary strategies provide the range and approach which children of this age really need?
- What should children learn during the primary phase?
- What kinds of curriculum experience will best serve children's varying needs during the next few decades? basics and cores for the primary phase be constituted?
- Do notions like 'basics' and 'core curriculum' have continuing validity, and, if so, of what should 21st-century basics and cores for the primary phase be constituted?
- What constitutes a meaningful, balanced and relevant primary curriculum?

Figure 16.1 Curriculum questions 1: The Cambridge Review (core questions).

Source: Alexander & Flutter 2009: 4

willingness to read. For those advocating phonics, for instance, this justifies closely restricting the reading environment that children are offered in the early stages of learning to read in order to reinforce a precise sequence in which particular letter–sound correspondences are taught. At the other extreme, within some whole language traditions, there is a contrary proposition that if teachers offer children fulfilling reading experiences in a rich reading environment, then the necessary skills will follow.

As the successive revisions to the literacy curriculum show, arguments over the teaching of reading have not abated. But the National Literacy Strategy (NLS) has created a new starting point from which such debate flows. There is now a general acceptance across research traditions that systematic instruction on the nature of the writing system and the way in which it encodes sounds is an essential part of literacy pedagogy (Lewis and Ellis 2006). And conversely, that developing comprehension requires attention to children's broader language skills (Stuart *et al.* 2007). Movement on these issues points to another perhaps more fundamental shift. The introduction of the NLS has helped establish a broad consensus in England over the value of explicit pedagogy for teaching key aspects of the literacy curriculum ranging across word-, sentence- and text-level objectives. Indeed, taken as a whole over the last decade there has been a general retreat from implicit pedagogy and its assumption that children can be expected to learn simply through immersion in rich literacy experiences. In the rest of this chapter I want to consider what has been gained and lost through this bigger shift in perspective, using ethnographic data collected in primary school classrooms.

Attending to classroom practice: the social organisation of reading in school

The data in this chapter were collected in a series of case studies conducted in five primary schools between 1995 and 2003, immediately before and some time after the introduction of the NLS. (These research projects were: The Fact and Fiction project, funded by the ESRC, 1996–1998 – research team, Gemma Moss and Dena Attar; and Building a New Literacy Practice through the Adoption of the National Literacy Strategy, funded by the ESRC, 2001–2003 – Project Director and researcher, Gemma Moss.) Of the four schools involved in the initial phase of the research, two had predominantly working-class and two predominantly middle-class catchments. The case studies explored children's development as readers between the ages of seven and eleven, working from a literacy as social practice perspective and using a range of ethnographic research tools. These included classroom observation, pupil, teacher and parent interviews, text analysis and parent questionnaires. A full account of the research can be found in Moss (2007). A primary aim of the research was to map the social contexts in which reading took place over the course of the school day. In practice this meant identifying the different ground rules associated with different kinds of literacy events, and analysing how such events variously defined what counts as reading for the children who participated in them. In this way the research highlighted how literacy is constructed in and through social interaction, and in relation to different kinds of resources.

By paying close attention to which texts got into which contexts for which readers, the research uncovered three distinct sets of ground rules for 'what counts as reading' routinely associated with different kinds of literacy events in all of the schools where the research was based. For instance, if a class were going to use a worksheet as part of planned curriculum activity, the teacher would read the worksheet to the whole class first, explicating any parts they might not understand before asking individuals to work with the text. In effect, the teacher takes responsibility for the reading, both de-coding it and making sure it makes sense. If children subsequently run into difficulties as they use the worksheet to guide their activity they are entitled to ask for help from peers or the teacher and any other adults in the class. Outside of exam conditions no penalty is incurred for doing this. This is 'procedural reading', reading to get other things done.

By contrast, teachers used different kinds of ground rules in events geared towards building and assessing children's levels of skills, most notably reading aloud from a text chosen specifically for that purpose: their reading book. In these literacy events, what matters is how well children read. Children are expected to take the full responsibility for reading and to do so unaided. Texts will be tailored to the precise level of competence children are seen to have achieved. Other choices cannot be made. If individuals cannot muster sufficient competence to make their way through the text without help, this will have consequences for what happens next: they may be asked to change their reading book, be assigned to a different reading group or given a different level of work. This is 'reading for proficiency'.

Still other kinds of literacy events put to one side the question of how well children read in favour of developing children's interests in reading as an end in itself. In these events, children would be free to react in a much more open way to the texts in question, without their responses being used to judge their skill. Sometimes teachers would choose texts they hoped their pupils would enjoy, and read them aloud to the class. At other times they would give children opportunities to choose texts for themselves, giving them access to a wider choice of reading materials in a context where they were far freer to choose what they then did with these texts. Neither of these activities would be formally assessed. This is 'reading for choice'.

Events exemplifying reading for proficiency and reading for choice would generally be recognised as part of the official reading curriculum. Teachers are expected to plan for both and in an ideal world students would be expected to move seamlessly between them, acquiring both the skills and the motivation to read. In practice, things are more complex than that. The role of the reading book provides a case in point. From the teacher's perspective, the reading book should match the child's level of proficiency in order to ensure they carry on shouldering the appropriate responsibility for the work of learning to read. Until they have reached the status of free or independent reader, a judgement that ultimately rests with the teacher, the kinds of choices children can make about what and how they read will ordinarily be constrained. Children are expected to take on the task of 'choosing wisely', invoking the same criteria as the teacher, rather than setting their sights on interests that are more diverse or which might take them in other directions. Proficiency and choice thus intertwine, invading and constraining each other's territory. Individual children navigate these potential tension points in different ways as they undertake tasks that represent reading as a particular kind of 'schooled' work imposed by others and tasks that represent reading as self-directed play (Solsken 1993). Moving from one form of pedagogy to another does not so much erase these tensions as present them in a new way.

Navigating the tensions between proficiency and choice prior to the introduction of the NLS

Prior to the introduction of the National Literacy Strategy, events that exemplified reading for choice, reading for proficiency and procedural reading would all happen as part of the literacy curriculum, but would probably take place at very different times of the school day. No necessary connection would be made between these different kinds of events. From a child's point of view the clear separation in space and time between events using different kinds of ground rules made the distinctions between them relatively easy to see.

In relation to reading for choice and reading for proficiency, their precise place in the literacy curriculum varied from school to school. At the simplest level, different schools committed more or less time or resource to one over the other. There was no consistency here. When they happened, literacy events geared towards reading for proficiency looked most similar. Whilst the frequency with which they were heard to read to the teacher varied, all children were expected to have a reading book, read it everyday, and take both it and a home reading record home so that parents could listen to children read too. Only one school made less official use of this final requirement in a context where almost all of the children in class were considered fluent readers.

There was less consensus over how teachers delivered on reading for choice. The events that constituted this way of reading were often less well defined, not least because a large part of the responsibility for this kind of activity was handed over to the children themselves. In each school there were opportunities for children to organise their own reading at some point during the school day. This was most likely to happen either during 'quiet reading time', time set aside for silent reading, or during episodes called 'finishing work', when children who had finished a particular curriculum task ahead of their peers would be expected to read until the rest of the class caught up. Although in some schools children were meant to be reading their reading book during this time, in others they were free to choose from a far wider range of materials. In any case, exactly what children did was never strictly monitored, with children allowed to move around the class and choose texts to read or change their books if they needed to. Provided noise levels didn't rise too high it was possible to talk to friends or share a book as well as read alone. Classrooms were set up in anticipation of this kind of activity with class libraries often placed in a carpeted area of the room along with a comfy chair or bean bag and soft drapes so that several children could congregate there together.

Only one of the four case study sites actively managed this activity as part of the curriculum. In this school, quiet reading time happened every day immediately after lunch as part of lesson time. The teacher expected children to choose a text from the extensive class library and read to themselves or in pairs or small groups. These different configurations happened on successive days, with children changing their texts according to the particular requirements. The classroom was well resourced with these changing purposes in mind, with the class library stock being chosen by pupils and teacher together from the central school library twice a term. Whilst children read to themselves, the teacher used the opportunity to listen to individual readers or work with reading groups. By contrast in one of the other schools, quiet reading time took place during the first 20 minutes of the school day when the teacher would also take the register and give out notices or send errands. In this class the children could either use the time to read their reading book or finish off homework, though if they chose to do neither this went largely unremarked.

The use children made of 'finishing work' time was even more lightly monitored. The following extract from field notes is not atypical in this respect. This episode happened towards the end of a Maths lesson and documents the kind of use children were able to make of the book corner before the teacher called the class together for the next activity.

> Harold's finished – told he can sit in the book corner. Harold asks 'Can I listen to a tape?' Martin and Terence in book corner too. Terence's looking through books right in the corner – takes picture book and flicks through. Does this with several books . . .
>
> 2.45 Sam and Terence now putting headphones on too. Jim and Peter looking through football magazines. Jim annoyed that Terence had headphones he wanted – gets them somehow. Terence goes back to going through picture books. Colin has a picture book too, sitting next to Terence. Peter's taken *Players* to his desk . . .
>
> 2.55 Peter's returned *Players*, has football sticker album.
>
> 3.00 In book corner and around the classroom: two football texts shared between four boys, plus one football text with one boy. Catherine, Suzy and Lynne are talking, starting up a unison recitation with a finger-clicking introduction. Organised by Catherine . . .
>
> 3.03 class all in book corner except for 3 girls and 3 boys finishing maths work . . .
>
> Farthing, Year 4

In this classroom most of the children had reached the status of independent readers. The teacher had placed a variety of resources in the book corner including an audio tape player, some story tapes and a variety of football magazines as a way of matching what she saw as the interests of the boys in her class. She was particularly concerned to encourage this group to read: 'I do think that with boys particularly, you have to meet them a bit more than half-way and if you want them to read you have to provide them with things that they want to read' (Farthing, Teacher Year 4).

The field notes give some idea of the kind of rapid movement in and out of the book area as children arrive and congregate, dip in and out of different resources and sort out with their friends what they want to do, and then depart. This range of resources and such a high level of activity can be justified in terms of developing children's interests.

In the run-up to the introduction of the National Literacy Strategy and at a point that was to prove crucial in the debates that immediately preceded it, a controversial Ofsted report into the teaching of reading in Inner London primary schools made a stinging attack on this aspect of teachers' practice.

> Reading was generally given a considerable amount of time each day and occupied a major proportion of the week. The actual amount of time allocated to reading ranged from two and a half hours per day to one hour per day with much of the time spent in free reading or listening to stories. . . . The long stretches of time allocated to reading . . . were poorly used . . . the pace was too slow and progress minimal. Most classes had a daily session of individual silent reading. In some of these sessions, relatively little progress was made. Children were seen changing their books too frequently and without purpose. Their behaviour in these aimless lessons often deteriorated so that by the end few would be reading anything at all.
>
> (Ofsted 1996: 22)

The activity of reading stories aloud to the class garnered little more support.

> For almost every Year 2 class, the final session of the day was devoted to hearing rather than to reading one or more stories. In these sessions, the actual text of what was being read was rarely seen by the pupils and consequently the sessions contributed little directly to teaching them to read. In nearly every case these story sessions required much of the class teacher but little from the pupils although they usually listened attentively.
>
> (Ofsted 1996: 23)

With low attainment already a cause for concern, this kind of description of current practice firmly located the problem in how little direct input from teachers children were receiving in many classrooms. Although the accuracy of the picture the report painted was hotly contested at the point of publication (Gardiner 1996) this onslaught effectively set the scene for the subsequent shift in pedagogic approach from implicit to explicit pedagogy as advocated through the NLS.

Navigating the tensions in the literacy curriculum after the introduction of the NLS

The NLS has had an enormous impact on the literacy curriculum, which has in large part survived subsequent revisions. This depth of change was engineered through: the combination of the NLS Framework document and its emphasis on what children should be taught; the accountability structures introduced with the NLS including a planning regime which committed teachers to covering the Framework objectives for a term through daily planning for the Literacy Hour; and the structure of the hour itself, with individual time slots committed to teaching text-, sentence- or word-level objectives. All these features produced a far more explicit pedagogy that depends upon specifying in advance exactly what the teacher will teach. The extent to which the pupils learn is presumed to follow directly from this.

In this kind of context it is difficult to justify finding pupils the time to learn indirectly from a process they control. Instead teachers plan for and place most emphasis on their own efficient curriculum delivery. In accordance with this view, time and space in the classroom are managed differently too. Classrooms are now organised to maximise the use of the space in front of the board, with whole-class teaching taking precedence over small group work. In many schools, book corners have disappeared altogether or been barricaded in by flipcharts or other resources destined for whole-class use. There are no longer opportunities to fully use them. Where once children finished at their own pace, activities are now designed to be completed in the fixed time-slots of the hour, with the pace of work kept high through close direction at the front of the class. Children have far fewer chances to read to themselves, whilst the concept of 'finishing work' at variable rates is no longer seen as an acceptable part of curriculum planning. There is less diversity and more uniformity in what the literacy curriculum covers and how it is organised, from classroom to classroom and from school to school. The switch to explicit pedagogy and such a strongly structured use of time has brought reading for proficiency and reading for choice into a different relationship. In particular far more of the available time is committed to assessing and building children's skills, with far less time available to allow them to direct their reading for themselves.

Putting skills first fits quite well with an arm's length management of the education system predicated on defining more closely what teachers should do and then using performance data to check whether or not they have lived up to their responsibilities. Skills can be itemised and listed, and their delivery as part of a curriculum programme can be assured as they are ticked off one by one. The skills themselves can be turned into clear learning objectives that can be identified at the start of a lesson. These can be drawn to pupils' attention so that they act as a clear reminder of their responsibilities in the coming session. All this now happens as a matter of routine at the start of most literacy hours. A typical example is the following notice pinned up besides the blackboard for the duration of a Year 3 lesson: 'Our Literacy Learning Objectives: To recognise and spell common prefixes and know what they mean'. In effect, such objectives act as imperatives. If the activity that substantiates this objective is undertaken then the work will have been done. This is teaching and learning as a kind of contractual obligation which pupils and teachers fulfil. Specifying what will happen at the outset is the first step in ensuring that such a contract will be discharged.

But those aspects of the reading curriculum which belong to reading for choice are much harder to manage in this way. It is not so easy to command children to 'like listening to lots of different stories' or 'enjoy reading and listening to different types of books'. Such responses are the child's own and cannot be determined in the same manner, or contracted in the same way. Whilst teachers may continue to seek to interest children in a range of texts, perhaps particularly those text types which the Framework document specifies, the space in which this might happen has changed. In the well-defined structure of the hour, the choice of text rests much more fully with the teacher, whilst the kind of reading that takes place will be tailored to the timings available and the tasks that will follow. With a planning regime geared to curriculum delivery, texts shrink to fit the teaching purposes they must serve. Self-directed reading as an objective within the curriculum disappears from view. (Indeed, it is not now part of the level descriptions for English.) In effect, the commitment to explicit pedagogy has extended the list of skills children must be taught to acquire, and postponed the point at which children take full responsibility for their own reading. In the current spate of curriculum revisions drawing attention to this omission only leads to calls for more skills to be taught sooner and faster (Rose 2009).

Making the transition from supported to independent readers

Traditionally in primary school practice, the teacher's direct support for and focus on children's skills would lessen as children's fluency in reading increased. Once they were deemed proficient readers, from there on in children would be expected to enlarge and refine their own reading skills through the increasing range of materials they would be expected to tackle. The teacher's role would change from instructor to facilitator, providing the appropriate resources to support this aim. This point of transition was marked by the term free or independent reader. Readers described in this way were deemed capable of tackling books of ever greater length and complexity. Even if in some cases they were left to do this pretty much on their own, the organisation of the curriculum provided opportunities for this to happen.

The switch to explicit pedagogy has made this end point of the curriculum much harder to see. There is no point at which children are now free of the list of yet more things they must learn. Whilst explicit pedagogy may make much clearer the nature of the work involved in learning to read, the current emphasis on curriculum delivery provides far less time and space for children to fully appropriate the skills they already have and use them for their own purposes. Instead government continues to fret over the benchmarks they have set for performance outcomes from the system as it stands and they tighten still further their prescriptions over what teachers should deliver.

Yet for children an important part of learning to read lies with discovering what reading can do for them. This includes finding out how to direct their reading for themselves. There is no reason why supporting such an endeavour should not form part of explicit pedagogy. Indeed, there are very good reasons why more direct support should be given to children at this stage as they move into independent reading, not least because they often seem to find this transition hard to manage without help. This parent's comments on her children's reluctance to read at home makes this clear. These children are both fluent readers, expected to use their reading record to log the books they were choosing to read for themselves:

> Parent: Hector sometimes, if I say to him, if I have a look at his reading record book and see that it's not up to date, I say "come on, let's, do you want to read something" and so he'll do it more at home if he hasn't done it at school, umm, and he likes the Roald Dahl books, so you know, he's been reading some of them at home. But it's hard work, I'd say with both of them, getting them to sit down and read and I suppose with Sarah really I've given up really because she obviously doesn't like it.
>
> (Farthing, Parent Year 4)

Input from school has a vital role at this stage in encouraging children to find things they think are worth reading. This is quite different from being asked to study texts in a more formal way in line with schools' requirements. Yet the revised Level 5 description QCA has drafted now focuses almost entirely on these kinds of formal skills in its attempt to capture for curriculum purposes what children should be able to show they can do:

> Pupils show understanding of a range of texts, selecting essential points and using inference and deduction where appropriate. In their responses, they identify key features, themes and characters and select sentences, phrases and relevant information to support their views. They understand that texts fit into historical and literary traditions.
>
> (QCA 2009: 3)

Recognition of the kinds of reading children might want to undertake for themselves is missing.

In supporting children to make the transition into independent reading, I have argued elsewhere (Moss 2000; Moss 2007) that teachers need to make time to promote different kinds of texts in ways that both extend and diversify the range of reading experiences that children will seek out. That means being much more aware of the different possibilities texts offer. The kinds of football magazines highlighted in the episode in the field notes above are absolutely appropriate for sharing in a group, and in that context may indeed encourage rapid turnover. It is hard to sit down for an extended read of a football sticker album, when the main function of this kind of text is to compare collections. There is an assumption that children should always want to spend time reading lengthy chapter books. Yet lengthy chapter books fit particular contexts – solitary and uninterrupted reading time. In a different context one might justifiably wish for time off from this kind of activity:

Trevor:	But I don't like reading, when I'm in a mood like, when I don't like to read chapter books, I just read baby books.
Interviewer:	What would you read if you weren't in the mood for a chapter book then, Trevor?
Trevor:	*Pathways* [Collins *Pathways* reading scheme], easy books
Interviewer:	Why would you read that?
Trevor:	Because if it's like a really hard book and it was a really long book, what I don't like doing is like halfway through a book, when you've got interested in it, and then having to stop.

(Farthing, Year 4, 'Can' reader)

Asking children to make choices about what and how they read inevitably means giving them more control over what they do. It also means pausing to understand the logic of the choices that get made rather than simply dismissing them as not worthwhile. Many of these issues can be resolved by making the widest selection of texts available and then encouraging children to talk about what they've chosen and extend their ideas by listening to each other. In this way direct support goes into creating a community of readers, who will exchange ideas and generate interest in new and different kinds of texts as a result of having the opportunity to sample them.

In many respects the NLS and its subsequent revisions have made the acquisition of skills central to the literacy curriculum. Explicit pedagogy driven by direct teacher input is seen as the main means of achieving this end. Schools quite rightly carry important responsibilities in this respect. But direct instruction in literacy skills is never going to be the whole story. Literacy gains its value from the many purposes to which it can be turned as children take control over the resources it represents. Anticipating from the classroom what those ends might be is difficult: the advent of digital and mobile technologies and the many uses to which they can be put amply demonstrate this. By stripping out of the curriculum the concept of the free reader and giving that role no room to thrive an essential pivot point has been lost in learning to read which needs to be restored.

References

Alexander, R.J. (2009) *Towards a New Primary Curriculum: A report from the Cambridge Primary Review. Part 2: The Future*, Cambridge: University of Cambridge Faculty of Education.

Alexander, R.J. and Flutter, J. (2009) *Towards a New Primary Curriculum: A report from the Cambridge Primary Review. Part 1: Past and Present*, Cambridge: University of Cambridge Faculty of Education.

Gardiner, J. (1996) 'Woodhead reading report is damned', *The Times Educational Supplement*, 25 October. Available at: http://www.tes.co.uk/article.aspx?storycode=19313 (accessed 26 October 2009).

Lewis, M. and Ellis, S. (2006) *Phonics: Practice, research and policy*, London: UKLA/PCP Sage.

Moss, G. (2000) 'Raising attainment: Boys, reading and the National Literacy Hour', *Reading*, 34, 3: 101–106.

Moss, G. (2007) *Literacy and Gender: Researching texts, contexts and reader*, Abingdon: Routledge.

Ofsted (1996) *The Teaching of Reading in 45 Inner London Primary Schools*, London: Ofsted.

QCA (2009) 'English: Revised level descriptions'. Available at: http://www.qca.org.uk/libraryAssets/media/95765_QCA_S_Levels_English_final.pdf (accessed 26 October 2009).

Rose, J. (2005) *Independent Review of the Teaching of Early Reading*, London: DfES.

Rose, J. (2009) *Independent Review of the Primary Curriculum: Final Report*, Nottingham: DCSF.

Solsken, J. (1993) *Literacy, Gender and Work in Families and in School*, Norwood, NJ: Ablex.

Stuart, M., Stainthorp, R. & Snowling, M. (2007) 'Literacy as a complex activity: Deconstructing the simple view of reading', *Literacy*, 42, 2: 59–66.

Part V

Teacher education

Chapter 17

The practical and political dimensions of teacher knowledge

Implications for reading teacher preparation and research on teaching

James V. Hoffman and Melissa Mosley

> There are known knowns. These are things we know that we know. There are known unknowns. That is to say, there are things that we know we don't know. But there are also unknown unknowns. There are things we don't know we don't know.
>
> (Rumsfeld 2002)

Knowledge is indeed tricky and Donald Rumsfeld was not the first to point this out. Centuries ago, Plato and Aristotle demonstrated that mapping the territory of knowledge would be a difficult task, even for the most gifted philosophers and their pupils. Teacher knowledge is no less difficult an area to navigate but we will attempt to steer a course away from the current trajectory. The structure of this chapter reflects our personal histories in researching teacher knowledge, our commitment and current work in the preparation of teachers, and a vision for researching teachers' thinking as they engage in effective literacy practices. Surrounding our treatment of this topic is an overarching concern for the policy contexts that currently exist for the study of teacher knowledge.

Background

The current focus on research in teacher knowledge is tied directly to the development of research in teaching. The history of research in teaching has been carefully documented in the four *Handbooks of Research in Teaching* (Gage 1963; Travers 1974; Wittrock 1986; Richardson 2001). The first generation of classroom researchers believed they could describe what effective teachers do and translate this into a curriculum for a teacher education program. By the late 1970s, it became clear that such a behaviorally focused, process-product driven, "what works" mindset yielded surface-level insights at best. Although policy-makers continue to be drawn to such lists of "best practices," the second generation of researchers moved on to examine the mental lives of teachers, asking questions such as: How do teachers make decisions in planning for teaching and during interactive teaching? How do teachers use the information they have about their students to adapt instruction? While this kind of research was useful in revealing the complexity of teaching – much to the dismay of policy-makers looking for certainty – it seemed to suggest that "expertise" in teaching was about more than just decision-making. Expertise seemed to be grounded in knowledge and wisdom. A new generation of researchers began to focus on questions of "What kinds of knowledge?" underpin effective teaching.

Today, we are being inundated with different ways of listing what teachers should know to be effective. These kinds of lists are then used to guide the development of, for example, standards-based teacher certification examinations, curricula for teacher education programs, and frameworks for teacher evaluation and supervision. When we look carefully at the benchmarks, rubrics, competencies and course objectives drawn from this framework, what we find are lists of declarative and procedural knowledge – facts and skills to be regurgitated or performed. This "reductionist" approach is reminiscent of the behaviorally focused findings of the 1970s and we fear, narrows the focus for research and obscures the much more important issues of how teachers use what they know in appropriate ways and how they gain new knowledge in and through the practice of teaching.

Our assessment of the current focus on teacher knowledge is quite simple. Based on years of studies of teachers and teaching, we understand teaching to be a complex, multi-faceted, creative, challenging and constantly shifting situation requiring differential application of knowledge and learning through practice in order to respond appropriately to students and contexts. Research in teacher education, and reading teacher education in particular, is stuck – perhaps even paralyzed – in its focus on the topic posed in our title: "What do teachers know?" or, a variation "What do teachers need to know to be effective in the teaching of reading?" or, another variation, "What do effective teachers know about the teaching of reading?" These questions are derived from a paradigm that constrains rather than expands our thinking and directs us away from the dynamic nature of teaching, away from the processes of becoming an effective teacher, and away from insights into effective teacher education. In short, we believe these are the wrong questions to be addressing today if we are to improve teacher education.

We know from years of studies of teachers and teaching that the best teachers do not implement knowledge in direct ways, rather, teacher knowledge evolves in the context of practice, or what Grossman (1995) calls the "crucible of the classroom," so that knowledge is applied differentially to meet the constantly shifting situations teachers face in the classroom. We certainly do not recommend ignoring research-based knowledge at all: knowledge is necessary but not sufficient. What we need is research on *how* teachers apply knowledge and how this knowledge gets reconstructed in practice. So in this chapter, we pose alternative questions about how teachers use what they know and on how teachers learn through practice. We have structured the chapter as an argument for an alternative approach to the study of teacher knowledge in four parts: the analogy, the anecdotes, the argument, and the advice.

The analogy

Most of us are familiar with the work of Lev Vygotsky (see Wertsch, 1985) and Jean Piaget (see Beilin & Pufall, 1992). Typically, scholars are so focused on the differences between them that we lose sight of their commonalities. Both scholars were troubled, at the same time, by the emerging field of psychology's focus on the measurement of intelligence. Piaget became fascinated, working in Binet's laboratory, with children's "wrong" responses to items that suggested an active construction of a mental model of the world that was in a constant movement from equilibrium to disequilibrium and then growth to a new equilibrium. He viewed intelligence as the act of reconstructing old meanings to new ones through experience, while Vygotsky believed the most important aspects of intelligence were to be found in the ability of the individual/the child to adapt to circumstances, to solve problems, to resolve issues and to overcome challenges by drawing on available resources. Vygotsky saw the attempts to measure intelligence with a focus on the "known" as less informative than a focus on assessing the learning activity that takes place in the zone of proximal development. They questioned measuring intelligence by computing the accumulation of knowledge and ventured into a more complex world of knowledge in action where doing, teaching and learning all became muddled, not isolated.

We suggest that creating taxonomies of teacher knowledge as an index of intelligence is analogous to the same flawed notion that intelligence can be measured by computing the accumulation of world knowledge. We challenge the teacher education community to ask, "Where in teacher education do we prepare teachers for the intelligence(s) that Piaget and Vygotsky envisioned? Where do we recognize that teachers come with knowledge that they can build on? Where do we prepare teachers to problem solve, to adapt to circumstances? Where do we support teachers to learn as they teach through their teaching?

The anecdotes

The anecdotes we offer are set in the context of our preservice teacher preparation program and a case study of Abby's (a pseudonym) learning as a preservice teacher over a three-semester preservice teacher education sequence. Data, collected using teacher-researcher methods, included our field notes of tutoring sessions in three practicum and student teaching, all of the written artifacts (online dialogue journals, coursework papers including case studies, and lesson plans from tutoring practicum), and one focus group interview with the preservice teachers of focus. We employed systematic analysis of all data sources, drawing on constant-comparative methods and discourse analysis of written artifacts to understand the construction of teaching knowledge in two of the three practicum (Hoffman et al. 2009; Mosley et al. 2010).

The first anecdote we offer takes place in a reading practicum in an elementary school program called *The Longhorn Readers*: pairs of preservice teachers and first or second graders engaged in reading and inquiry twice a week for one hour. Abby, an American preservice teacher in her second semester of professional coursework, is tutoring two male first graders in reading with another university student. The boys are sprawled on the floor with Abby. Jim, the first author of this chapter, is also on the floor, observing the lesson. The boys are both Hispanic American English-language learners, attending a school that serves a low-income community, and this is about all they have in common. David is extremely shy, easily distracted and does not talk much. Marcos, on the other hand, has taken to reading and writing quite easily and never stops talking.

While appreciative of Marcos, Abby is trying to make the read-aloud segment of the tutorial more conversational, modeling thinking while reading without relying on interrogation. Abby is dynamic with the students: her face lights up with excitement in the good parts of the story; she smiles and leans in when the children are talking, and her words are carefully chosen to illustrate her love of reading, inquiry, and emotionally connecting to others and literature. On this day, Abby opens the session by saying,

> Today, we are going to read a great book that I chose because you are both interested in scary stories and I think I found the perfect one for you to enjoy. There are lots of surprises in this book. The author is tricky so you are going to need to stay on your toes with your thinking and we are going to need to help each other at times with our ideas. Before I start reading though, I want to explain a new way that we are going to read. You know how sometimes when I am reading you a story you comment on what I am reading or you ask a question? Or, I talk to you about what I am thinking? [The boys nod.] Well today we are going to do this differently. I brought each of you a pad of sticky notes and a marker. As we are reading the story today, rather than saying what you are thinking or wondering about, I am going to ask you to jot down a note of what you are thinking and post it up here on the poster board chart. Is that OK?

David nods. Marcos does not respond and has already started writing his first note. This is likely the only clue you will need to know what happens next. Abby starts reading and Marcos continues to write furiously. He is posting notes at a rate of three or four per page of the read-aloud. Based on what he is posting it is clear that Marcos is barely attending to the story at this point, he is just commenting on anything that comes to mind. David notices what Marcos is doing and begins to write as well, but it is clearly a struggle for him. He interrupts Abby's reading to ask about spelling words. He has stopped listening and is intent now on copying one of Marcos's post-its.

Jim could see Abby's frustration building, and at this point she stopped the reading and said to the boys,

> You know how sometimes you have this idea and you think it is a really great idea and then you realize along the way that it wasn't such a good idea? [The

boys nod. Even Marcos pauses in the writing of his tenth sticky note.] Well, that's kind of like me today with you. I am going to collect your post-it notes and markers now, and instead we are going to go back to reading the story like we have been. We'll just talk along the way.

The boys went along with the new plan without a pause and the story came back to life.

There was something about this particular event, on this particular day, with this particular student that stood out to me (Jim) as extremely powerful. It was not the knowledge that Abby possessed, although she did bring forward some knowledge she had constructed from our methods courses. It was learning I was seeing. It was active use and reconstruction of knowledge to "think like a teacher." In Vygotskyan terms, Abby was drawing on available knowledge and available resources in active ways. She approached the situation as a problem-solver with a willingness to take on a challenge, to take risks, and to learn as she was teaching.

The short anecdote is only part of the story. There was planning, all of the activity that went on after the lesson and before the next one, and the scaffolding that Jim provided in past interactions. He had taken time to build trust with Abby as Abby had taken time to build trust with her students. Jim set an expectation for the flexible use of practical knowledge and was available to follow up in subsequent interactions with Abby and support her in the construction of alternatives in the future. But, to our main point, propositional or declarative knowledge was not at the center here. The event illuminates her learning and thinking, not her knowledge. When Abby as a teacher faces situations such as these in the future, she will have the problem solving and reflection strategies we nurtured within the program.

The argument

We have been researching over the past several years learning to teach at the preservice level with a particular focus on the qualities and impact of practicum experiences on learning to teach. The words and concepts we draw on are familiar to most teacher educators: experience, reflection, and practical knowledge. These are good words but a lot has been lost, ignored or rendered meaningless through lip service in our programs. Our argument will be focused on changing our focus from nouns to verbs (from knowledge to knowing); from the static to the dynamic (from the codification of knowledge to thinking like a teacher); from the procedural to the conditional (from the behavioral routines to the beliefs and moral dimensions of action in teaching).

We will use the term practical knowledge not as a kind or type of knowledge but as a source of knowledge that may, at some point in time, be recognized as declarative, procedural or conditional knowledge. Drawing on the work of van Driel, Beijaard, & Verloops (2001) in the area of science education, we view practical knowledge (at least initially) as action-oriented, personal and context-bound, tacit in nature, integrated (not isolated or fragmented), imbued with beliefs and valuing dimensions (see also Verloop, van Driel, & Meijer, 2001).

If we are to support learning to teach reading then we would argue we need to conceptualize practice as the center of our teacher education efforts with a deep understanding of how practice accompanied by reflection and support leads to learning and not just practice that leads to automaticity (Britzman 2003).

The Learning to Teach through Practice Cycle

We have been developing a conceptual model to illustrate what Learning Through Practice might look like, to build on the concepts of the development of practical knowledge. We refer to the model as the "Learning to Teach through Practice Cycle." It consists of seven components that are interactive between and across and not as sequential as the visual display may suggest. Here, we will briefly describe the seven components and continue to use the case introduced in the

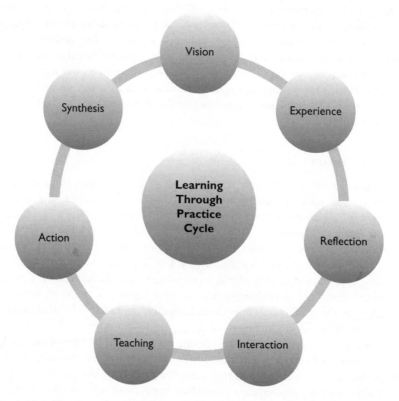

Figure 17.1 The Learning to Teach through Practice Cycle.

previous section to illustrate the features of the model as we have observed them in practice.

Visioning

A teacher's vision is messy and multidimensional. It includes beliefs, values, ideology, knowledge, temperament, motivations, mythology, images, metaphors, purposes, expectations, biases, prejudices, stored narratives, skill-sets, identities, and more (Duffy 2002; Squires & Bliss 2004). It is the starting point and the ending point for the practice cycle. It is personal and is (or should be) in a state of constant reconstruction as expertise is developed. It is a world-view specific to the act of teaching, the role of teacher and the aims of education.

The Learning through Practice cycle begins with the activation of the teacher's vision – in much the same way we activate prior knowledge in learning new concepts. In order to support teachers' visions, we need to listen carefully to what they say about themselves and their desires for their students. We heard one such statement from Abby early in her practicum work.

> I still love to read. I love getting involved in stories that weren't mine to begin with and making them my own. I especially love reading to kids as I was read to at their age. I love it so much because I get to give them a chance to become part of a story that they might remember for their entire lives, as I have.
>
> (Myself as a Reader Essay, May 7, 2008)

Abby believes that a love of reading is something that an influential person shares with a child; but more importantly, a love of reading comes when a child sees himself in the story. It is memorable experiences with texts that are valued, both for the child and for the person who shares her love of reading with another.

For the expert teacher, a vision is activated typically in the planning stage for teaching, but is actually always in operation throughout the teaching cycle. For the novice teacher, the vision element may need to be activated in order to achieve the maximum learning through practice effect (i.e. revisioning).

Experiencing

The desired practicum experience is educative in the sense of Dewey's (1966) concept of continuity. In designing these experiences we are concerned with such factors as quantity, quality, focus, intensity, contexts, support, and distribution of these experiences across a preparation program. There are two essential requirements across all of these features. The first is authenticity – first-hand teaching experiences with students around learning outcomes. Tutorials, small-group work, whole-class direct instruction, guiding readers and writers workshops, and conferencing can all count. The second feature is a "problem." There must be something within the experience that presents a challenge to the existing "vision" and is recognized as a challenge to be addressed.

Reflecting

Reflection, within the context of teacher education, is one of those dangerous words. Our quick response is often, "We do that." We ask preservice teachers to reflect constantly. But do they really? We treat reflection as a "moment" (typically of recording) and then move on without any further consideration. "They reflected." But when do we teach them how to reflect? How do we teach them the processes of reflection? How do we support them to learn through reflection to knowledge construction in the ways that scholars like Zeichner (1992) and others (see Milner 2003) have recommended? We found throughout our research that the preservice teachers reflected when we asked them to do so, after reading or having a particular experience. We do not always know, however, when and how reflection occurs when it is not an assignment.

Schön (1973, 1983, 1987), perhaps the most cited and least read advocate of reflection, argued that reflection is critical to professional life. There are two kinds of reflection: that which occurs during the act of teaching and requires flexibility and adaptability to achieve successful outcomes (reflecting *in* practice) and reflection *on* practice that occurs after teaching. Across six cases we analyzed in our larger study, and in Abby's case particularly, in online postings, the most common source of influence on practice was a reflection on previous practice. This is one of the most critical parts of the reflection process that requires the consideration of "governing" variables that shape or place constraints on action and may be regarded as outside the teacher's control now or in the future. Or, by re-evaluating the governing variables new possibilities emerge. This is Schön's (1987) double-feedback-loop system that, in the model we are using, is represented in the teacher's vision.

The initial reflection can be written or oral, immediate (best for capturing the in practice reflection) or delayed (best for capturing the on-practice reflection). The reflecting process can be done by memory alone or by stimulated recall (e.g., viewing a video clip). Returning to the anecdote of Abby, what is essential is the use of reflection to begin the process of constructing new knowledge. In the post-it example, she drew on her vision of making reading memorable for students by asking them to connect with the book. Abby had the notion that at every moment in the practicum, she and her students were constantly revising their ways of interacting with texts in line with this vision of making personal connections with and through literature. She wrote about Marcos, ". . . he made the comment that 'It feels like we're just getting started!' How right he is! I feel like we've just begun! There's such a friendship and bond that we've developed through literature and inquiries . . ." (Lesson Plan Reflection, April 22, 2008). We believe that this sense of "just getting started" relates to the constant revisions that are underway when reflection and visions are linked.

Interacting

The socialization of experiences according to Piaget is essential for learning. Sociocultural learning theory, drawing on Vygotsky and Bakhtin (see Wertsch 1993) features the importance of social mediation. In the end, it is not the quick-write reflection that makes the difference (although this may facilitate the process), it is the opportunity for social interaction and problem solving. The interaction might be face-to-face or written or virtual (as in a message board or chat rooms) or some combination of all of the above.

In a focus group interview at the end of the third practicum, Abby and her peers who were student teaching at the same elementary school sat together to watch a few videos of practice and talk about their own processes and experiences over the course of the semester. The video clips were representative of the problems of practice I (Melissa) saw while observing reading instruction in their classrooms. Abby's clip was an example of how she led her third-grade students in character analysis while reading aloud a chapter book. The following is an excerpt of this conversation around this clip:

Tamara: And the way, the questions that you asked, . . ., and the way you led the conversation. It reminded me of what we have been reading about, what we've been learning about, how to ask these open-ended questions, like well, why. We want to look deeper into these characters. . . .

Abby: And that's so hard too, because there are some students where, they aren't at that level of thinking yet. I want to pose these questions but I want to know like, certain students' limits. . . . They were really struggling with thinking deeper, and so I didn't want to just accept that.

Tamara: But you were scaffolding them really well.

Abby: Thanks.

Tamara: The individual students.

Kacey: It is hard to know, how far to push them before it's too much . . . to make sure that everyone is engaged, at least most of the time.

All: yeah

Abby: Especially in discussion, which we all know is really important to comprehension and enjoyment of a book together. But it, yeah, discussion is hard because you have one kid who's like thinking very deeply but a few students where it's like, "How do I draw you into this."

(Focus Group Interview, May 4, 2009)

This set of interactions is interesting because we see that reflection and visions are folded into the conversation, as Abby says how important discussion is to comprehension and this "enjoyment of a book together," which also relates back to her vision of having interactions around texts that support relationships with reading. However, Tamara's voice adds another dimension: the teachers have been moving towards the development of teaching knowledge together – reading together, talking together – and that these interactions have supported their teaching. We notice the use of "and" and "especially" in Abby's entrée into the conversation each time, which shows how she builds on her peers' ideas to make sense of what was happening. Kacey's turn reiterates the problem of practice: Abby's students were entering into the character analysis differently, and allowed Abby to expand on her reflection. She ends with a re-voicing of her own reflection in the moment, "How do I draw you into this," providing another window into how reflection happened both in the moment and in this current interaction.

Teaching (or scaffolding)

While the goal of the Learning to Teach through Practice Cycle is to lead to independent and autonomous learning, the teacher educator plays a critical role as facilitator and mediator of the reflection process. We are particularly drawn to Golombek's (1998) notion of the role of the teacher educator as a kind of moral agitator:

> Recognizing the moral and affective ways of knowing in personal practical knowledge requires teacher educators to manage teachers' potentially unsettling reflections and articulations because they may resist questioning their assumptions or contradictions in their thinking and behavior. Teacher educators, within a supportive community of teachers, can pose questions; draw links among experience, instruction practice, and knowledge; and suggest instructional strategies while modeling self-reflection in their own teaching and in meetings with teachers. In this way, teachers can pursue self-exploration to discern how emotions and moral beliefs influence their sense-making processes.
>
> (Golombek 1998: 462)

The teacher educator is sometimes the agitator, the counselor, and the resource person. He or she insures that the cycle is completed, that learning through practice occurs; but also guides the teacher through the new practice experience based on what came before. The teacher educator guides the revision of the teacher's vision through this process (as he or she comes to know the vision, how the reflection and vision interact, etc.)

We are not arguing that the traditional kinds of things done in teacher preparation programs outside of practice be abandoned. Course lectures, readings, project-based learning activities, observations of teaching, service learning projects, teacher inquiry or action research projects are critical in the ways they can help shape a teacher's vision.

Action

For Freire (1995) acting on and reflecting belong together. Human beings, as unfinished persons, are always in the process of becoming particular kinds of people – social actors, teachers – as they respond to problems in the world. For us, this phase of the cycle marks the return into practice, for example testing out a new strategy that may become later a part of a revised vision. Acting on knowledge, we shape possibilities and roles for ourselves and others, working towards more satisfying and joyful ways of being in the world. Freire's emphasis on the interaction between experience, reflection and action is embodied in his use of the term "praxis" (see Hoffman-Kipp, Antiles & Lopez-Torres 2003).

Abby's initial vision of providing experiences towards personal connection with a text played out when she put Marcos's name into a poem or song, or implemented an inquiry project that built on his interests. In Mosley *et al.* (in press) we discuss the ways in which Abby, in connecting narratives about instructional practices with Marcos, her first-semester practicum student, moved from observation to action, and were also places where she identified dilemmas of practice. In the following narrative, Abby reflected on a common dilemma: when do we follow a student's lead, and when do we introduce a new topic?

> I originally had wanted to do a research project on animals. But after making a few more observations and conclusions on Marcos's learning style and developmental direction, I can see that he does really well in things that he's super comfortable in and loves exploring topics that he already knows about. So I started wondering how I could challenge him, and I thought about all the times I'd brought in a new activity, and how he was a little hesitant to get involved. My thought is to challenge him . . . but still set him up for success by exploring new topics for research.
>
> (Tutoring Reflection, March 3, 2008)

Course assignments in our teacher education program were crafted to evoke the "looking backwards" reflection, telling stories to better understand the nature of literacy acquisition and identity. Abby's observations thus caused her to reconsider her initial plans. She brought her new ideas to Marcos for input, and captured his responses verbatim (as she often did),

> I asked him what he thought about the idea of exploring new topics for a research project and his first response was, "What's a research project?" After we explained and wrote down the concept in his wordbook, he smirked in a shy way and said, "I think that'd be fun. I really like learning."
>
> (Tutoring Reflection, March 3, 2008)

In the sessions that followed, Abby responded to Marcos's feedback by carefully selecting nonfiction texts, offering choices, working on strategies for reading more challenging information words, and planning future inquiries that incorporate technology.

In this anecdote, Abby learned that in action, her vision might look and sound differently depending on the interactions that transpire. Often, revisions of teaching happen in the moment, in response to a student's reaction. When Abby experienced hesitancy from Marcos, she did not give up on him. Instead, she believed that she could act in ways that would change Marcos's vision of himself. Her report that he said, "I like learning," is evidence that she felt as though she was changing and shaping possibilities for Marcos, ways that he might respond to reading instruction as someone who likes learning.

Synthesizing

Out of this next iteration in practice comes a synthesis of knowledge that leads to accommodation and a revised vision or world-view. This is the Piagetian disequilibrium to equilibrium cycle of learning replayed within a professional life. The revised vision will satisfy only till the next cycle of teaching practice reveals another challenge that cannot be addressed with the "old knowledge" and the cycle will be set in motion again. In our model of Learning through Practice we actually introduce another teaching moment where the teacher educator engages the teacher's vision prior to practice as a way of setting the teacher up for learning.

In each instance of Abby's practicum work, she drew on her peers, her own reflections, her readings, and her interactions with her instructors to think through problems of practice, as we saw in the anecdotes in this chapter. The ongoing learning was evident in the changes in her practice, her sense of efficacy in her teaching, and her shifting visions of what kinds of reading would happen in her instruction. However, there were few moments when it seemed that Abby was tying up the loose ends, or moving to some greater truth or discovery. In the focus group interview, after the close of her teaching, she did not take the position that she had solved all of her problems of practice. Instead, she continued to replay the events of the read-aloud, noticing and naming what was challenging and the complexity of leading a group of students in literature discussion. Indeed, she is just getting started.

We know that the synthesis dimension of our model may be the trickiest. There are points when the teacher educator steps in to discussions and debriefings, not "telling" but planting the important questions for teachers to ask of themselves as they plan for, enter into, engage in and reflect on practice. We look for examples in our research of how we engaged in synthesizing that doesn't tie up the loose ends but instead, tries to understand the nature of the knot. This is the part of the cycle that promotes autonomy and independence as a professional. The synthesizing step leads to a revised vision that is carried forward into the next teaching experience.

Our current research is exploring how each of the components of this cycle function in learning to teach. Clearly, the components are much more interactive than can be represented in a simple diagram. While there is danger is depicting such a complex process in a model like this, we feel such a representation is useful in grounding our research. We are interested in the ways this cycle changes as beginning teachers move into different kinds of teaching contexts. What are the qualities of the local context that support the processes of learning through practice? What are the qualities of the local context that subvert, modify or replace this process? Our current research is a longitudinal study following a group of students, including Abby, through their first years of teaching.

The advice

If teaching was simple we could certainly continue along the path of creating lists of knowledge and skills necessary to teach reading. We could train teachers to do what we expect. But teaching is complex. While training might be appropriate in some aspects of teacher preparation, we must eventually focus on the education of teachers to prepare them to meet complexity, adapt to it and learn from it. Our advice for those who would engage in teacher preparation and those who would study teacher education is toward the complex. We must move from studying categories of knowledge to studying how teachers, in the context of practice, use knowledge in dynamic and problem-solving ways and learn from that experience. We must move teacher education away from knowledge bites delivered in courses, to programs that create opportunities for teacher educators to scaffold on top of what exists into new understandings.

These shifts are particularly challenging in a policy context that values simplicity, certainty and control. The requirements, in the United States for example, to base teaching and teacher preparation on narrowly defined scientifically based practices has encouraged reductionist research and reductionist teacher education. This policy context is based on an ideology that privileges control over professional prerogative. This agenda seeks to remove significant decision-making from the professional teacher and replace it with a set of standardized practices. Under this ideology there will continue to be a favoring of research that produces lists of "best practices" and "necessary teaching knowledge." The alternative is complex. The policy context for research needs to shift from the ideological to the pragmatic. The pragmatic policy context is open to the inherent complexity and ambiguity that surrounds teaching, learning to teach, and teacher preparation. The pragmatic policy context is not "anything goes" but rather a demand for evidence of effectiveness – a standard that all teachers, researchers and teacher educators can embrace. The pragmatic policy context, in contrast to the current ideological context, is not atheoretical. Our current work focused on the development of practical knowledge both theoretical and pragmatic.

We offer this advice in the spirit of Dewey's notion of truth. Dewey challenges the correspondence to "how things really are" with the rejoinder: "how are they really?" In other words, how is it that "the mind can get out of itself to know a world beyond, or how the world out there can creep into consciousness?" Or, stated another way, as problems change, the truth changes. Thus our search for truth in teaching is not the quest for absolute or fixed truth. It is the individual and collective quest for coherence in practice and thus our model, the Learning to Teach through Practice Cycle, is grounded in vision, experience, reflection, interaction, teaching, action and synthesis. Our search for truth will lead us, we can hope, to understand the wisdom of practice (Shulman 2004) as more than just accumulated knowledge but as a vision, a disposition toward action, and a process for growing.

References

Beilin, H. & Pufall, P. (eds) (1992) *Piaget's theory: Prospects and possibilities*, Hillsdale, NJ: Erlbaum.

Britzman, D. (2003) *Practice makes practice: A critical study of learning to teach*, Albany, NY: SUNY Press.

Dewey, J. (1966) *Democracy and education: An introduction to the philosophy of education* (1st Free Press paperback ed.), New York: The Free Press.

Driel, J., Beijaard, D., & Verloop, N. (2001) 'Professional development and reform in science education: The role of teachers' practical knowledge', *Journal of Research in Science Teaching*, 38, 2: 137–158.

Duffy, G. G. (2002) 'Visioning and the development of outstanding teachers', *Reading Research and Instruction*, 41, 4: 331–344.

Freire, P. (1995) *Pedagogy of the oppressed* (new rev. 20th Anniversary ed.), New York: Continuum.

Gage, N. (1963) *Handbook of research on teaching*, Chicago: Rand McNally.

Golombek, P. R. (1998) 'A case study of second language teachers' personal practical knowledge', *TESOL Quarterly*, 32: 447–464.

Grossman, P. L. (1995) 'Teachers' knowledge', in L. W. Anderson (ed.), *International encyclopaedia of teaching and teacher education* (20–24), New York: Pergamon.

Hoffman, J. V., Mosley, M., Horan, D., Russell, K., Warren, H. K., & Roach, A. K. (2009) 'STELLAR tutoring in preservice teacher preparation: Exploring video-case support for learning to teach', in J. Richards & C. Lassonde (eds) *Evidence-based quality literacy tutoring programs: A look at successful in-school, after-school, and summer programs* (7–20), Newark, DE: International Reading Association.

Hoffman-Kipp, P., Artiles, A., & Lopez-Torres, L. (2003) 'Beyond reflection: Teacher learning as praxis', *Theory Into Practice*, 42, 3: 248–254.

Milner, H. R. (2003). 'This issue – Editorial', *Theory into Practice*, 42, 3: 170.

Mosley, M., Hoffman, J. V., Roach, A. K., & Russell, K. (2010) 'The nature of reflection: Experience, reflection and action in a preservice teacher literacy practicum', in E. G. Pultorak (ed.) *The purposes, practices, and professionalism of teacher reflectivity: Insights for 21st century teachers and students*, New York: Rowman & Littlefield.

Richardson, V. (2001) *Handbook of research on teaching* (4th Edition), Washington, DC: American Educational Research Association.

Rumsfeld, D. (2002) 'Donald Rumsfeld known unknowns'. Available at: http://www.youtube.com/watch?v=Sq5mQLArjmo (accessed 26 October 2009).

Sailors, M., Keehn, S., Martinez, M., & Harmon, J. (2005) 'Early field experiences offered to and valued by preservice teachers at Sites of Excellence in Reading Teacher

Education programs', *Teacher Education and Practice: Focus on Global Practices*, 18: 458–470.

Schön, D. A. (1973) *Beyond the stable state: Public and private learning in a changing society*, Harmondsworth: Penguin.a

Schön, D. (1983) *The reflective practitioner: How professionals think in action*, London: Temple Smith.

Schön, D. (1987) *Educating the reflective practitioner*, San Francisco: Jossey-Bass.

Shulman, L. S. (2004) *The wisdom of practice: Essays on teaching, learning, and learning to teach*, New York: Jossey-Bass.

Squires, D. & Bliss, T. (2004) 'Teacher visions: Navigating beliefs about literacy learning', *The Reading Teacher*, 57: 756–763.

Travers, R. (ed.) (1974) *Second handbook of research on teaching*, Chicago: Rand McNally.

Verloop, N., Van Driel, J. & Meijer, P. (2001) 'Teacher knowledge and the knowledge base of teaching', *International Journal of Educational Research*, 5: 441–461.

Wertsch, J. V. (1985) *Vygotsky and the social formation of the mind*, Cambridge, MA, and London: Harvard University Press.

Wertsch, J. V. (1993) *Voices of the mind: A sociocultural approach to mediated action*, Cambridge, MA: Harvard University Press.

Wittrock, M. C. (1986) *Handbook of research on teaching* (3rd Edition), Washington DC: American Educational Research Association.

Zeichner, K. M. (1992) 'Conceptions of reflective teaching in contemporary U.S. teacher education program reforms', in L. Valli (ed.), *Reflective teacher education: Cases and critiques* (161–173), Albany, NY: State University of New York Press.

Index